Critique of Religious Thought
First Authorized English Edition
of *Naqd al-Fikr ad-Dini*

Other Books by the Sadik J. Al-Azm Published by Gerlach Press:

SADIK J. AL-AZM

SECULARISM, FUNDAMENTALISM
AND THE STRUGGLE FOR THE MEANING OF ISLAM
Collected Essays on Politics and Religion
With a Foreword by Stefan Wild

3 Volume Set
Total No of Pages: 627
ISBN: 978-3-940924-20-9

Also available as individual Volumes:
Vol. 1 - On Fundamentalisms
191 pages
ISBN: 978-3-940924-22-3

Vol. 2 - Islam – Submission and Disobedience
191 pages
ISBN: 978-3-940924-24-7

Vol. 3 - Is Islam Secularizable? Challenging Political and Religious Taboos
245 pages
ISBN: 978-3-940924-26-1

www.gerlach-press.de

Sadik J. al-Azm

Critique of Religious Thought

First Authorized English Edition of *Naqd al-Fikr ad-Dini*
With a New Foreword by the Author

Translated from the Arabic
by George Stergios and Mansour Ajami

 Gerlach Press

First published 2015
by Gerlach Press
Berlin, Germany
www.gerlach-press.de

Cover Design: www.brandnewdesign.de, Hamburg
Printed and bound in Germany by
Freiburger Graphische Betriebe
www.fgb.de

British Library Cataloguing in Publication Data.
A catalogue record for this book is available from the British Library.

Bibliographic data available from Deutsche Nationalbibliothek
http://d-nb.info/1049547675

ISBN: 978-3-940924-44-5 (this hardcover volume)
ISBN: 978-3-940924-45-2 (eBook)
ISBN: 978-3-940924-94-0 (ePUB)

Contents

The numbers in square brackets in the text indicate the pagination of the original Arabic book published by Dar at–Tali'a, Beirut, e.g. [A 12] refers to Arabic page 12.

Translator's Acknowledgements

Having just completed *Self-Criticism after the Defeat* to his satisfaction, I was asked by Sadik al-Azm if I was interested in completing a translation of the book you are reading, the *Critique of Religious Thought*. I jumped at the opportunity and soon received a manuscript in various degrees of completion.

The second chapter, "The Tragedy of Satan (Iblis)," had already been impeccably translated by Dr. Mansour Ajami and published in a volume dedicated to Al-Azm called *Orientalism and Conspiracy*. I have done no more than change a word or two in that translation in order to maintain a uniformity in vocabulary across the book.

All the other chapters required more work, but I always had the advantage of a draft, which made my work much easier. I want to express my gratitude to all of those who contributed to this project. All remaining errors and infelicities, of course, are mine.

George Stergios

Boston, Massachusetts, Autumn 2014

A critique of every aspect of contemporary Arab society and its traditions – a rigorous scientific and secular critique combined with a deep and penetrating analysis – is one of the fundamental obligations of the revolutionary socialist vanguard in the Arab homeland. Only such a critique is capable of preparing the conditions for the possibility of the uprooting of all the negative, inhibiting, and disabling aspects of our social heritage. Exploding the traditional frames of Arab society will lead precisely to an acceleration in the pace of work on the construction of a completely modern Arab society. Without this exploding, the possibility of a systematic, speedy, and revolutionary development of the traditional intellectual and social structures of the Arab people becomes questionable, if not impossible. At the same time, this will cast its negative and disabling shadows on swift and serious Arab economic development.

Yasine Al-Hafez

Introduction to the English Edition

This book has been on the market in the Arab world without interruption for over a half century. While it has been formally banned in every Arab state save Lebanon, it is available to anyone, in any Arab country, who wants to read it (or burn it). Its first edition (Beirut, December 1969), sold out almost immediately: the remaining copies were confiscated by the Lebanese authorities at the behest of the Grand Mufti of Lebanon. Consequently, the Attorney General referred author, publisher and book to the appropriate court for trial on charges of "inciting confessional strife" in the country.

The book sparked the most sensational Arab literary scandal of the second half of the 20th century. Reviewers immediately compared it to the two most famous such scandals in the first half of the same century:

(a) Ali Abdulraziq's daring book "Islam and the Foundations of Governance" (Cairo 1925), which argued from inside Islam for the separation of state and religion in contemporary Muslim societies and, in effect, justified Ataturk's abolition of the caliphate in 1923.

(b) Taha Hussein's unorthodox volume on Jahili poetry, i.e., on pre-Islamic Arabic poetry (Cairo 1926), which upset much of the received medieval wisdom and approaches to the subject.

Critique of Religious Thought eventually generated about 1,500 pages of controversy, polemics, rebuttals, refutations, and responses—and some rare defenses.

The main thrust of all these rejoinders was first to reaffirm and fortify the traditional narratives of Islam against my skeptical criticisms and rational questionings, and second to "prove" again the veracity of those elements of the scriptures and faith that I described as myth. By the way, the problem of the meaning and role of "myth" in Islam (and by implication the possibility of demythologization) figured prominently in the trial and in the rejoinders and refutations.

This went on for many months, especially in Lebanon. In a formal declaration (not quite a Fatwa), the Mufti of Lebanon condemned author and book for blasphemy against Islam, and apostasy and atheism.

Interestingly enough, no disturbances of the peace occurred anywhere in protest against what was portrayed, then, as a vicious attack not only on religious thought but also on religion itself. At the time, Arab popular opinion and attention were still stupefied and paralyzed by the devastating Arab defeat in the Six Days War with Israel in June 1967.

Throughout the commotion, author and book were denounced in many a mosque in the course of the Friday prayer sermons. This went on for several months, especially in Lebanon.

At the height of the scandal, I was approached by some colleagues and fellow Arab intellectuals in Europe proposing the translation of the book into English and French. I was skeptical then about the value of such a translation for European thought and intellectual interests. I responded by saying my book is a Marxisant Enlightenment critique of religious thought, something very *déjà vu* in English, French and most of the other European languages.

The assertive rise of Islamic fundamentalism after the Arab-Israeli War of October 1973 revived interest in the book both locally and beyond. In the wake of the 9/11 attack, it was an American colleague, Blair Gadsby, of Scottsdale, Arizona, who proposed again a translation of the book into English to make it available to as wide a readership as possible. I am deeply indebted to him for initiating this translation project, eventually completed by George Stergios and myself. In an explanatory note, Blair wrote the following: "We suffer from a dearth of translated works from Arabic into

English... The hope here is that *Critique of Religious Thought* will be deemed one additional, if significant, corrective to this reality. To have a growing access to the full spectrum of ideas of cultural, socio-economic and political voices of the Arab World in English should go a long way toward reducing our knowledge deficit, helping us understand that Islam is not the only resource which has been tapped by Arab thinkers in the modern age. May this be the beginning of a trend."

I take this opportunity to express my gratitude to another colleague, Mansour Ajami of Princeton, for his superb translation of the "Iblis" essay and for much linguistic and literary advice received over the years. It was a pleasure indeed working with another American friend of Syrian origins, George Stergios of Boston, Massachusetts, in reviewing and finalizing the translation.

The first two chapters of the book go back to the early 1960s and reflect deep political and intellectual dissatisfaction with the continuing inertness and conservatism of Arab thought and culture at a time of decolonization, progressive socio-economic changes and third-world projects of modernization, growth and catching up with the developed world.

Questions about the role of modern science and technology in our underdeveloped societies were very much on the agenda, especially their possible impact on traditional culture, inherited systems of belief and the conventional religious understandings of the world. Ideas were circulating then about the urgent need for the critical reinterpretation and updating of Islam's theology, law and conventional narratives; above all, undoing the overly literal reading and comprehension of scriptures.

A good example is my use of belief systems internal to Islam to rework the Koranic story of the fall of Satan (Iblis) in terms of modern concepts of tragedy and the drama of trying existential choices. Not unexpectedly, the result scandalized orthodoxy in the Arab World, both Muslim and Christian. When these two chapters were given as lectures in Beirut and Damascus, they gave rise to quite a bit of healthy discussion, criticism and debate, but not the widespread scandal they provoked when they entered the sensitive parts of the public sphere.

The chapter on the apparition of the Virgin in a Cairo church in 1968 sought to expose the manipulation and politics of deceit of the Egyptian military-security establishment, which exploited the "miracle" to deflect popular attention away from the defeat itself. This essay bears all the painful marks of the devastating trauma experienced by the sixties generation in the Arab world after that defeat. The trauma signaled the precipitous collapse of the reigning politico-cultural amalgam of Arab nationalism, populism and third-world enthusiasm.

In my contribution to Arab self-criticism after the defeat, I sensed that some form or other of conservative revivalist Islam would proceed to fill the resulting vacuum. The politico-cultural center of the Arab World was already shifting from "progressive" Nasserist Egypt to "reactionary" Wahhabi Saudi Arabia. I had assumed at the time that the returning Islam would be more escapist and consoling than aggressive and violent.

After discussions and consultations with my left-leaning publisher in Beirut and with various friends and fellow intellectuals, I concluded that collecting my critical essays – those from before and after the defeat – and publishing them in a book could form a stimulating and challenging contribution to the debates and controversies raging in the Arab World over the defeat and its consequences for the Arabs and their future. I did not assume or anticipate that the book would result in a literary scandal of such proportions.

The Sunni clerical establishment in Lebanon and its allies spearheaded the campaign against the book, referring both author and publisher to the courts on various charges. The Christian clerical establishment was divided. One part disapproved thoroughly of the book on the grounds that any criticism of and/or skepticism about religion is dangerous and destabilizing in our societies as it undermines the basic belief systems of the common people. The other part cautiously welcomed the book and the resulting affair as a positive and refreshing development inside a stale and stagnant system of Islamic thought and belief.

Since the critical questionings and skeptical approaches of the book dealt primarily with Sunni religious thought, the Shi'i clerical establishment in Lebanon assumed a well-calibrated and measured position of tolerance and understanding towards the book and the attendant polemics. For example, the most venerable Shi'a 'Alim and theologian in the country at the time – Mohammad Jawad Moughniyya – wrote saying that he disagreed with all the ideas and arguments of the book, but that he believed that if Islam failed to take serious account of the issues, dilemmas and problems raised by Al-Azm, then Islam was the loser. Lebanon's chiefs and politicians contributed their bit to the controversy and sensation. The statements they made and positions they took concerning the controversy were often motivated, however, less by principle than by their internal rivalries and personal animosities.

After my brief imprisonment in Beirut, the case was brought to trial in the spring of 1970. It was a sensational political trial par excellence. Four of Lebanon's most eminent lawyers volunteered to take on the case and act as the defense on behalf of author, publisher and book.

The point of the whole exercise was to placate the Mufti and the Sunni clerical establishment. Kamal Jumblatt, Lebanon's chief Druze leader and Minister of the Interior at the time (himself a cultivated ascetic intellectual and Lebanon's most prominent personality in the Arab world and internationally), was attacked by his foes for seeming partial to the book. He certainly acted to protect me from harm and from being deported out of the country immediately after the imprisonment. I remain grateful to him to this day.

Another interesting reaction was that of the premier Sunni political leader and six-time Prime Minister, Saeb Salam, who refused to condemn the book and privately advised the opposite side to write a book of refutations instead of stirring up this whole commotion.

In the end, the court dismissed the case and the prosecution decided not to appeal the verdict in spite of calls to do so from various clerics and their followers.

An informal public opinion bloc had formed in Lebanon made up of secular Arab nationalists, left-wing forces and parties, professional associations, liberals, secularists, militant Palestinians, progressive intellectuals of all stripes and much of the local press. There was informal support from similar blocs made up of similar elements in other Arab countries. The spontaneous pressure of these blocs contributed greatly to my acquittal and the prosecution's waiving of appeal.

It is worth mentioning that the book created an embarrassing dilemma for communists and those on the left. On the one hand, criticism of religion impedes the ability of the left to organize the popular masses. On the other hand, Karl Marx called religion "the opium of the people" and regarded the criticism of religion as "the criticism of that vale of tears of which religion is the halo." For Marx, the criticism of religion is the beginning of all other criticism of contemporary society, economy and life. The left-wing press and chiefs navigated the quandary by floating above it, affecting something close to neutrality in covering the book, the controversy, and the political and ideological fallout. In other words, the left acted as a reluctant supporter of the book and author in spite of their Marxism, while the informal popular opinion bloc tended to defend the book on principle without adopting its content.

I believe that my book will remain significant and relevant within the Arab-Islamic universe of discourse for a long time. The centers of Islamic study and learning (Al-Azhar in Cairo, Zeitouna in Tunis, and the Shari'a schools attached to the Arab national universities) are no less sterile today than they were when I wrote my series of critiques. Islamic thought has rarely benefited from its attempts to come to terms with modernity, particularly with modern science and modern socio-political institutions. Over the last two centuries, these attempts take the form of a descending historical dialectic, a series of desperate steps backward deeper into the past, ignorance, and violence.

For example, the movement of reform in Islamic theology, thought and law of the end of the 19th century regressed from Afghani's revolutionism to Mohammad Abdo's mere latitudinarianism and cultural adaptism, an adaptism that gave way in the next generation to the theological conservatism and political reaction of Rasheed Rida (a student of Abdo). That conservatism slid further back into the restorationism and fundamentalism of Hasan Al-Banna and the organization he founded in 1928, the Muslim Brothers, and then, in the next generation, even further in Sayyed Qutb's jihadism against the "jahiliyya" of the 20th century, as explained in his famous and very influential book "Signposts."

The descending dialectic reaches its logical and practical nadir in the four following phenomena: a) Abdusalam Faraj's seminal tract "Jihad: the Absent Commandment" (Cairo 1981), (b) the extravagant violence of the Islamic "Gama'at" in Egypt in the 1980s, (c) Bin Laden's spectacular terrorism on a global scale and (d) the blind jihadism and barbarism of his children and inheritors. Given this historical descent instead of ascent, shocking books, critical ideas, challenging interpretations and provocative readings like *Critique of Religious Thought,* remain both relevant and necessary.

There have been other thinkers and other works that share the critical spirit of my book, often writing from within Islam, and who represent glimmers of vitality and hope within the dominant narrative of regression and despair. The most prominent instances are the following:

(a) Egypt's Nasr Hamid Abu-Zeid (1943-2010) and his historical re-readings of Islam, Shari'a and the Koran itself, as in his famous book Critique of Religious Discourse (Cairo, 1994), which provoked a significant Egyptian and Arab literary scandal leading to his exile in the Netherlands for many years. Also, his very engaging volume Al-Tafkir fi Zaman Al-Takfir (Trying to Think in an Age of Apostatization) (Cairo, 1995).

(b) Syria's Muhammad Shahrur and his semantically and linguistically based radical re-interpretation of Islam, Shari'a and the Koran, mainly in his first book: The Book and the Koran: A Contemporary Reading (Damascus, 1990). Shahrur's work provoked censure, attack and refutations from orthodox and fundamentalist Islam (a Shahrur "Reader" is now available in English: The Qur'an, Morality and Critical Reason: The Essential Muhammad Shahrur (Brill 2009)).

(c) Algeria's Mohammad Arkoun (1928-2012) and his attempt to apply French discourse theory and postmodern semiotic methods and approaches to the re-reading of the Koran, Shari'a and Islam in general. Arkoun's books also incited much heat from the orthodoxy while shedding much light within contemporary Islamic thought.

It is especially telling and noteworthy that none of these three theological thinkers emerged from the traditional centers of Islamic learning, and that nothing that has emerged from those traditional centers has approached the works of these three thinkers in terms of political courage or intellectual interest.

Sadik Al-Azm
Berlin, October, 2014

Introduction

(First Edition 1969)

The reader will find in the following pages a collection of studies that undertake, I hope, a contemporary, secular, and scientific examination of several aspects of the religious thought that still prevails, in various and sundry ways, in the Arab world today. I need not add that this kind of thought dominates, to a great extent, the mental and emotional life of Arabs, whether implicitly and unconsciously or explicitly and consciously.

The method I have employed in composing these studies relies on approaching "religious thought" in one of its specific meanings: deliberate, conscious, intellectual productions in the area of religion, as expressed openly by a number of writers, institutions, and advocates. This sense of "religious thought" is only the conscious surface layer of the gelatinous, amorphous mass of ideas, conceptions, beliefs, objectives, and customs that we give names like the "religious mentality," "supernatural ideology," or "salafist spiritual mentality," etc. In this sense, the "religious mentality" is characterized by the dominance of spontaneous acceptance of and unconscious submission to the confines of the prevailing and implicit "supernatural ideology."

Among the chief functions of the deliberate and conscious intellectual production of religious thought are the elucidation of the contents of the implicit supernatural ideology, theorizing, justifying, and rationalizing its contents by giving them a consistent, coherent, and orderly appearance. In other words, it aims to raise religious ideology, as much as possible, from the unconscious, spontaneous, and implicit to something resembling the clear, organized, intellectual, conscious, and logical. In contrast to the functions *[A 7]* performed by religious thought, there is analytic, scientific thinking that is presumed to practice, among other things, constant criticism of the prevailing supernatural ideology at every level. What is the state of the latter type of thought in contemporary Arab intellectual life?

After the Arab defeat in June 1967, a number of progressive Arab writers undertook a critique of some aspects of the intellectual and traditional social structures of Arab social life, and their legacy. However, most of the time, the critique of the superstructure and higher layers of life in Arab society (thought, culture, legislation, implicit supernatural ideology, etc.) remained feeble and weak. Especially feeble was the treatment of the "religious mentality," although everyone acknowledges its importance, its comprehensiveness, and the seriousness of its influence. In truth, most of the criticism did not surpass the repeating of some broad generalizations and exhausted clichés in denouncing the "helpless supernatural mentality" and "faith in the supernatural, myths, and belief in miraculous solutions," along with the imploring of the Arab people and its leaders to adopt a "scientific attitude" and a "rational methodology" in dealing with affairs, and to erect a contemporary technocratic state!

However, none of these critics and implorers proceeded to undertake a critique of the supernatural religious mentality that they rejected, based on a direct, rational, scientific examination of the living and tangible instances of its productions, claims, and explanations of events. I hope that I am not entirely wrong when I say that I have tried in the following studies to practice this kind of concrete criticism of the religious thought that is so common to Arab public opinion.

On the other hand, it became clear as well, after the defeat of 1967, that religious ideology, whether conscious or spontaneous, is the basic "ideological weapon" of Arab reaction in its open war and secret maneuverings against the progressive and revolutionary forces in the Arab world. Some progressive Arab regimes even found in religion a crutch to lean on for pacifying the Arab masses and for concealing their failure and impotence as exposed by the defeat, by going along with the religious and spiritualistic explanations given, then, for the victory of Israel and the defeat of the Arabs; and by remaining silent concerning the resignation, at the time, to awaiting a new victory from the Almighty.[1] Another progressive regime found in religion an effective demagogic instrument to console and pacify the masses concerning the defeat with all its dimensions, consequences, and means of countering it, as happened with the story of the miracle [A 8] of the apparition of the Virgin in Egypt last year (1968). The reader will learn from these studies how religious thought plays its role as "the ideological weapon" mentioned above by falsifying reality and the consciousness of its truths: a) falsifying the truth about the relationship between Islam and modern science; b) falsifying the truth about the relationship between religion and any type of political regime (for example, the formula, then, of a socialism that is Arab, scientific, Muslim, believing and revolutionary all at the same time; c) falsifying the truth about the strict revolutionary classification of enemies and friends in international relations during this current critical stage (at the Islamic Summit Conference, for example); d) falsifying the truth about the current social struggle in the Arab world between the rising revolutionary social forces and obstructive reactionary ones, between the trampled, exploited forces of rebellion and the forces of the dominant ruling class (for example, in the calls to build bridges between the classes in the name of righteousness, reconciliation, love, and other spiritual values). This process of falsification undoubtedly works to the benefit of a group of narrow, dominant class interests, striving desperately to maintain itself and its status by imposing its religious ideology and its deceptive mythological perspective on society as a whole and on the entirety of its intellectual and cultural life.

Everyone knew that religious thought was an ideological weapon in the hands of the Arab reactionaries and their allies across the world even

---

1   On June 7, 1967, in the heat of the ongoing battle, President Abdel Nasser sent a telegram to King Hussein that, in part, read: "In the history of nations there is give and take, progress and regress. May whatever we choose in this decisive moment, even if the choice is harsh for us, be a step from which we can advance. This is the will of God and perhaps there is something good in His will for us. We believe in God and that He cannot abandon us, and perhaps in the days that follow He will give us victory." Sa'd Jum'ah, *Al-Mu'amarah wa Ma'rakat al-Masir [The Conspiracy and the Battle of Destiny]* (Beirut: Dar al-Katib al-Arabi, 1968), 239–240.

before the defeat of 1967. However, the Arab liberation movement never concerned itself with the obligation to confront intellectually and scientifically this weapon by means of a critical scientific analysis, exposing the types of falsification and alienation that religious ideology had imposed on the Arabs. This conservative attitude is part of a general lack of enthusiasm on the part of the Arab liberation movement and its political and intellectual leadership for criticizing the Arab social and intellectual heritage and re-evaluating its superstructural levels against the great material changes taking place in the infrastructural levels of society. The Arab liberation movement considered the upper cultural layers—along with what they contain of backward mental habits, values dating back to nomadism and feudalism, deeply regressive human relationships, and quietistic, apathetic, supernatural life-views—as worthy of its respect and veneration. It granted them an aura of holiness that pushed them beyond the reach of scientific criticism and historical analysis.

The Lebanese thinker Munah al-Sulh identified this phenomenon and gave it the following clear diagnosis: "one of the things that damaged the Arab revolution was the extreme simplification in the understanding and application of the idea that 'If you change the economic and social condition of man, then man himself changes.'" Munah al-Sulh elaborated on this in the following way: "We cannot say: If the economic and social conditions have undergone change, then man's view of himself, life, and the world will also have changed. This is an illusion; for a cultural and intellectual effort is required to complement the economic and social effort in order to hasten the achievement of correspondence between the thought and the interest it represents." He then exposed the failure of the progressive Arab regimes as the representatives of the Arab liberation movement, by saying: "The progressive regimes have yet to address in a deep manner the mind and conscience of the individual and this is why the mind and conscience have yet to *[A 9]* change in the same proportion as the social and economic conditions have changed."² The phenomenon that Munah al-Sulh defines with clarity and

---

2   "Al-hazima wa al-thawra" ["The Defeat and The Revolution"], an interview with Munah al-Sulh, *Mawaqif* [*Positions*] magazine, (Beirut: May-June, 1969), 154–155.

precision is known in Marxist circles as the deviation of "economism." The danger of this inclination lies in how it leads to "tail-ism," where one part of the general social whole (the superstructure) becomes merely a negative and ineffective mechanical appendage of the other part (the base) of the same whole. However, sound revolutionary practice requires a dialectical view of the complex social whole that takes into serious consideration every layer and structure in the "whole" as something constantly active and entailing shifts in the basic centers of contradiction among them. Consequently, these shifts require constant revolutionary effort to exert pressure on the social whole (in differing degrees) and to deal seriously with all layers and levels, particularly the superstructural ones, since they are more likely to be the object of neglect. Thus, the importance of what Munah al-Sulh said about the role of the intellectual and cultural efforts that complement the changes in the lower levels, a role that the Arab liberation movement had ignored and neglected in its visions and plans.

When we push this analysis to its furthest extent it becomes clear that the error that the Arab liberation movement made was not how it drifted into the current of the "economistic deviation," as it appeared at first, but how it introduced a novel distortion into the "economistic deviation" itself. If the Arab liberation movement had only fallen into the deviation of "economism," then it would have changed the economic and social conditions and then awaited an automatic matching change in "man's view of himself, life, and the world," in the words of Munah al-Sulh, without the need for further revolutionary effort or struggle. The fact is, however, that the Arab liberation movement did change some of the Arab social and economic conditions but then, at the same time, placed all available obstacles and impediments in the way of any complementary changes and developments in the Arab's mind and conscience, and in his "view of himself, life, and the world." Even the "tail-ism" of the "economistic deviation" was undesirable to the Arab liberation movement, both officially and in the thinking and practice of its intellectual and political leadership. The "extreme simplification" in understanding the dimensions of the idea of changing man for which Munah al-Sulh reproached the Arab liberation movement is nothing but an expression of the "tail-ism" distortion (related to the economistic deviation) and the determination of the liberation movement to preserve the superstructural layers of the social whole as they are. Nevertheless, some adjustments at the superstructural level did take place, *[A 10]* some imposed by urgent necessity because of their very direct relation with the success of vital economic changes, and some imposed merely by the passage of time and the accumulation of partial changes that are transformed afterwards into a clear qualitative change.

In other words, the liberation movement stood "on its head instead of its feet" (whereas "economism" stands on its feet but in an unstable, skewed manner) in the sense that it wanted to place the revolutionary changes that it introduced into the economic situation and some of the social conditions, along with the benefits drawn from modern science and technology, in the service of the dominant social relationships, class divisions, and prevailing ideological trends. All of this instead of expecting, at the least, the emergence of the necessary changes in the superstructure that would match the economic changes, and the like, that took place in the infrastructural elements. This standing "on the head instead of the feet"[3] finds expression, for example, in the Arab liberation movement's cultural policies, for example, and also in its very superficial and conservative concern with heritage, tradition, values, and religious thought, all of which led to the obstruction of the desired changes in the Arab himself "and in his view of himself, life, and the world." Under the pretext of protecting the traditions, values, art, religion, and mores of the people, the cultural effort of the liberation movement was converted into the preservation of the supernatural ideology, its regressive institutions, its culture stemming from the Middle Ages, and its mode of thinking resting on the falsification of facts and reality.

In addition to this inverted stance, the liberation movement abstracted the "colonialist factor" in the life of the Arab nation from the

---

3   This inverted stance has, no doubt, its radical social causes and specific class explanations. However, I am not concerned here with explaining the phenomenon but only describing and diagnosing it.

sum of historical conditions and Arab social circumstances with which it was intertwined and surrounded to such a degree that "colonialism" emerged as the sole immediate reality standing over and steering the course of events in the region. In other words, there was a basic imbalance in how the liberation movement viewed itself and its society and how it viewed its enemies and the outside world in general. This process of abstraction simplified to no end the complicated historical reality and to such an extent that "colonialism" (and sometimes world Zionism) emerged as the one force controlling, directly or indirectly, the movement of Arab society and the environment provoking its reactions. This shortcoming led to an almost total neglect of the superstructural forces, institutions, organizations, and mental efforts that are always present in the Arab social whole and continually affect its life, and that play a great role in determining its reactions and its individual and collective patterns of behavior. Indeed, the other side of abstracting the colonialist relation in this way is the chauvinistic acceptance of the great idealist delusion that the ideology of the supernatural and *[A 11]* the conscious religious thought that emerges from it (along with the values, customs, and traditions attendant on it) is the product of the true, authentic, and pure Arab spirit that has been constant across the ages, never having been affected by changing economic conditions, social forces that rise and recede, or class structures that are subject to constant historical change, possessing only a relative stability.

Therefore, I hope that this book will be a modest first step towards eliminating this and similar delusions. It goes without saying that traveling this road will be long and onerous for any Arab with revolutionary socialist persuasions.

Sadik al-Azm
Beirut, October 1969

Chapter One

Scientific Culture
and the Poverty of Religious Thought

Cure me with that which was itself the disease.

Before I broach the main part of the subject, I would like make some introductory observations to clarify the purpose and contours of this study.[1]

1) When I speak about religion in this study, I do not mean it in the sense of a purely spiritual phenomenon associated with the lives of the few, such as saints, mystics, and some philosophers. By religion I mean a tremendous power that penetrates the core of our lives, that influences our essential mental and psychological structures, that determines our way of thinking about and reacting to the world in which we live, and that forms an integral part of the behaviors and habits with which we grew up.

Therefore, we shall consider religion as the complex of doctrines, regulations, ceremonies, rituals, and institutions that circumscribe the life of a human being, in some cases almost entirely. Religion also comprises a large number of stories, myths, tales, and opinions about the emergence of the world

---

1 I presented a part of this study as part of lecture at the Arab Cultural Club in Beirut. Refer to the club's magazine *Al-Thiqafat al-'Arabiyyah* [*The Arab Culture*], May 1965.

and its structure, about the origins of man and his destiny, and about history, its events, and those who played a role in steering those events. Religion enters the innermost life of the great majority of people in this manner and not as a pure spiritual essence that touches, in fact, only the few. *[A 13]*

2) When writing about faith or belief in this study, I do not mean the faith of the elderly or the phenomenon of naïve, simple surrender that characterizes the position of most people in everything that touches on their religion. I am concerned here with a contemporary person (let us call him "X") who inherited Islam with all its doctrines, stories, myths, and tales as an essential part of his intellectual and psychological formation. Since "X" is self-aware and enjoys some degree of sensitivity, he attempts to examine closely the foundations on which his inherited doctrines rest as a condition of accepting them. He also tries to elucidate the extent to which these doctrines are compatible with other convictions he has acquired from sources outside that tradition. Thus, "X" must confront the following question: Can I persist in accepting these inherited doctrines when they are not consistent with the other convictions I have acquired without betraying the principle of intellectual integrity and without sacrificing the unity of my thoughts and their internal cohesion? My study also concerns a contemporary Arab society that inherited religion as an integral part of its existence and yet attempts to reject the phenomenon of naïve, simple surrender and to examine closely the foundations on which its inheritance rests through its intellectuals, scholars, writers, and artists, particularly when they have progressive and revolutionary convictions. "X," the subject of this study, does not have a concrete existence, but is a construct, and thus an abstraction. However, from another point of view, "X" is, to some extent and to varying degrees, every one of us and therefore a matter of great importance to us.

Towards the end of the 19th century, the philosopher William James published a study that gained wide fame under the title "The Will to Believe." In it he tries to defend the right of a person who grew up amidst a modern scientific culture to religious belief. His thesis is that scientific evidence and rational argument are insufficient in themselves to confirm the existence or non-existence of God. Thus, a person has the right to hold a position that is compatible with his emotions and feelings and to disregard his scientific and logical incapacity to settle the issue decisively.

The questions that should stir our concern are the following: Why did James address this problem at the end of the 19th century? Why did he provide this kind of answer? Is there anything more obvious and firmly established than that the universe has an Almighty, Most Wise, All-Hearing, and Most Generous Creator (along with all the other characteristics we are used to attributing to Him)? Is it possible to doubt that the astonishing system of nature requires an organizer, that products require producers? Do not these considerations create definitive and tangible evidence about the existence of a creator for this universe? Are not the religious scholars and theologians of the revealed religions able to infer with ease the existence of God by considering Him the first cause of all things? Are they not able to prove that the soul is immortal and that God performs miracles, bringing old bones to life *[A 14]* and calling His creations to account on Judgment Day?

James clearly does not believe that the scholars and philosophers of religion have succeeded in these attempts. Nor does he believe that the natural system suffices to prove the existence of God, or else why does he resort to the emotional nature of man to decide the issue and provide an answer to his perplexing question?

Let us reformulate our question: How do we explain the transition from a sharply affirmative attitude towards religion, as exhibited by the scholars and philosophers, to one of apprehension and hesitation, as expressed by William James? How do we explain this transition from the old position, one flush with intellectual confidence and spiritual optimism, to the new position heavy with hesitation and indecision concerning religion and religious doctrines, knowing that James was not expressing his personal opinion alone but rather was reflecting the mood and culture of twentieth-century civilization? What happened during the period that separates the position of religious scholars and classical philosophers from that of James that forced him to consider the issue of religion as an emotional one falling outside the scope of science and the intellect?

The answer to these important questions is summarized in five developments experienced by the peoples of the Mediterranean Basin, and their neighbors:

1. The Renaissance Movement that started out in Italy in the fifteenth century and spread to every corner of Europe.
2. The Scientific Revolution, which officially started with the publication of Nicolaus Copernicus' book about the solar system and reached its peak with the publication of Isaac Newton's book *The Mathematical Principles of Natural Philosophy*.
3. The Industrial Revolution that began in the seventeenth century and continues until today.
4. The publication of Charles Darwin's book entitled *On the Origin of Species* in 1859 and Karl Marx's book entitled *Capital* in 1867.
5. The intense interaction between these four movements and their spread beyond the European continent. Indeed, those who do not reside in Europe, and especially the Arabs, have inherited the results, products, and influences of these movements in a much more condensed form. We are undergoing right now the great transformation that descended on Europe over a period that exceeded three centuries, but at a stunning speed and in a brief period.

The old religious position, once flush with serenity and optimism, is on its way to total disintegration. We are passing through the stage of an important renaissance: a total scientific and cultural upheaval along with a radical industrial and socialist transformation. For we have been strongly affected by the two most important books published during the last two centuries: *Capital* and *On the Origin of Species*. For us, the strict and positive attitude towards religion and its problems has perished. It vanished with the remnants of traditional feudal society shredded by the machine and disintegrated to the bone by modern forms of social and economic organization. *[A 15]*

Two problems loom large in this frantic atmosphere: the first is of a general cultural and intellectual nature and has to do with the conflict between science and religion (which, in our case, is primarily Islam). The second is more particular and concerns those whose culture has been influenced radically by the scientific culture that has permeated their society and environment, forcing them to confront, once again, a simple question: "Can I accept, in all honesty and sincerity, the religious doctrine of my forefathers without betraying the principle of intellectual integrity?" This is the question latent in James' article and his queries.

There is a widespread opinion that claims that the conflict between science and religion is only apparent and that the conflict between scientific knowledge and religious beliefs is merely superficial. The proponents of this opinion also claim that the spirit of Islam as such cannot enter into conflict with science and that the conflicts cited are really between science and the outer husk that has thickened around its spirit and obscures its view. I want to elaborate a little in order to examine this view, criticize it, and explain the opposing point of view, that religion, as it has entered the heart of our lives and as it influences our psychological and intellectual formation, is entirely at odds with science and scientific knowledge, in spirit and in word.

First: We need to keep in mind that in Europe science required more than two-and-a-half centuries before it was able to triumph fully and decisively in its long war against the religious mentality that had dominated this continent and finally establish its place in its cultural heritage. Science is still fighting a similar battle in most developing countries, including the Arab world, a battle that continues out of sight and only manifests itself to all sporadically.

Second: The Islamic religion includes opinions and doctrines on the development, structure, and nature of the universe, and on the origin, history, and life of man through the ages that are integral to it. I need not stress that these opinions and doctrines are clearly at odds with scientific knowledge on these topics. However, these conflicts over particular beliefs concerning particular subjects are less significant than the deeper conflict concerning the recommended method for gaining knowledge and conviction concerning these subjects, or the means of ascertaining the veracity or falsehood of these beliefs. Here, Islam and science diverge completely. For Islam (as for other religions), the correct methodology for arriving at knowledge and conviction is to return to specified texts considered sacred or revealed, or to go back to the writings of the wise men and legal scholars who studied and explained these texts. As for the justification of the process as a whole, it rests on faith and blind trust in the wisdom and infallibility of the sources of these texts. *[A 16]*

It goes without saying that the scientific path to knowledge and conviction concerning the development and nature of the universe and man and his history is entirely incompatible with the deferential methodology that prevails in religion. For the scientific method rests on observation and inference and its sole criteria for truth is the degree of internal logical coherence and conformity with reality.

Third: Among the essential matters stressed by the Islamic religion is that all the basic facts that touch the core of man's life and all the knowledge connected with his destiny in this life and the next were revealed at one specific and decisive moment in history (the revelation of the Qur'an and perhaps other books that preceded it). For this reason we find that the gaze of believers is always directed backwards to that time in which they believe that God revealed these truths and this knowledge through angels and messengers. As a result, the role of the believer, sage, philosopher, and scholar is not to discover new essential truths or gain important fresh knowledge. It is, rather, to work towards a deeper view and more comprehensive understanding of the revealed texts, tying together and interpreting their parts so as to reinterpret the interpretations in order to extract the buried meanings and bring the facts and knowledge hidden in them since eternity to the surface. This work is necessary and indispensable, based on the Qur'anic verse: "Nothing have we omitted from the Book."[2] Hence, we should not be surprised to find that the intellectual history of religion is always composed of interpretations and explanations, and explanations of explanations of explanations. The scientific spirit is far removed from this logic and religious view: science does not acknowledge the existence of texts that are not subject to objective criticism and rigorous

---

2   *Qur'an* 6:38. Trans. Abdullah Yusuf Ali.

study. The most conspicuous characteristic of scientific activity is the notion of discovery. It is what makes science a dynamic discipline that constantly goes beyond its previous achievements. When the dynamic spirit of science weakens and the logic of discovery fades, science and the scientific methodology will be ready to expire. As for religion, because of the nature of its firm, stable, and circumscribed beliefs it still lives among eternal verities and looks backward to seek inspiration in its infancy. Thus it has always provided the metaphysical and obscurantist justification for the social, economic, and political status quo, and it has always formed and continues to form the best bulwark against those who expend great efforts to make a revolutionary change.[3]

Religion was in Europe an ally of the feudal organization of social relations and still plays this role in most of the backward countries, especially in the Arab world. In fact, Islam has become the official ideology for the reactionary, backward forces within the Arab world and outside of it *[A 17]* (Saudi Arabia, Indonesia, Pakistan) and is overtly and directly tied with the new colonialism steered by the United States. Religion is also the chief source of the justification of monarchical regimes since it has promulgated rulings stating that the right of the monarch to rule is derived from the heavens not the earth. It has also become the primary ally of the bourgeois capitalist economy and the chief defender of the belief in private property and its sanctity so that it and its institutions have become one of the strongest bulwarks of rightist and reactionary thought. Religion is predisposed to play this conservative role and has played it in every era with brilliant success by means of its utopian notion of another world in which dreams of happiness come true. All of this applies as much to Islam as to other religions.

There is a similarity between religion and science in that both attempt to interpret events and determine causes. Religion is an imaginary substitute to science: the problem arises when religion claims for itself and

---

3   This does not prevent religion form being revolutionary and progressive when it first
     spreads, depending on the historical period it appears in.

its doctrines a kind of truth that is not possible for an imaginary substitute. The attempt to efface the contours of the conflict between religion and science is nothing more than a desperate attempt to defend religion, one that religion resorts to whenever it is forced to surrender one of its traditional standpoints or when it is forced to withdraw from an outpost it previously occupied.

This process occurs in a familiar manner: it begins with a violent collision on some subject between the new scientific vision and the more widely accepted religious vision. After a conflict that might last for many years, the new scientific vision wins the battle, prevailing among the major thinkers and spreading throughout the intellectual classes, at which point science is about to pass to a better view. At that time, the supporters of the religious perspective claim that the conflict was unnecessary from the very start because the discord was never between the essence and spirit of religion, on the one hand, and science, on the other, and that religion does not incur any harm in surrendering to science on issues that do not affect its spirit. It would be fair to state, however, that this line of thinking covers up a long series of important and decisive retreats that religion had to make when it was confronted with science. Despite this pretty language about the spirit of religion and its essence, religion has never retreated in the face of science before fighting a brutal battle, or under increasing pressure from modern scientific culture, or because of the dire necessity to adapt to the wave of secularism and progress that eventually force themselves on the life of societies.

Let us touch upon the nature of this disparity between the old religious vision and the scientific vision that supplanted it. We shall look at a specific example that clearly demonstrates the manner in which scientific research guides us towards convictions and rationales that are incompatible with the prevailing religious beliefs and rationales, and which will compel us to make a definitive and final choice.

The reader is surely familiar with the traditional Islamic explanation of the nature, development, and fate of the universe: God created this universe during a specific period by ordering it to be, and it was. The reader will also recall how the expulsion of Adam and Eve from Paradise marked the beginning of man's history on earth. At the heart of religious doctrine is that God cares for his creatures, hears their prayers, sometimes answers their *[A 18]* supplications, and from time to time interferes in the natural system in the shape of miracles. As for nature, it has maintained its central characteristics since God created it, that is, it still contains the same celestial bodies and animal and plant species since creation day. Scientific theory, however, neither acknowledges creation from nothing nor a nature unchanged since its beginnings. The contemporary British scientist and philosopher Bertrand Russell expressed this scientific view in a beautiful literary piece entitled "A Free Man's Worship"[4] in the following words:

> To Dr. Faustus in his study Mephistopheles told the history of the Creation, saying:
>
> "The endless praises of the choirs of angels had begun to grow wearisome; for, after all, did he not deserve their praise? Had he not given them endless joy? Would it not be more amusing to obtain undeserved praise, to be worshipped by beings whom he tortured? He smiled inwardly, and resolved that the great drama should be performed.
>
> For countless ages the hot nebula whirled aimlessly through space. At length it began to take shape, the central mass threw off planets, the planets cooled, boiling seas and burning mountains heaved and tossed, from masses of cloud hot sheets of rain deluged the barely solid crust. And now the first germ of life grew in the depths of the ocean, and developed rapidly in the fructifying warmth into vast forest trees, huge germ springing from the damp mould, sea monsters breeding, fighting, devouring, and passing away. And from the monsters, as the play unfolded itself, Man was born, with the power of thought, the knowledge of good and evil, and the cruel thirst for worship. And Man saw that all is passing in this mad, monstrous world, that all is struggling to snatch, at any cost, a few brief moments of life before Death's inexorable decree. And Man said: 'There is a

---

4   "A Free Man's Worship," in *Mysticism and Logic* (London: Allen and Unwin, 1951), 41.

hidden purpose, could we but fathom it, and the purpose is good; for we must reverence something, and in the visible world there is nothing worthy of reverence.' And Man stood aside from the struggle, resolving that God intended harmony to come out of chaos by human efforts. And when he followed the instincts which God had transmitted to him from his ancestry of beasts of prey, he called it Sin, and asked God to forgive him. But he doubted whether he could be justly forgiven, until he invented a divine Plan by which God's wrath was to have been appeased. And seeing the present was bad, he made it yet worse, that thereby the future might be better. And he gave God thanks for the strength that enabled him to forgo even the joys that were possible. And God smiled; and when he saw that Man had become perfect in renunciation and worship, he sent another sun through the sky, which crashed into Man's sun; and all returned again to nebula.

"'Yes,' he murmured, 'it was a good play; I will have it performed again.'" *[A 19]*

This extract from Russell summarizes the natural scientific view on the following issues: the development of the universe and its evolution; the development of life and its evolution; the origin of man and his development and evolution; and the development and evolution of religions, forms of worship, and rituals. Finally, he stresses that evanescence and nothingness are the inevitable end of all things, where no hope remains for any living thing: from the nebula it has come and to nebula it shall return.

On another occasion, when Russell was asked if there was a life for humans after death, his answer was negative and he explained it as follows: Upon examining this question from a scientific point of view and not through the mist of emotions, we find it difficult to discover a rational justification for the continuation of life after death. It seems to me that the widespread belief that we live after dying has no scientific support or basis. I do not think that such a belief would have developed and spread but for the emotional repercussions that the fear of death causes within us. There is no doubt that our belief that we shall meet in the hereafter those whom we love is our greatest consolation at their death. However, I do not find any justification for our assumption that the universe is concerned with our hopes and wishes. We, therefore, have no right to ask the universe to accommodate itself to our emotions and hopes, and I do not consider it right and wise to embrace opinions that are not based on clear scientific evidence.

Let us attempt a comparison between this cold, harsh, and bare scientific theory and the warm, comforting, and beautiful Islamic religious story with which we are familiar. We find that transcendental powers, angels, prayers, miracles, and spirits comprise an integral part of the religious explanation of the development and nature of the universe. The same applies to the history of man and his destiny. As for the scientific view, it was best expressed by the French philosopher and mathematician Pierre-Simon LaPlace when he offered his book *The System of the World* to Napoleon. The Emperor asked him: "What place does God occupy in your system?" La Place replied: "God is a hypothesis that I do not need in my system." Is it then surprising to hear Nietzsche in the past century announcing the death of God? Can we deny that the god that died in Europe is at the point of death everywhere under the influence of scientific knowledge, industrial progress, rational methodologies for pursuing knowledge, and revolutionary trends in society and the economy? Of course, when we agree with Nietzsche that God has died or is dying, we do not mean that religious doctrines have faded from the conscience of people but rather that the scientific understanding of the universe, society, and man is free from the mention of God, just as LaPlace stated.

Stating that God is dying in backward societies symbolizes the state of revolution, ferment, and dislocation that these societies are suffering in their attempt to reach a kind of provisional balance between the new scientific ideas (and their practical and industrial applications) and their remote religious heritage without renouncing entirely and all at once the transcendental values of their past.

Hence, we always hear these loud echoes: Even if we were to *[A 20]* surrender entirely to the scientific perspective, the problem of the original source of the universe would still remain. Assuming with Russell that the universe began from the nebula does not inform us about the source of that nebula: it does not explain to us the source of the original matter from which everything developed. Eventually, science must meet religion.

However, posing this question in such a way reveals to us the extent to which our religious upbringing and obscurantist heritage controls our thinking. Let us assume that we concede that God is the source of the original matter. Is the problem solved? Does this assumption answer our question about the source of the original nebula? No, of course. You ask after the cause of the original nebula and reply that it is God, and I ask you, in turn, what is the cause of the existence of God? You will answer that God is uncaused. Here I will reply why don't we assume that the original matter is uncaused and close the subject without recourse to the transcendental world and spiritual creatures whose own existence is unproved?

The ancient philosophers, including the Muslim ones, always leaned towards this opinion when they spoke about the eternity of the world. However, they were compelled to be evasive and agreeable due to the religious fanaticism against the philosophical view of this subject. In fact, we need to confess in all modesty our ignorance about all issues pertaining to the problem of the original source of the universe. When you tell me that God is the cause of the original matter from which the universe is composed and I ask you, in turn, what is the cause of God, the fullest answer you can provide is "I only know that God is uncaused." When you ask me about the cause of the original matter, the fullest answer I can provide is "I only know that it is uncaused." In the end, each one of us acknowledges his ignorance regarding the original source of things. However, you needed a step more than I did, and you introduced transcendental elements unnecessary for solving this problem.

In summary, whether we state that the original matter is eternal and uncaused or that God is eternal and uncaused, we will have acknowledged that we do not and will not know how to solve the problem of the original source of things. It is better, then, to confess our ignorance frankly and directly instead of in roundabout ways using pompous words and phrases. There is no disgrace in acknowledging our ignorance since the frank acknowledgement of what we do not know is one of the most important elements of scientific thinking. You know that a scientist is obliged to suspend judgment when he lacks sufficient evidence, testimony, or proof to corroborate or disprove a matter. This is the minimal necessary condition of intellectual integrity in the rigorous search for knowledge and truth.

After treating in some detail the issue of scientific culture and religious belief at the level of the conflict between religion and science, I want to shift now to treating the subject at the level of what we called the particular problem. The question around which our study revolves can be summarized as follows: How will someone who has been exposed to scientific culture and been radically affected by it regard religious and traditional doctrines and the institutions that embody them? Can he persist in believing in Adam and Eve, heaven and hell, and that Moses divided the Red Sea and transformed his staff into a serpent? How will someone who had *[A 21]* a religious upbringing and accepted it thoroughly regard a natural-scientific view of life, universe, and man? It is difficult to find someone among us who enjoys a bit of sensitivity or just a modest share of intelligence and scientific education who does not feel at some stage of his life and development the tension that surrounds this question and the worry it provokes. The intellectual and psychological state that this question expresses has become a basic part of our makeup. Sometimes it floats on the surface of consciousness and we feel its existence strongly. Other times it hides deep in our selves where it affects our conduct and thought imperceptibly but effectively.

For example, I have noticed that students I have known through my profession as a teacher were affected by this issue and suffered from the anxiety and disquiet that these questions provoked. However, they were unable to identify the issue that was the source of their intellectual anxiety and disquiet, and it remained at the level of murky and repressed feelings for them. I noticed also that a certain minority of these students unconsciously sought a solution to this problem by recourse to a religious perspective that was dogmatic and extreme in its fanaticism and excessive in its adherence to the minutiae of religious observances. This minority expressed on every occasion its boundless hostility to any progressive or scientific thoughts and its rejection of any critical perspective on its heritage and anything that disturbed the ways of traditional life. I also noticed that another minority of these students took the opposite direction, being unusually receptive to progressive and secular thinking and to scientific culture in general. It became clear to me that although the doubts that afflicted them concerning religious doctrines and the heritage hovering behind them were increasing with time, they were unable to clearly express their perspectives, emotions, and doubts, which only further entrenched the problem. As for the remaining majority of the students with whom I became familiar, they were vacillating aimlessly between the two groups. They felt the problem but only unconsciously, having murky intimations that went unacknowledged. Their general attitude was characterized by indifference and apathy.

On several occasions I asked some of them: Don't you sometimes feel the existence of clear contradictions between what you are learning in your philosophy and science classes and what you are learning in your religion classes? They all answered in the affirmative. Then I asked them: What do you do when you are confronted with such contradictions? They replied that although it silently disturbed them, they, for practical reasons, just repeated to their religion teacher what he had taught them and repeated to their science teacher what he had taught them, or else they would fail the exam. As for serious thinking about these contradictions and the connection between the two sets of views, it was not an issue for them. This schizophrenia is a very dangerous phenomenon since if it swelled and surged it could generate a kind of intellectual and practical paralysis that could preclude someone from being productive and effective, even if this kind of cognitive disintegration and artificial isolation among thoughts and information does not lead to the blunting of the growth of systematic objective scientific thinking *[A 22]* in the students. Let us go back to our initial question, which has to do with how someone who has been exposed to scientific culture will regard religion, and how someone with a religious upbringing will regard science. I will dedicate the remainder of my study to address some of the answers or solutions provided for this question, evaluating each in turn.

The First Solution

The first solution is the attempt to reconcile inherited religious doctrines and scientific views and knowledge. This solution includes some concessions made by religion to science on the condition it retains its principles and essential doctrines intact. This is an example of a general phenomenon that flourishes whenever there is a clash and struggle in history between two ideological systems that differ in how they conceive reality, the universe, and man—the phenomenon of reconciliatory thinking that attempts to bring into harmony incompatible systems and contradictory thoughts and that can only succeed by distorting and obscuring the matters to be reconciled. This kind of thinking is of special concern to us because Arab and Islamic thinking is infatuated by it and Arab and Muslim thinkers have been fearless in engaging in reconciliatory thinking. The most important of these is the classical attempt to reconcile reason and faith or wisdom and the Sharia. Among the characteristics of modern reconciliatory thinkers is garrulity concerning the spirit of religion and how it is truly progressive and in full harmony with modern scientific methodology. Some of these thinkers go as far as deriving scientific methodology from the spirit of Islam. Likewise, we find them going on about basing religious doctrines on new principles that harmonize and keep pace with the scientific view of things. These attempts have always failed in the past and I have no doubt that they must fail in our time too due to the following considerations:

To a great extent, religious doctrines form a cohesive, internally consistent systems, and thus if you accept one part you must accept the rest—if you wish to remain internally consistent. The moment we begin to make concessions to science or philosophy, for example, concerning some of these doctrines, we will find ourselves logically compelled to concede the balance of the religious doctrines. For example, if we renounce our belief in Adam and Eve for the scientific version of the origin of man then why not renounce also the belief in heaven and hell, since these doctrines form an indivisible part of what is revealed in the Qur'an? Moreover, if we renounce our belief in heaven and hell, how can we justify our belief in the immortality of the soul? If we follow the logical progression of these renunciations we will find ourselves, in the end, renouncing all religious doctrines, unless we make an arbitrary and capricious decision to stop at a particular point beyond which we will perform no other renunciations. Such a decision will certainly satisfy us emotionally. However, our mind cannot settle at such an arbitrary, unjustifiable decision. In other words, logical thinking requires us either not to cede any religious belief to science or to cede everything to science. As for the notion of reconciling them, it is nothing but a fable to which some thinkers in certain well-known historical periods appeal since they are neither *[A 23]* able to renounce their religious doctrines nor able to pretend to ignore science, scientific applications, and the natural view of things. Thus they find in reconciliatory thinking a means to evade the tension caused by this clash just as they find a kind of comfort in the thought of bringing harmony to the inharmonious.

It is widely recognized that the notions of reconciliation lauded in one generation appear to the following generation a naïve simplification of complicated concepts and issues and an exercise of mental acrobatics to establish contradictory doctrines and views by making them appear as other than what they are, conflicting and incompatible. Let us review some real examples from the repertoire of the great contemporary scholars of reconciliatory thinking.

Rhetorical Reconciliation

Muslim clerics and writers acknowledge that there is at least an apparent incompatibility between modern science, and its culture and methodologies, on the one hand, and Islam, and its doctrines and creeds, on the other hand. Therefore, we find that most books written by this set of thinkers begin with this acknowledgement in order to announce and accentuate that the incompatibility is only apparent since modern science and Islam are entirely harmonious and completely reconciled. One of the authors in this group begins his book with the following question: "Is there an estrangement, even if spurious, between science and religion?" His answer: "No theorist or thinker doubts the existence of an estrangement between science and religion. As for whether the estrangement is spurious, only the obstinate and imposters of science and knowledge deny it." [5]

The author, then, asserts the existence of a clash between religion and science in the Christian West:

> As for the Muslim East, the situation differs completely. There is neither a clash nor a rift between Islam and science. In the Muslim East, we are not satisfied to offer half-solutions or advocate some kind of peaceful co-existence, but we aim to eliminate the specious rift between science and religion. For religion is from God, and God is Truth, just as He called himself, and nothing emerges from the Truth but the truth, and science is the truth, and the truth is not estranged from itself. Thus, there is no estrangement between science and truth, for science is truth by the nature of things. [6] *[A 24]*

Note that this Muslim writer is ready to admit the existence of an incompatibility and estrangement between Christianity and modern science, but reluctant to admit it for Islam. This line of thinking is extremely widespread among this type of writers, whether they declare it or not. Second, note that the writer of this passage has settled the matter and drawn his conclusions about the inexistence of an estrangement between religion and modern science through a strict declarative rhetoric that plays with certain words like "truth" and "science" as if a list of rhetorical passages suffices to corroborate the truth and validity of an inference.

---

5   Muhammad Ali Yusuf, *Al-Jafwa al-Mufta'ala baina al-'Ilm wa al-Deen* [*The Spurious Estrangement between Science and Religion*] (Beirut: Dar al-Hayat, 1966), 5.
6   Ibid. 6.

Dr. Sheikh Subhi Al-Saleh makes a similar argument in the following text, trying to reconcile Islam and modern science by simply declaring it with enough rhetorical force. According to the Doctor, Islam cannot refuse:

> To test its beliefs, traditions, and revelations against reason and the objective perspective...for the simplicity of its beliefs, the straightforwardness of its conceptions, and the austerity of its meanings give Islam absolute self-confidence when its teachings are tested against analytical, historical, critical, philosophical standards. For human nature finds in the Muslim creed what conforms to its spiritual longing for discovering the unknown and its intellectual inclination to discern the value of the human being in existence and his dignity before God. The researcher finds here what comforts his heart and nerves and what pleases his thinking and philosophy regarding man and the purpose of his existence, the nature of life and its relationship with its creator, and the scope of the absolute, divine will and the motion of the human will within it...[7]

If Dr. Al-Saleh is right when he says that the researcher finds in Islam "what comforts his heart and nerves and what pleases his thinking and philosophy" about mankind, the nature of life, and freedom of will within the divine will, then the problem will have dissolved by itself and we have no need for all this clamor about the harmony of Islam with modern science, the attacks on atheism and atheists, and all this attention, argument and discussion about the problems that Muslim youth face with the challenges of contemporary life and the twentieth-century.

His Eminence Sheikh Mousa Al-Sader has the same inclination for declarative rhetoric in reconciling Islam and modern science. In a lecture entitled "Islam and the Culture of the Twentieth-Century," he states the following:

> The culture of Islam motivates human beings constantly towards advancement in the various fields of intellectual development. It

---

7   "Al-Masihiya wa al-Islam fi Lubnan: Adwa' wa Ta'amulaat" ["Christianity and Islam in Lebanon: Highlights and Meditations"] in *Al-Masihiya wa al-Islam fi Lubnan [Christianity and Islam in Lebanon]* (Beirut: Publications of the Lebanese Club, 1965), 208.

embraces everything new and all knowledge with an eager heart, regarding *[A 25]* it as an approach to God, knowledge of Him, and the fulfillment of man. Islam views science with respect and appreciation and considers it as a way for human beings to achieve the purpose of their creation, their original perfection, the office of God's deputy on earth, and knowledge of God. Therefore, progressing along this path is a sacred duty.[8]

It is clear that the words of those who promote rhetorical reconciliation always remain (by design) at the level of the general and bombastic so as not to disturb anyone or threaten anyone's position. Can anyone be against "truth," "science," and "knowledge?" It is the logic of blandishments and consolation that pleases all sides and disturbs no one. For that reason, such orators avoid dealing with any specific issue that might force them to interrupt their boasting of the virtues of Islam and its scientific merits in order to undertake a thorough investigation of the problem that has been raised. In fact, their discourse lacks the most rudimentary tools of intellectual analysis and ignores the simplest methodological rules for empirical verification and scientific thinking. Even Descartes' methodological rules for valid inquiry, which he composed in the 17th century and which are now considered rudimentary and outdated, have no influence on their rhetorical reconciliatory writings. Among those rules is to identify the problem to be solved in a definite form, to systematically divide it into the smaller parts of which it is composed, and then to work on the simpler parts before working on the more complicated parts, and so on to the rest of the Cartesian account taught even in high schools.[9]

This means that instead of making vast generalizations about Islam and science and speaking of their compatibility in broad and general terms, we should break the question of compatibility between them into specific issues and from there derive the degree of compatibility or incompatibility between them. I shall bring up a few relevant examples.

---

8   "Al-Islam wa Thaqafat al-Qarn al-'Ishreen" ["Islam and the Culture of the Twentieth Century"] in *Christianity and Islam in Lebanon*, 129, 141.

9   See Descartes *Rules for the Direction of the Mind*.

Those who claim that Islam and science are entirely compatible emphasize that Islam is a religion free from legends and superstitions, considering it and science to be one. Let us examine this allegation with some precision by carefully analyzing one specific issue. According to the Qur'an, for instance, God created Adam from clay, then ordered the angels to prostrate themselves before him, which they all did except for Satan, which is why God expelled him from paradise. Does this story constitute a legend or not? We want a definite and decisive answer from our reconciliatory orators rather than a speech. Should a Muslim, living in the second half of the twentieth-century, believe that such an incident really occurred in the history of the universe? If this Qur'anic story is entirely veracious and true to the facts and history of the world (for it is revealed), it is clearly incompatible with our scientific knowledge, and thus we must conclude that *[A 26]* modern science has gone astray in this case. However, if this Qur'anic story is not true to the facts, what can it be (for the reconciliatory orators) but a beautiful myth?

Should a Muslim today believe creatures such as jinns, angels, Satan, Harut and Marut, and Ya'juj and Ma'juj truly exist (though not always visibly) just because they are mentioned in the Holy Qur'an, or is he allowed to consider them as mythological creatures like the Greek gods, mermaids, ghouls, and griffins? How much better it would have been had these reconcilers between Islam and science handled such specific issues and stated their opinion clearly and honestly, instead of orating about the complete compatibility between Islam and science. On one occasion, His Eminence Sheikh Nadim Al-Jisser actually tried to approach the problem of angels and jinns and how belief in them conforms to modern science and its knowledge of the universe. The conclusion reached by His Eminence is summarized in the following statement:

> Imagining angels and jinns was more difficult in my time, before the discovery of the Laws of Light. Today, however, after knowing about light waves, their visible and invisible types and their many spectral regions (only one of which houses the visible world), one would have

to be stubborn and disputatious to deny the existence of angels and jinns.[10]

I am not aware of the nature of the relationship that His Eminence Sheikh Al-Jisser finds between the theory of light and the existence of jinns and angels. According to the science of physics, the speed of light waves is 300,000 kilometers per second, and these waves are natural physical (material) phenomena subject to strict mathematical measurement. How is this connected to transcendental spiritual creatures such as angels and jinns? There is no doubt that light waves appear in many spectral regions (due to the length of the wave and frequency), some visible and others invisible. However, we can ascertain the characteristics and nature of the invisible ones by means of scientific equipment that detects these waves. Does His Eminence mean to hint at the existence of scientific equipment that could detect light waves specific to angels and jinns, determining the nature of these creatures with empirical and mathematical precision?

Allow me to raise another specific case. His Eminence Sheikh Mousa Al-Sader describes the Islamic conception of the nature of the universe in the following manner:

> The universe is a single creation imbued with spirit and beauty. It is organized, balanced, proceeding towards lofty goals based on the principles of truth and justice, harmonious, its elements in concord with one another and with their Creator.[11] [A 27]

Obviously, this Islamic view of the universe is a teleological one that depends for its explanation of the nature of the universe on final causes and "lofty goals," as well as moral notions such as "truth and justice." Is such a teleological perception of the universe and life in harmony with the scientific outlook that prevails in the contemporary world and its culture? If we go back to the scientific explanations of the universe, from Newton

---

10 "Raka'iz al-Tafkir al-Islami" ["Pillars of Islamic Thought"] *Al-Nahar*, March 12, 1967, 15.

11 "Islam and the Culture of the Twentieth Century," 121.

to Einstein, do we find among their central ideas phrases like "lofty goals" or "truth and justice" or "spirit, beauty, and the Creator?" Are these religious moral concepts ever mentioned in the Theory of Relativity or Quantum Mechanics, for example? This is a question that at least deserves investigation, clarification, and explanation. However, reconciliatory orators do not like to embark on such straightforward questions for the simple reason that it would expose their rhetorical-declarative solutions to the basic issues at hand.

When we address the issue with such simplicity and specificity, it appears that there is clear contradiction between the teleological Islamic view of the universe, as recounted by His Eminence Mousa Al-Sader, and the scientific view as it crystallized with the development and advancement of modern science. Whoever reviews the history of modern science quickly discovers that its founders and philosophers waged a war without pity on the dragging of final causes and moral conceptions into scientific explanations of natural phenomena. They refused the teleological perspective entirely, considering it a product of the mythological imagination of man and an obstacle to the progress of science and the spread of natural explanations of phenomena of all kinds. We find this hostile attitude to teleology, from the outset, among the thinkers and philosophers who firmly established the foundations of modern science: from Francis Bacon to Bertrand Russell via Descartes, Spinoza, Galileo, Darwin, Pavlov, Durkheim, Freud, and Marx, and so on to the end of the long list of names. What is the clearly defined view of the reconciliatory orator on this clearly defined question? The practical translation of Dr. Subhi Al-Saleh's claim about testing Islam and its beliefs, traditions, and revelations against objective theoretical reason and analytical, historical, critical, philosophical standards begins with a clear and rigorous examination of the issues and not with the mere preemptive assertion that Islam must emerge a winner when this test takes place. For the conclusive result does not precede but follows the experiment.

Among the Qur'anic verses that reconciliatory orators love to repeat when speaking about the compatibility of Islam and modern science is the following Qur'anic description of the origin of man and his evolution:

> Man We did create from a quintessence (of clay); Then We placed him as (a drop of) sperm in a place of rest, firmly fixed; Then We made the sperm into a clot of congealed blood; then of that clot We made a (fetus) lump; then we made out of that lump bones and clothed the bones with flesh; then we developed out of it another creature. So blessed be Allah, the best to create! *(Qur'an 23: 14)*

According to this Qur'anic description, the process of the growth of the human cell depends on direct and continuous intervention by God to convey it from one stage to another. *[A 28]* In other words, the transformation from a sperm to a clot of congealed blood requires a new process of creation, and the transformation from a clot of congealed blood to an embryo requires another process of creation, and so on. In summary, the growth of the human cell is a divine miracle that has no explanation except for God's absolute ability to create and His direct intervention in the course of the world.

Does this description and account correspond to our scientific knowledge on the subject and what embryology tells us about the development of the human cell in its primary stages? Of course not. For embryology does not leave any room to doubt that the cell grows organically from one stage to another according to specific laws of nature, where the later stage grows from the core of the preceding one and on the basis of its primary givens. All this occurs in way that allows us to predict the development of the cell and the future stages it will pass through, and enables us to control its growth, whether by delaying it, speeding it up, or deforming it (if we wish to do so) by exposing it to specific chemical substances or specific types of radiation. I wish that these religious-scientific believers in reconciliation had not stopped at citing the Qur'anic description of the growth of the cell but rather continued on to clarify how this description sits with our unshakable scientific knowledge about this natural phenomenon.

Among the sayings repeated by reconciliatory orators to confirm their claim is the prophetic tradition that states "seek knowledge, even if it is in China," and various other Qur'anic verses that spur man to ponder and comprehend things and to pursue science and seek knowledge, etc. These citations are meant to demonstrate that Islam's concern for science and the intellect extends back to its beginning. Naturally, these thinkers give an absolute sense to these Islamic expressions, as if they do not belong to a particular time or place and can be separated from the historical circumstances in which they were stated and the contexts that determined their meaning and sense at that time. It is clear that the sciences that Islam spurs one to seek are in essence the religious and legal sciences, and what is associated with them or derived from them, not physics and chemistry, for example (see the Book of Knowledge in the first part of Al-Ghazali's *Revival of the Religious Sciences*).

The intellect that Islam appeals to man to use has its aim in attaining knowledge of God from pondering His works and creation, as did Hayy ibn Yaqzan in the story written by Ibn Tufayl, not in formulating the theory of dialectical materialism, Durkheim's theory on religious rituals and worship, or the theory of a curved universe. There is no harm in that. For in those days, the religious sciences were considered the most significant, the most powerful, and the ultimate goal of all those seeking knowledge.

In this regard, it is worth noting that the vast majority of these reconciliatory orators know next to nothing about modern science, its methods and methodologies for conducting research, and what we might call the "scientific breath" or "scientific spirit." However, they stand baffled and dazzled by the achievements of science and its practical applications and are compelled to interact with its products in their daily lives. Thus, they have no choice but to pronounce the perfect harmony and total compatibility between their Islam and this new awesome power *[A 29]* that moves, drives, dominates, and controls.

All that they know about modern science is that it rests on observation, experimentation, and induction. Can anyone be against observation, experimentation, and induction? Then modern science and Islam are in total harmony and concord! No wonder, then, that they fall into strange contradictions. We have already cited an excerpt from the book *The Spurious Estrangement between Science and Religion,* in which the author announces that the Muslim East has been in complete harmony with modern science since its beginnings, because God is Truth, the Truth is one, and nothing emerges from the Truth but the truth, and so on. However, the same writer states on the following page concerning the role of religion in secondary education:

> The main purpose of religious curricula, especially in secondary schools, is to detect snares and traps in the other subjects that they study—the theory of evolution in the life-sciences, universal freedoms in history classes (especially the French Revolution), that the earth is round and revolves on its axis in geography classes, and so on. The religious curriculum is the vigilant true guard that stands ready against all the forays from the armies of atheism that creep into the minds of the students from their "public" and "cultural" surroundings.[12]

The snares that the Islamic religion must detect and protect minds from are the theory of evolution in the sciences, universal freedoms in history classes, especially the French Revolution, and that the earth is round and revolves on its axis. If the facts about the roundness of the earth and how it revolves on its axis constitute a danger for the minds of Muslims then where is the total harmony and complete compatibility between the Muslim East and modern science that the author extolled on the previous page?

The Islamic thinker Sayyid Qutb displays the same contradiction, though with less naiveté. Qutb hails science and scientific methodology, on the one hand, claiming that there is an old concord between Islamic methodology and science and industrial civilization. On the other hand, he goes even further in his reconciliatory thinking and derives the scientific method of experimentation from the spirit of Islam, considering Islamic methodology the foundation for the modern scientific experimental view.

To evaluate the success of this comprehensive harmony between religion and science, we need only to follow Sayyid Qutb as he thinks. For

---

12 *The Spurious Estrangement between Science and Religion,* 8.

after boasting that Islamic methodology is the foundation of experimental methodology, he rejects entirely the most import attainments of this methodology because they contradict religious beliefs. He rejects the theory of organic evolution although it is the crown of scientific research in biology, and Freudian theory, although it is one of the most significant products of scientific research in the field of psychology. He also rejects Marxism or scientific socialism, although it is the most important comprehensive theory *[A 30]* in the social and economic sciences in the modern era. In other words, Qutb derives the foundations of scientific methodology from Islamic methodology but he wants to absolve both from the historical responsibility for what emerged from the rise of science and to reject all the consequences associated with its great advances. In a similar manner, we see that he resists everything that scientific methodology has borne in terms of social, economic, political, and scientific systems and theories despite his certainty that their historic roots extend back to Islamic methodology.[13]

It is rather entertaining to go back to what I have mentioned earlier about the inclination among this group of Muslim reconcilers to insist on the existence of a major contradiction between Christianity and modern science and their sharp denial of the existence of such a contradiction and conflict between Islam and science. However, there is a Christian thinker who contradicts the opinion of Muslim reconcilers and claims that Christianity also harmonizes completely with modern science, presenting a declarative rhetorical reconciliation between Christianity and science in the manner of the rhetorical reconciliators we mentioned. Father François Dupré La Tour states the following:

> First and foremost, I take it upon myself to demonstrate that it is impossible for us to discover any conflict between Christianity and modern science, just as the Christian authorities affirm to us whenever they get a chance. Then we see how religion supports the efforts of

---

13   See *Al-Islam wa Mushkilaat al-Hadara [Islam and the Problems of Civilization]* (Cairo: Issa Al-Babi Al-Halabi and Partners, 1962), 165.

the Christian researcher and how he, in his turn, helps the devout to observe God and pray to Him.[14]

Naturally, the existence of such a conflict between Christianity and modern science does not in any way depend on the assertions made by Father La Tour or the Christian authorities themselves, notwithstanding the forceful, emphatic, declarative tone. The establishment of the existence of contradictions depends on the factual evidence and history and not on pronouncements on the part of Christian priests or assessments made by higher church authorities.

Reality and history are just the two things that these people would like to ignore so that they can reconcile according to their whim. If there was no conflict between Christianity and modern science, as is claimed by Father La Tour, then what was the subject of the conflict between the church and science[15] that lasted three centuries? If there was no conflict between Christianity and science, *[A 31]* then why did the church burn Giordano Bruno, force Galileo to admit that the earth is fixed at the center of the universe, make such a stir (which has not yet settled down in some places) about Darwin and his theory of organic evolution, and place most scientific and philosophical books that expressed the new scientific spirit on the list of proscribed books, including the works of Descartes, who was a pious Catholic believer? Did the church do all this out a love of destruction and just to oppress and tyrannize or because its theory of the universe was in complete contradiction with the discoveries of modern science and the ideas it generated about the nature of things,

---

14 "Al-Masihiya wa al-ʿIlm al-Hadith" ["Christianity and Modern Science"] in *Christianity and Islam in Lebanon*, 76.

15 On the social level, which is the main level, the conflict was between the feudal system that found in the church its last bulwark and the middle class, whose thinking, institutions, and new organizations were rising, However, I limit myself to discussing the subject on the level of the conflict between the superstructures (scientific theories and religious doctrines) so as to be able to respond to reconciliatory figures (and other idealist and obscurantist thinkers) according to their assumptions and methods of dealing with the subject matter.

and thus it was compelled to defend its position desperately using all the means available to it? Was this brutal conflict merely a simple slip that the church discovered three hundred years later, when it suddenly became apparent that modern science did not conflict with Christianity at all? Does not our intellectual and historical integrity impose on us the frank acknowledgement that Christianity did not discover, in a moment of truth, that modern science was not in conflict with its teachings, but rather that Christianity and the church were forced to retreat continuously in their battle against these new contending powers? When it finally became clear that Christianity could not win the battle, it changed its mind about the issue and decided to join the ranks of the victorious, shifting to the camp of the supporters and heralds of modern science. The church adopted this new position because it had no choice, that is, under the pressures of need and historical necessity, not willingly in its hour of strength. It is fine if the church changes its well-known traditional stance concerning modern science in order support it. However, it rankles when it justifies this conversion through a view whose basis falsifies history and confuses the facts.

Rationalizing Reconciliation

This type of reconciliatory thinking between Islam and contemporary life is concerned with justifying the social and political conditions that exist, no matter what they may be, on the basis of their complete harmony with the true religion and its teachings and law. A league of thinkers and Islamic clerics supervise this operation of defending the status quo and its personalities and policies. They make great efforts to wrap Islamic law around the political and social order with which they are associated, no matter what it may be. We see here the conservative, and even reactionary, tendency in contemporary Islamic thought and practice.

In the Arab states that have declared a liberationist and revolutionary politics, we find that those who are responsible for the Islamic institutions there declare the total harmony of Islam with the policy of the particular state and with its political slogans "derived from the spirit and law of Islam" (according to its fatwas). For Islam is always "revolutionary" and "liberationist."

However, if *[A 32]* we take a look at the reactionary, backward Arab states that wage war against the liberationist revolutionary direction (Saudi Arabia), we find that Islamic imams there are in the vanguard of those rationalizing the policy of that reactionary state and those defending social conditions steeped in backwardness, exploiting Islamic institutions to defend and protect them. Between these two extremities, we find that every Arab system of government, no matter what type, is not lacking esteemed Islamic institutions ready to issue *fatwas* declaring that its policy is in complete harmony with Islam and contradicts it in nothing. It goes without saying that the Islamic institutions in each of these states amass Qur'anic verses, prophetic traditions, and legal opinions to demonstrate that the position of the given country is just.

Let me provide some typical examples. There is an active reconciliatory movement regarding the issue of scientific socialism and its application in the Arab world. When the Nasserist revolution in Egypt proposed its own special version of socialism (Arab socialism), thinkers undertook to prove that the socialism of the Revolution of July 23rd, 1952 emerged from the heart of our Arab tradition and our Islamic spiritual values. The religious minds and Islamic institutions in Egypt and other countries actively sought to rationalize the policy of the socialist revolution by demonstrating its complete compatibility with Islam, based on the claim that Islam is the first to have laid the foundations of a socialism that is, all at once, scientific, Arab, rightly-guided, and believing. Many articles were written clarifying that this strand of socialism is based on three principles, the first being the belief in God.[16] At this moment I do

---

16 See Dr. Salah Eddine Abd Al-Wahhab, "Al-Ishtirakiya al-'Arabiya wa Al-Ishtirakiya Al-Yaminiya" ["Arab Socialism and Right-Wing Socialisms"] in *Al-Majalla*, Cairo (Jan. & Feb. 1964), and Muhammad Ahmad Khalafallah, "Al-Qur'an al-Kareem

not remember the second principle, but I would not be surprised if it were fidelity to Adam Smith. I have no doubt that such an impure mix would not be truly palatable to the believer, and that the real socialist would not be pleased to find that one of the most important principles in his creed is the belief in God.

Continuing along the path of this rationalizing thinking, Dr. Sheikh Subhi Al-Saleh derives the socialism of the "petty bourgeoisie" proposed by the revolution in Egypt from Islam in the following manner:

> It does not deny any of the mature views that fill our volumes of Islamic jurisprudence, whether those concerned with economic systems, the principles of social justice, or a constructive, faith-based socialism that does not renounce spiritual values.[17]

Even those Arab states that swung to the extreme left (and even if this extremism has more to do with words than deeds) by declaring themselves to be popular democratic republics found a place *[A 33]* for fatwas among their tools and gear in order to rationalize their position and not only render it in harmony with Islam but derive it from the teachings of Islam, which are progressive in all times and places. In other words, it appears that Islamic teachings are wide and baggy enough to comprehend Arab socialism, Arab popular democratic republics, and regimes steeped in reaction, salafism, and backwardness like those of King Faisal in Saudi Arabia and Suharto in Indonesia.

Recently, an Islamic call was released "to establish a Caliphate and an Islamic council" because "seeking a Caliph who establishes the rule of Islam is one of the most important duties of Islam, and the Muslim who does not pledge allegiance to the Caliph deserves to suffer on earth and afterwards."[18] This call goes on to clarify its position by frankly stating that "Faisal Bin Abd Al-Aziz was acknowledged, in a practical manner, as Caliph in Saudi

---

wa al-Madamin al-Ishtirakiya" ["The Holy Qur'an and Socialistic Meanings"] in *Al-Katib*, Cairo (July 1966).

17 *Christianity and Islam in Lebanon*, 196.

18 *Al-Mufakkir al-'Arabi* [*The Arab Thinker*] magazine, Beirut, N°. 4 (May 1969), 22.

Arabia, and it is the duty of the Islamic legal scholars to make this decree clear to all Muslims and to obey the Caliph."[19] This Islamic call claims the following in order to justify the regime of King Faisal and support him:

> The legal scholars of the Islamic nation and those striving to lift up Islam and spread its call to the people must pronounce this Islamic decree in all mosques on Fridays and feast days in order to hasten Muslims to acknowledge their pledge of allegiance to Al-Faisal, for such a pledge has now become a necessary and inevitable obligation after the legal scholars of the Kingdom of Saudi Arabia have established it. These legal scholars should attest to their standing as legal scholars by supporting Al-Faisal as the Imam for the Muslims and calling upon him to establish a Caliphate government, just as it is their duty to call the rulers to hasten in joining the proposed council of the Caliphate until such time when all the Islamic countries are incorporated within the Caliphate.[20]

In the wake of these words, we are curious to know whether Islam inherently harmonizes and agrees with the socialist system as it took shape in Nasser's Egypt or with the caliphate that Saudi Arabia is trying to establish. Naturally, Islamic institutions in Egypt, as a practical matter, form a part of "Arab revolutionary progressive socialism" and are associated with Nasser's system, just as Islamic institutions in Saudi Arabia, as a practical matter, are part of the reactionary ruling approach and are associated with the tribal monarchical system. Each side has its own group of reconciliatory thinkers who demonstrate the total compatibility between Islam and the system of rule with which they are associated and find ways *[A 34]* to rationalize everything no matter what.

Not only have "Arab socialism" and the revival of the Caliphate both been reconciled with and rationalized by Islam but there is a band of reconciliators who have taken upon themselves to demonstrate the harmony and compatibility between Islam and the western liberal democratic system. This category of reconcilers and advocates claim that democracy in the western sense is not only in harmony with Islam, but is inherent

---

19 Ibid. 31.
20 Ibid. 32.

in its teachings and laws and does not at all differ from the Islamic adage that governance is "consultation." This rationalizing reconciliation reaches its peak in the writings of the Lebanese Dr. Hassan Sa'ab, who derives all the pillars of the bourgeois capitalist system and all principles of liberal thinking from Islamic law. In a lecture entitled "Islam and Contemporary Economic and Social Issues," Dr. Sa'ab wrote the following about the subject:

> We establish legal, political, economic, and social structures with the divine aims of the happiness and welfare of human beings, which the first Islamic legal scholars derived from the Book of God and the goals of the Shari'a. These include the following:
> First: preserving and protecting the human self.
> Second: preserving religion, that is, freedom of worship.
> Third: preserving the family.
> Fourth: preserving the mind, that is, freedom of thought and its dignity.
> Fifth: preserving wealth or private property promoting welfare.
> These are the goals that God has imposed on us according to the Islamic legal scholars. We are free to choose the forms, organizations, and means that will realize the goals.[21]

It is very clear that the rationalizing and reconciliatory mission in Lebanon can only be to the benefit of bourgeois and liberal ideas (private property, wealth, the family, and individual freedom in the bourgeois sense), considering that this is the official line of the state in Lebanon, as imposed by the interests of the ruling capitalist class. Dr. Sa'ab, however, does not want to offend anyone outside of Lebanon, whether that means the Arab revolutionary regimes or the reactionary tribal monarchical regimes. Therefore, Sa'ab works diligently to categorize all Islamic countries, despite their conflicting social and political systems, within the framework of Islam and democracy in such a way that Islam and democracy become compatible with any system regardless of its type. According to Dr. Sa'ab, the system in Indonesia is a "directed democracy"; in Pakistan, a "fundamental

---

21 *Christianity and Islam in Lebanon*, 156.

democracy"; in the *[A 35]* United Arab Republic, Algeria, Syria and Iraq, a "socialist democracy"; in Saudi Arabia, a "salafi democracy"; in Turkey, a "Kemalist democracy"; and in other countries, a "liberal democracy."[22] Islam and democracy are as inseparable as Siamese twins. As long as a country is Islamic, the system of rule could only be a pleasant and tolerant democracy. That is, the rationalizing reconciliatory logic of Dr. Sa'ab leads to the dangerous result that there is no system or rule that cannot be rationalized and granted legitimacy by Islam.

Arbitrary Reconciliation

This method of reconciliation between Islam and modern science is epitomized in the deriving of all the modern sciences, their theories, and their methodologies from the Holy Qur'an, that is, the arbitrary and simple-minded exercise of cramming every bit of modern science, great and small, into verses of the Qur'an, then claiming that the Qur'an contained all science from the beginning. In other words, the proponents of this current lie in wait for every breakthrough in scientific theory and every scientific discovery and then rush to identify a verse in the Qur'an that they claim has contained the theory and the discovery for fourteen centuries, if not forever! The most unfortunate attempt along these lines is that which we find in the book of Yousef Muruwwa, which is introduced by two Islamic clerics prominent in Lebanon.[23]

Mr. Muruwwa decided that the Holy Qur'an contains sixty-one verses on the science of mathematics, sixty-four verses on the science of physics, five verses on nuclear science, sixty-two verses on the theory of relativity, twenty verses on climatology, twenty verses on geology, and so on to the end of the standard list of the branches of modern science. Mr.

---

22 *Al-Islam tujah Tahadiyaat al-Hayat al-Mu'asira* [*Islam Confronts the Challenges of Contemporary Life*] (Beirut: Dar Al-Adab, 1965), 21.

23 *Al-'Ulum al-Tabi'iya fi al-Qur'an* [*Natural Sciences in the Holy Qur'an*] (Beirut: Muruwwa Scientific Publications, 1968, with an introduction by His Eminence Sheikh Mousa Al-Sader and Sheikh Mustafa Al-Ghalayini.

Muruwwa rationalizes this purely arbitrary reconciliation in the following words:

> However, when physicists, chemists, astronomers and geologists read the Qur'an, they do not find any contradiction between their researches and experiments and the scientific thoughts and aims found in Qur'anic verses in the areas relevant to their fields of expertise. This is because the Qur'an is a divine book that "leaves out nothing small or great, but takes account thereof," *(Qur'an* 18: 49) and "Nothing have we omitted from the Book." *(Qur'an* 6: 38) *[A 36]*

Contrary to Mr. Muruwwa's claims, I do not believe that geologists would be entirely comfortable from the point of view of their science with the Qur'anic verses that reveal how Moses divided the Red Sea with his rod. It is also untrue that physicists and chemists will not find any contradiction between the laws of their sciences and the Qur'anic verses that reveal how fire was transformed suddenly into cold, and peace upon Abraham! Furthermore, astronomers (not astrologists) will undoubtedly find it difficult to reconcile their scientific data about meteors and shooting stars with the Qur'anic verses that teach us that shooting stars are there to stone devils and Djinns when they try to ascend to heaven in order to eavesdrop on the conversations of the angels. However, the proponents of reconciliatory thinking have accustomed us to their amazing, sweeping, general judgments without close investigation of specific issues that discomfit them and their claims.

Mr. Muruwwa classifies the following Qur'anic verse under the science of physics:

> It is He Who doth show you the lightning, by way both of fear and of hope: It is He Who doth raise up the clouds, heavy with (fertilizing) rain. Nay, thunder repeateth His praises, and so do the angels, with awe: He flingeth the loud-voiced thunderbolts, and therewith He striketh whomsoever He will. *(Qur'an* 13: 12, 13)

It has escaped Dr. Muruwwa that man observed the existence of thunder, lightening, clouds and thunderbolts long before Judaism, Christianity and

Islam, leaving his observations about them in his legends, folklore, engravings and drawings. Recording such general observations about a few natural recurring phenomena does not mean that we have discovered physics or penetrated the core of scientific methodology for studying natural phenomena.

We find such extremely fundamental truths about thunder, lightning, clouds, and night and day in the legends of Mesopotamian civilization (such as the Epic of Gilgamesh), the Old Testament, the Iliad, and the Chinese and Hindu holy books, as well as the Qur'an. Moreover, thunder, lightening, clouds, and thunderbolts in Qur'anic verses are all attributed to the Divine Will and serve it. I do not believe that physics takes such a primitive view of natural phenomena and their explanation. I will not elaborate further on Mr. Muruwwa's classifications of Qur'anic verses under each of the sciences because his work does not conform to any specifiable logic, but is closer to the Theater of the Absurd and the irrational (ceding that this comparison disparages avant-garde theater). For that reason, I will be satisfied giving only a few examples from his book in order to expose the excesses that this kind of contemporary religious thinking in Islam has reached.

Mr. Muruwwa classifies the following verse under the science of physics: *[A 37]* "From God, verily nothing is hidden on earth or in the heavens." (*Qur'an* 3: 5) Why the science of physics in particular? I do not know. The writer does not explain his classifications but rather announces them, and no more. The mere mention of earth and heaven is the reason for including this verse under the science of physics! Muruwwa also classifies the following verse under the science of acoustics: "It was no more than a single mighty Blast, and behold! They were (like ashes) quenched and silent." (*Qur'an* 36: 29) He classifies the following verse under the science of nuclear explosions: "Then watch thou for the Day that the sky will bring forth a kind of smoke (or mist) plainly visible, enveloping the people: this will be a Penalty Grievous." (*Qur'an* 44: 10-11) He also categorized the following verse under rocket science: "Ye shall surely travel from stage to stage." (*Qur'an* 84: 19) And this verse under meteorology: "For We sent against them a furious wind, on a Day of violent Disaster." (*Qur'an* 54: 19) As for the famous verse, "Then shall anyone who has done an atom's

51

weight of good, see it! And anyone who has done an atom's weight of evil, shall see it," *(Qur'an 99: 7-8)* he entered it under nuclear science. Of course, it escaped Mr. Muruwwa that the "atom" in the verse is no more than a symbol of very small particles such as a grain of sand or a speck of dust. Finally, he classifies the verse "Those whom God (in His plan) willeth to guide,- He openeth their breast to Islam; those whom He willeth to leave straying,- He maketh their breast close and constricted, as if they had to climb up to the skies" (*Qur'an* 6: 125) under the conquest of space! No one can match Mr. Muruwwa's ability to grasp the linguistic metaphors, and the proof is the way he interprets the phrase "as if they had to climb up to the skies" as concerning the conquest of space by sending rockets to the moon!

One of the most important achievements of Mr. Muruwwa's arbitrary reconciliatory thinking is to calculate the speed of "divine light" just as scientists calculate the speed of light. Mr. Muruwwa managed to determine the meaning of "the divine day" and the "divine second" mathematically, based on the general theory of relativity! From there, this exceptional scholar managed to measure the speed of divine light.[24] According to him, the "divine day" equals 86,164 "divine seconds," which is equivalent to 31,556,926,000 earthly seconds. Mr. Muruwwa states the following about his brilliant scientific discoveries:

> If the normal light circles around the earth seven and half times per second, then the divine light circles between 277.5 to 13,875 *[A 38]* times around the earth per second (the speed of normal light is 300,000 kilometers per second). In light of this evident truth, we can now understand many things that have appeared in the Qur'an that the human mind was unable to understand before, since they conform to the concepts of relativity theory and this was unknown prior to this century.[25]

According to his claims, Mr. Muruwwa had finally achieved what human minds had failed to achieve until now: he established a theoretical and

---

24 *Natural Sciences in the Holy Qur'an*, 180-198.
25 *Natural Sciences in the Holy Qur'an*, 183.

mathematical basis for the mechanics of the heavenly host. I suggest calling all this the "Muruwwaian Mechanics," in analogy with the long-standing scientific tradition that has provided such nomenclature as "Newtonian Mechanics" and "Einsteinian Mechanics."

On the other hand, this exceptional mind has failed to note that assimilating divine light to light (that is made from material waves) and determining its speed in this way is blasphemous and a deviation from the teachings of the religion he is defending. For it is not only a deviation from the principle of divine transcendence and a lapsing into assimilating divine attributes to material events, but a lapse into the most extreme form of anthropomorphism, which attributes corporeality to God. In religion, the divine light is an infinite, unlimited, spiritual energy (that is, it cannot be determined quantitatively and mathematically in the Muruwwaian manner) and its essence can only be grasped through faith, the soul, and the inner light. As for this material, mathematical conception of the nature of divine light and the talk about the number of times it is able to circle around the earth in a second, as if it were a ray of normal light, they both would be rejected by any sincere Muslim (or Christian or Jew) with a remnant of sanity.

There is another method of arbitrary reconciliation between Islam and modern science similar to that of Muruwwa but more prevalent. It is represented in a book published by the Dar Al-Ma'aref in Egypt in two editions under the title *The Scientific Exegesis of the Cosmic Verses in the Qur'an*. It contains innumerable examples of extraordinary reconciliatory thinking—I will offer just a few.

The author of this book concludes from the Qur'anic verse "It is He Who maketh the stars (as beacons) for you, that ye may guide yourselves, with their help, through the dark spaces of land and sea" (*Qur'an* 6: 97) the scientific fact that the stars are the original light in the sky, and that the light of planets is not original, but rather derived from that of the stars. The writer states the following, word for word:

> However, the expert researcher in the realm of the stars finds that God Almighty had given special mention to the stars (in the verse above) rather than the planets, although they emit light like the stars. We

can infer from this that the special mention is an indication that the stars are the original source of light in the sky, is and that the light of the planets *[A 39]* not original but is derived from starlight and therefore need not be mentioned. Do you see the wisdom in this special mention? It is the wisdom of the Almighty.²⁶

The author also comments on the verse "And marks and sign-posts; and by the stars (men) guide themselves," (*Qur'an* 16: 16) by stating the following:

> The researcher finds that the saying of the Almighty "by the stars, men guide themselves" means to let yourselves be guided, and be guided by the stars, the "by" here is a causal "by," as instanced in the statement "by the pen he writes," and that the guidance resulting from those stars themselves means that their light is from themselves, or in other words, as can be seen from the phrase "by the stars," there is a strong indication that the light of the stars comes from within them, emitting outwards.²⁷

With all fervor and seriousness, the author of this book comments in the following way on the Qur'anic verse "Blessed is He Who made constellations in the skies, and placed therein a Lamp and a Moon giving light" *(Qur'an* 25: 61)*:

> From a scientific point of view, and based on the specific meaning given to the word "light" in the Qur'an, any body that lends itself to the transformation of various types of energy to light without changing its composition is called a luminous source, such as the following: 1. platinum wires that illuminate through conducting heat or an electronic current; 2. tin chloride compounds that illuminate in the dark after being exposed to a sufficient amount of sunlight; 3. compounds of cyanide platinum and barium that illuminate under gamma radiation; 4. compounds of rare elements from which are formed the wicks of common electric light bulbs and that illuminate

---

26 Hanafi Ahmad, *Al-Tafsir al-'Ilmi lil-Ayaat al-Kawnia fil-Qur'an* [The Scientific Exegesis of the Cosmic Verses in the Qur'an] (Cairo: Dar Al-Maaref, 1960), 25.
27 Ahmad, 35.

when conducting an electric current. Some of these luminous sources can be employed economically in daily life whereas others are too difficult or expensive to produce.[28]

Lebanese Reconciliation

I addressed the views of a number of Islamic clerics in Lebanon concerning the relation between religion in general, and Islam in particular, with modern science and the culture it generates. It is worth noting that within general reconciliatory thinking there is an approach with a special Lebanese stamp represented by what is called the "Islamic-Christian dialogue." As an attempt at reconciliation, this phenomenon of dialogue deserves close examination. For it reveals again the extent to which this type of complacent thinking has infiltrated the minds of those responsible for religious affairs [A 40] in general and how it dominates their concerns. Moreover, some of the writers among the religious clerics whose views we have cited take part in the lecture series delivered at the Cénacle Libanais, whose basic purpose is to promote Islamic-Christian dialogue in Lebanon.

Following the common pattern of reconciliatory thinking, Islamic-Christian dialogue is steeped in rhetorical expressions that lack any explicit meaning and in generalizations concerning a long-established harmony between Islam and Christianity. For example, Dr. Sheikh Subhi Al-Saleh states the following:

> I did not miss a single word of what was said in the lectures concerning these two revealed and universal religions, even if what I had heard or then read carefully did not increase my faith in the proximity of Christianity and Islam, for this proximity, as I will demonstrate to you, has been evident throughout the generations. Islam has established—because of the similarity of religions in the understanding of the phenomenon of revelation—its basic maxim as the necessity of the

---

28   Ahmad, 149.

constant meeting of all spiritualities, even if it has greatly favored the Christians, since, as we have seen earlier, they are the closest people in friendship to the faithful.[29]

His Christian counterpart, Father Joachim Mubarak, stated the following:

> The establishment of a special secretariat to engage in dialogue with Muslims by His Holiness Pope Paul VI should be considered an invitation to worthy discussants who are able to speak in the name of Islam both for its various divisions and as a global indivisible whole.[30]

In accordance with the tactics of reconciliatory thinking that we became familiar with earlier, none of the thinkers among the participants in the dialogue raised even a single well-defined and specific issue in order to explore its dimensions and to what degree Christians and Muslims could agree on it. To the contrary, all of the participants in the dialogue strove to disregard all well-defined, essential, doctrinal points in the two religions in order to indulge in flattery, sophistry, and generalizations that do not hurt anyone's feelings or provoke anyone's wrath.

Father Joachim Mubarak hinted, obscurely and tersely, to the issues around which the dialogue should revolve: "a purely theological encounter"[31] between Islam and Christianity (that is, comparative theology). Then he claimed that "whenever something of a misunderstanding arises between Christian and Islamic beliefs, it is an indication that we should return to the sources; these sources bring us closer and do not take us further apart."[32] None of the participants in the dialogue objected to the words of Father Mubarak or *[A 41]* even discussed them. I would like to show Father Mubarak that intellectual integrity requires of us that we make clear that entering the heart of the matter of the dialogue as he understands it (a theological encounter) will not lead to merely "something of a misunderstanding" between the two parties, as he remarked with politeness

---

29 *Christianity and Islam in Lebanon*, 193, 206.
30 Ibid. 186.
31 Ibid. 175.
32 Ibid. 185.

and good manners. Integrity requires that we acknowledge the existence of radical theological differences and profound doctrinal disagreements between Islam and Christianity (as a rigorous theological comparison would inevitably prove) that cannot be overcome by obscure, utopian formulations concerning a "return to the sources." For that reason, reconciliatory thinkers who participated in the dialogue avoided any real and serious invitation to a "pure theological encounter" and its consequences.

To move away from the realm of generalizations, I shall provide a brief and straightforward example of a theological encounter between Christianity and Islam in order to introduce some clarity. In other words, I shall do the work that was supposed to have been done by the participants in the dialogue with some depth and accuracy.

A Christian believes in Original Sin, while a Muslim opposes it totally and considers it a curious tale at best, finding it strange that some believe in it although it has always been "illogical." A Christian believes in the Holy Trinity, while a Muslim considers this Trinity a clear deviation from the Oneness of God, that is, nothing other than blasphemy. A Christian also believes that God is incarnated in Christ, while a Muslim considers this the essence of blasphemy and a deviation from all logic, reason, and sound religious sentiment concerning the attributes of God. A Christian believes that Jesus is the Son of God, while a Muslim clearly responds: "Say: He is God, the One and Only; God, the Eternal, Absolute; He begetteth not, nor is He begotten; And there is none like unto Him." (*Qur'an* 112: 1-4) A Christian holds a number of specific beliefs such as the Crucifixion of Jesus, His Resurrection, and His being the Savior; while we find that a Muslim rejects the Crucifixion and the Resurrection and does not acknowledge anyone to be the Savior. I present this modest theological comparison to Father Joachim Mubarak and all the participants in the dialogue with the following note: as long as the participants in the dialogue prefer rhetoric, sophistry, flattery, reconciliation through generalizations, noble sentiments, and the "proximity between the two religions since generations," their efforts remain meager and without great results, whether we agree or disagree with them on these results.

In the absence of any realistic and scientific approach to religion, it is inevitable that the dialogue descends to repeating a number of familiar clichés, such as the previously cited statement that we all, Christians and Muslims, worship one God. Dr. Sheik Subhi Al-Saleh, citing the words of the Pope, stated that "His Holiness does not miss any opportunity to address all believers in the One Almighty God," and then adds, 'He is the God whom we worship as well.'"[33]

It seems to me that the core *[A 42]* of the Christian-Muslim dialogue should clarify this point in particular. Is it true that the God worshiped by Muslims is the God worshiped by Christians as well? Is the God composed of the Father, the Son and the Holy Spirit, and Who was incarnated on this earth and sent His Son to save humanity, the same God worshiped by Muslims? I personally do not believe so. All that remains for us is to find out what the advocates of the Muslim-Christian dialogue think on the basis of a real argument and straightforward discussion and not on the basis of civility, collaboration, and reasoning based on equivocation, intimations, and consolation.

Unless the critical scientific historical methodology becomes our guide in studying religion in general, the Muslim-Christian dialogue will remain closer to the "dialogue of the deaf" than to any form of dialogue worthy of esteem. The critical approach to studying the phenomenon of religion entails starting on neutral grounds, that is, standing on a strict scientific and secular foundation. It also means looking at religious doctrine as a purely personal and subjective matter that is up to the free choice of the individual according to his disposition and convictions. It is therefore more suitable and appropriate that understanding and dialogue among the Lebanese be based on the principle of civic belonging and shared interests than sectarian affiliation and religious classification.

In the absence of this scientific environment, each partner in the dialogue has generated endless absurdities in its conception of the religion

---

33   *Christianity and Islam in Lebanon*, 203.

of the other partner. Some of these absurdities include, but are not limited to, the attempts made by some Islamic legal scholars to prove that the Bible predicted the mission of the Prophet Muhammad (Ahmad), who would follow Issa [the common name for Jesus in Islam, trans. note] at a determined time. These scholars cite the Gospel of Barnabas, although it is rejected by all Christian churches, because it allegedly mentions the Prophet Ahmad. They therefore claim that the current Gospel held holy by Christians is a corruption of the "original Gospel" that God revealed to Issa, which mentioned the Prophet Muhammad. How can there be a dialogue between Christians and Muslims if Muslims continue to fabricate theories about the holy texts of their counterparts, and intrude into their internal matters?

From another perspective, we find that some Christian thinkers who have studied Islam work diligently to prove that the Qur'an admits to the divinity of Christ, which would bring the two religions closer together and make the dialogue more productive. However, how can this dialogue take place when Christians make up views about the contents of the Qur'an and the meaning of its sayings about Jesus? The absence of scientific methodology in studying the phenomenon of religion inevitably leads to such absurdities or to pure sentimentality and extravagant expressions of noble emotions. The following is a section written by Father Joachim Mubarak, which clearly demonstrates the level of sentimentality at which the dialogue between Christians and Muslims in Lebanon concludes. Father Mubarak was responding to the criticism directed at Christianity for not giving the Prophet Muhammad the status he deserves, both historically and theologically:

> I want to demonstrate during my reflections and prayers this evening that even if this religious vision of things has yet to prevail, *[A 43]* there is more than one Christian soul among those I know or interact with at a distance who knows how to maintain a place for the thought of Mohammed in the depths of their prayers. I have contemplated this occasionally and brought him to mind in various popular Islamic shrines that I have visited, both humble and

illustrious. I did this in Jerusalem, between Al-Aqsa Mosque, the traditional site of the Mi'raj, and at the Dome of the Rock, the site of Abraham's sacrifice. I remembered him at the Imam Al-Shafi'i in Cairo, where the southeast corner of the poignant City of the Dead (which the shrine of the prince of lovers overlooks) stands out. I did it on the way to Mecca on the road that the Egyptian mahmal followed in old times, and by the tomb of Uqba [Ibn Nafi'], one of the first companions of the Prophet. I did it in Bouake, on the Ivory Coast, near a humble mosque situated at the border between the Great Forest and the Green Sahel, in the very heart of Africa. At the time, I thought of the desert of the Arabian Peninsula, which Massignon recalled in these nostalgic words "the sad heart of Islam." I did it many times in the Maghreb, especially in Moulay Idriss, that exalted sacred place from where the word of Islam spread throughout the region at the hands of the ruler who bore that same name. I also did it in Tinmel in the heart of the High Atlas Mountains of Morocco that overlook Marrakech from the Tizi-n-Test Pass, from where the Great Muwahed Movement was launched by Muhammad Bin Tumert and his student Abd Al-Mu'min. I often did it recently in the vicinity of the Islamic cemeteries in Morocco, which formed large plots of land in the big cities or were scattered neglected in rural areas. There is a tradition there that says that on Friday evenings, when Muslim women are allowed to head to the cemeteries, the spirit of Mohammed returns to inhale the aromas of the valley, exactly as flocks of thirsty birds return to drink from the goblets that the pious and merciful hands of the loved ones lying awaiting the Day of Resurrection prepare for them.[34]

This kind of talk continues to absorb more than three and a half pages from Father Joachim Mubarak's lecture, although it is nothing but a steady drip of rhetoric without positive or (negative) import, and entirely vague. It is the textbook example of how the patrons of the Islamic-Christian dialogue respond to every embarrassing point or pertinent criticism: Unequalled excess in the rhetorical expression of noble sentiments and subjective emotions.

---

34 *Christianity and Islam in Lebanon*, 188-189.

Naturally, this reconciliatory movement represented in the Christian-Muslim dialogue *[A 44]* has its own principles, implication, and social objectives, whether participants of the movement are aware of them or not. It is known that in the 1960s, the Lebanese public began to feel keenly and increasingly the pressure of class struggle in their society. One of the tangible realities in Lebanese society in general is that the majority of Muslims belong to the poor, the working classes, and the lower middle class. Christians, on the other hand, feel that the existing social structure belongs to them, since they, more than others, exploit it for their own interests. Under these circumstances, socio-political slogans such as "national solidarity," "the higher interest of Lebanon," "building bridges between classes," and "mutual understanding, brotherhood, and love" are circulated among the Lebanese regardless of their sect, dispositions, and degree of wealth or poverty. Of course, the Muslim strata that are financially comfortable and likely to benefit from the existing regime play a major role in promoting the aforementioned slogans.

When we translate these slogans into the language of religion and sectarianism, the result is the Christian-Muslim dialogue, reconciliation between the sects, harmony between the various religious beliefs, and whatever else is currently in circulation. The ultimate aim of all these efforts is to preserve the existing sectarian system with all its social, economic and political implications in the name of religion and other things. The Christian-Islamic dialogue is an attempt to reconcile the leaderships of the social classes, whether Christian or Muslim, that own the wealth and the means of production in the country, and thus have power and influence (for example, on the Muslim side, the Sunni bourgeoisie). In the final analysis, it is clear that the Christian-Muslim dialogue merely sanctifies sectarianism in all its current social implications, camouflages the raging class struggle within Lebanese society, and creates a diversion from it.

In the course of his participation in the Muslim-Christian dialogue, Father Joachim Mubarak strives to justify sectarianism in Lebanon with words that are elegant but free from any positive and tangible meaning. According to Mubarak, the state of Christianity and Islam in Lebanon is ideal and unsurpassable. It is a "predicted outcome of a long history, "a harbinger of solidarity between these Mediterranean peoples," and the site of "increasing solidarity." Father Mubarak writes the following:

> As Islam and Christianity exchange peaceful theories and prepare to shake hands across the expanse of water that joins them more than it separates them, we see that this has already been achieved in Lebanon and that something more than an encounter has taken place, their increasing solidarity. Lebanon appears at this time as if it were the foretold outcome of a long history of centuries and the harbinger of solidarity between these Mediterranean peoples with whom the churning of relationships and struggles between Muslims and Christians have played havoc. It is the firstborn child of peaceful coexistence between Islam *[A 45]* and Christianity.[35]

Father Mubarak continues his intellectual acrobatics to prove to us that Lebanese sectarianism constitutes the most solid basis on which to build a real democracy and its social and political systems. He states the following:

> I do not mean by this that the spiritual, holy or religious element cannot be made the firm basis for a modern democracy. When we examine democracies around the world that have the strongest traditional principles (I have in mind the Netherlands and Switzerland), we notice the opposite, that sectarianism, or its ethnic or cultural counterpart, is able to blend completely into a coherent and flawless democratic system.[36]

Then Father Mubarak explains that present-day Lebanon is the model after which Muslims and Christians seek and strive. The important thing is to maintain the balance between Lebanese sects (and we know for whose benefit this balance works) and continue with the Muslim-Christian dialogue, since the latter is one of the tools that maintains the balance and serves the status quo. Father Mubarak writes the following:

---

35 Ibid. 167.
36 Ibid. 168.

However, if Christianity and Islam are necessary for each other, then Lebanon is necessary for Christianity and Islam, and for the world. It is important to be very aware that if Lebanon wants to be purely Christian or majority Christian, it would lose its raison d'être and condemn itself as Israel has done. And if Lebanon wants to be purely Muslim or majority Muslim, it would also condemn itself and make of Islam an ethnic chauvinism jealous of its identity, exclusive of all other identities, and unable to survive in the context of a unified, pluralistic nation. However, Lebanon, as it is, as it wants to be, and as enlightened Muslims love it, is a glittering argument for Islam before international public opinion.[37]

Like Father Mubarak, Dr. Sheikh Subhi Al-Saleh also expresses his opinion that the process of drawing Christianity closer to Islam in Lebanon is very important to the whole world. According to Dr. Al-Saleh, what is important is the necessity of confronting modern culture and its "atheistic" inclinations, or more precisely, confronting scientific socialism, or even more precisely, the Soviet Union itself! Indeed, this is the logic of proponents of the "the Islamic Alliance"[38] that found its earlier and most zealous supporters in the representatives of the Lebanese Christian capitalist [A 46] bourgeoisie that considers the alliance of the "spiritual powers" necessary to confront secularism, communism, atheism, and so on. Dr. Subhi Al-Saleh wrote the following excerpt explaining this perspective:

The reasons for conciliation multiplied as a result of the overwhelming wave of atheism and the candor of Nietzsche's followers in announcing the death of God in the world of sensations and carnal appetites in the middle of the nineteenth century. The announcement of the death of the Living and Everlasting God (the most astounding announcement in existence for the Being whose existence is necessary) had effects, for example, in smothering the holy glow in the hearts of the wavering among the weak of faith. Soviet Russia completed the symphony of

---

37 Ibid. 183-184.
38 An alliance led by the Saudi Monarchy against President Nasser of Egypt and his political program at the time [trans. note].

atheism with its denial of the existence of God and its urging the people to a paradise on earth rather than in heaven. The communist "ideology" had a skill in dialectical argument that convinced many to substitute Moscow's revelation for God's revelation and turned the others—after sloughing off religion—towards rushing into empirical currents: economic with the economists, nationalistic with the nationalists, and regional with the regionalists! It was only logical, after the ruin of conscience, the death of the heart, and the disruption of standards, that the church should turn towards the ecumenical councils in order to bring the scattered Christians back into the fold. It did not see any obstacle to cooperating with other religions, above all Islam, to ward off the deceptive corruptions of the atheism and materialism prevailing among the people.[39]

It does not occur to Dr. Al-Saleh to question the reasons behind what he calls an "overwhelming wave of atheism" or discuss its justifications lest he find himself confronted by a possibility he would rather ignore: that it is not a crisis of atheism but essentially a crisis of religion and faith in an age in which science, secularism, and scientific socialism are in ascent.

The Second Solution

The second solution is the complete rejection of scientific theory and all its associated ideas and opinions and the complete retreat within the walls of the religious view to defend it at all costs. However, adopting such a solution is harsh whether at the individual or collective level because in extreme situations it forms a kind of intellectual and mental suicide. In less extreme situations, it leads to a gradual rupture between a person and the world around him. It is a kind of escapism that spares someone the difficulties of confronting facts that are incompatible with their psychological, emotional, intellectual, and religious make-up. No human being enjoying a measure of intelligence and perception would be able to bear such a psychological and religious isolation since the world he is forced to live in every day is radically

---

39 Ibid. 200–201.

affected by science and applications of science that he must confront and co-exist with wherever he goes and however he tries to escape. He lives in *[A 47]* a world affected by the rhythm and speed of the machine. If he is unable to bear this contradiction between his internal and external world, he will manifest the symptoms that lead in some cases to a total nervous breakdown, other forms of collapse, or to a kind of general paralysis that impedes his undertaking any productive or fruitful work. For he is highly vulnerable to the burden that the culture of the past and his religious heritage place upon him and unable to adapt to the new conditions surrounding him. In order to expose, at the practical level, the nature of this dogmatic religious perspective toward everything external to it, we can turn to the book of Sheikh Dr. Muhammad Al-Bahi, *Modern Islamic Thinking and its Connection with the Imperialism of the West*.[40] In this book, hardly an Arab or Muslim writer influenced by scientific methodology is spared the author's assault, slander, and disparagement even when the intentions are good and the Islam is pure, for he attributes everything in the views of others that is at odds with his dogmatic position to deception and apostasy.

The Third Solution

The third solution distinguishes between the temporal dimension and the eternal or spiritual dimension of religion by saying that all that we find in religion about nature and history, etc. falls under the temporal dimension, which can be ceded completely to science. The spiritual dimension, on the other hand, has absolutely no relation at all to science. It is the realm of eternal truths, the transcendent, faith, and mystical experience.[41] The proponents of this perspective say that that the scientific method and knowledge do not extend beyond the scope of nature and thus it is not possible for them to investigate

---

40 (Cairo: Wahbi Library,1964).

41 One of the first people to spread this opinion in the Arab East was Sheikh Ali Abd Al-Raziq in his book *Al-Islam wa Asul al-Hukm* [*Islam and the Principles of Rule*] *(*Cairo: 1925).

religious beliefs that are supported by pure faith rather than the intellect and its arguments and science and its proofs. In other words, the proponents of this perspective say that religious knowledge differs in kind from scientific and intellectual knowledge. Therefore, we always find that we fail when we try to apply logic to religious knowledge since it always contradicts logic and is inconsistent with the scientific mentality. For this special type of knowledge emerges from mystical experience or a leap of pure faith, and the like.

Undoubtedly, mystics and those who have made leaps of faith have deep personal experiences and fixed convictions that rest on these experiences. However those who lack such experiences, or anything similar, must answer this question: Do the statements of mystics and their descriptions of their personal experiences provide sufficient and convincing proof for the existence of God, since He is the Being with whom the mystic communicates and unites? We are unable to undertake the long process of examining all of the many responses proposed to this question here. Therefore, we shall limit our exertions to discussing an exemplary response, by the French philosopher Henri Bergson in *[A 48]* his book *The Two Sources of Morality and Religion*.

Bergson states that the man who is concerned with this problem either believes the testimony of the mystic, considering it sufficient proof of the existence of a higher spiritual truth or follows the mystic along the rocky road in order to verify the truth or falsity of the testimony. He adds that we are not obliged to resort to such procedures because most of the time we believe the testimonies of people and religious scholars without passing through the same trials and experiences that they do. For the sake of clarification, Bergson provides the following analogy: When the famous explorer David Livingstone journeyed into the jungles of Africa and discovered the lake that was the source of the Nile, the whole world believed him upon hearing about his discovery without anyone following his trail and undergoing the same trials and experiences that he underwent. Only a few were beset with such doubts about the veracity of the famous explorer's testimony that they could only be convinced of its truth by being sent along his path to see it for themselves. In fact, the path taken by Livingstone appeared on maps before scientific missions were sent to that area to verify the details of the discovery.

Bergson compares the mystic with this explorer because he is a man who strikes a particular spiritual path and travels along it in order to reach a special type of knowledge and discover a new truth. If you are beset by doubts about the veracity of his testimony about the existence and nature of the fact sitting at the end of the road, then it is only fair that you do not judge the mystic before you make the same journey that he did.

While at first glance this analogy seems reasonable and persuasive, it is not. It does not take into consideration that we believe the testimony of Livingstone and those who followed him because they returned to us with uniform descriptions of what they found at the end of their journey. However, this does not apply to the testimony of mystics and the descriptions they give of the truth they reach at the end of their spiritual journey. Undoubtedly, mystics who belong to a single religious heritage and a single mystic order do not strongly disagree in their descriptions. However, when we compare the testimonies of mystics who belong to different religions, we find they differ radically in how they describe what they find at the end of their spiritual journey. This indicates that consistency in the opinions of mystics about this subject arises not from a common mystical vision but from the unity of the religious tradition to which they belong and from the meanings and texts they use to ascend to the desired goal. Therefore, we have the right to doubt the existence of a single spiritual truth that all mystics are in touch with, whatever their differences in religion and whatever their distinct spiritual tendencies.

Let us return to Bergson's analogy: Imagine, for example, that the missions that were sent, one after the other, to study Livingstone's discovery returned to us with inconsistent reports on the nature and character of the discovery. *[A 49]*

The first mission claimed that it found a lake with salt water, the second that it found a lake with fresh water, the third that it did not find a lake at all but only a green mountain, and so on. Would we not be entitled at this point to doubt the testimonies of these missions and to refuse to consider them sufficient and convincing proof for the existence of a lake with a set of specific, definite characteristics? The inconsistency of mystic testimonies about the existence of a spiritual truth called God, and about its nature and characteristics, fills me with deep doubt as to whether they are sufficient and convincing evidence of His existence.

Moreover, I must also note that the testimony of a mystic on the nature of God is always embedded in the concepts of the religious heritage to which he belongs. In other words, the mystical experience in the view of its adherents does not form a proof for the existence of God but rather presumes His existence. Thus we find that the effort of the mystic is based on establishing a special relationship between God and himself after having had accepted His active existence since the beginning. If he has not, he loses his reason for embarking on his path in the first place. The mystical experience, by its very nature, is unable to prove anything because it is a personal and spiritual intensification of religion and its transformation from a bare doctrine to personal feelings. It packs its empty formalities with a flow of intense passion that the mystic uses to supersede the rituals, formalities, ceremonies, and external appearances in which everyone participates in order to elevate religion to a special personal experience that he shares with no one else and that he experiences with his flesh, blood, and whole being.

We mentioned a group of thinkers who say that religious knowledge radically and completely differs from knowledge in the intellectual and scientific sense, and that is why we always find it in contradiction with logic and at odds with the intellect. The proponents of this school of thought say that the human mind is incapable of knowing the nature of the deity or understanding it, even partially. The human mind is unable to imagine it or express its nature. Some express this view of God with the statement "He differs from whatever may come to your mind."

There are a number of objections to this view. First: Am I able to establish any serious relationship between myself and this God whose nature absolutely surpasses my logic, emotions, thoughts, imagination, and hopes? Am I able to find consolation in an awesome God when the only thing I know about him is that he is entirely different from however I may conceive or describe him? The existence or non-existence of such a God is all the same to me. This God is nothing but an abstraction void of all meaning and content, and the will of a human being cannot relate to a pure abstraction that exceeds by degrees the abstraction that Aristotle posited under the name of "the Prime Mover." For even if you are able to offer supplication and prayer to "the Prime Mover," you surely will not be able to offer it to a God whom you cannot describe at all since he is in His very nature counter to every thought that occurs to you or any description you can utter. Second, if God cannot be described or conceived by human beings, what do we mean when we say that He is "merciful and just?" When we describe God as merciful and just, what do we mean by these attributes? Isn't there any similarity between mercy and justice *[A 50]* as attributed to God and our human conception of these attributes? If the answer is negative, then are our minds bare of all meanings and associations when we characterize God as merciful and just? Do we attribute to Him words that lack any meaning at all in relation to human beings? We find ourselves in a difficult place on this issue, because either we attribute justice to God in accordance with a conception that bears some dim resemblance to our human understanding of justice or our talk of justice is free of any meaning or content. In other words, we are obliged either to make an analogy with all its consequences or to maintain a total de-anthropomorphism with its consequences.

There is a traditional solution for this bundle of problems and contradictions: to just accept and believe the literal meaning, entrusting the knowledge of its inner truth to God Himself, that is, belief without knowledge and faith in the way of aged people. The best example of this approach is the following classical conundrum: The believer is supposed to resign himself for better or worse to predestination and divine decree from God Almighty *and* to believe in rewards and punishments *and* to believe in Divine Justice, despite the obvious ethical and intellectual contradictions among these principles. Proponents of this view justify their position by asserting that the human intellect is entirely unable to grasp the nature of

Divine Justice and its relation to accountability and fate and divine decree since these issues do not submit to human logic and thus they appear contradictory and contrary to our standards of morality and fairness.

However, the question that I am confronted with is the following: Am I, the son of this century and the stepson of its culture and science, able to have the faith of aged people when I see blatant contradiction and incoherent and inconsistent positions knowing that my faith or lack of it would not blunt or diminish the contradiction. If I accept this blatant contradiction, what will then hinder me from accepting all the other contradictions that we find in all religions, legends, and tales? This call for naïve acceptance of matters that appear contradictory leaves the door wide open to things that modern science has struggled for many years to expel from the human intellect. Every attempt to reinstate them sabotages scientific values and distorts objective methodology and its application in solving the great and challenging problems of humanity. Therefore, I have no choice but to completely reject this intellectual anarchism that allows one to believe in whatever one wishes to believe in, in spite of all the considerations that make one's faith untenable. For example, imagine a man approaching you and saying: "In paradise, there is a married bachelor!" Undoubtedly, you would immediately inquire about what he means, and warn him that the sentence he uttered contradicts itself. Imagine, also, that he answers you in this way: "But, my friend, this married bachelor exists in paradise and thus he is radically different from bachelors on earth, and it is possible for bachelors in paradise to be bachelors and married at the same time." He then elaborates stating: "Certainly, it might seem to you that there is a blatant contradiction in this statement, but the bachelor in paradise is not subject to the considerations of human logic in the least, and the human mind is unable to comprehend this eternal truth. Therefore, all you need to do is surrender to this truth through faith, *[A 51]* or accept and believe its literal meaning while entrusting the knowledge of its inner truth to God Almighty."

What is your view of this claim and of this eternal truth that exceeds human logic and science? As for myself, I would answer that if this married bachelor is beyond the limits of logic, the intellect, and comprehension, then

I have absolutely nothing to do with it—considering that I am human—and am unable to pay any attention, negative or positive, to it.

Those who solve the contradictions standing within the heart of religious doctrines through pure faith do not differ significantly, upon examination, from the one who brings up this married bachelor. But they adorn these incompatible doctrines with a pleasing, alluring, emotional language that hides for a moment the inherent contradictions and exploits our psychological and emotional nature to attract us.

The Fourth and Last Solution

We will now proceed to tackle the solution provided by William James in the article cited at the beginning of this study under the title "The Will to Believe." In this article, James establishes a general principle to guide our assent to opinions and judgments placed before us: We are not allowed to accept or reject any particular opinion unless sufficient evidence and testimony is provided for its truth or falsehood. When these conditions are not met, we must suspend judgment. In the same way, our commitment to and defense of a particular opinion should be proportionate to the strength of the argument and the weight of evidence attesting to its truth.

This principle certainly forms an ideal that one can only achieve in varying degrees, no matter how intelligent or free from prejudice and passion he is when he forms his considered opinions on the various subjects of life. In fact, this ideal is an ethical principle that sums up the bases of what is called "the ethics of belief." In other words, the general ethical principle that James establishes forbids us from believing in an opinion unless we have satisfied ourselves as to the truth of this opinion on the basis of data, evidence, and scientific testimony sufficient for its truth, and vice versa. James then asks himself if there are exceptional cases in which someone would be right to believe the truth of some matter despite a clear lack of evidence and corroboration for its truth or falsity. He answers that religious belief or faith in the existence of God is one of these cases.

According to James, the person who faces the difficult choice between belief in the existence or inexistence of God will not find any intellectual corroboration or scientific evidence proving the one or the other. James then asks himself what will this person do, does he postpone judgment forever or does he have the right to adopt a particular position—whether negative or affirmative—on this issue despite that scientific evidence and intellectual proofs do not favor either of the two choices? Here James affirms *[A 52]* the right of this person to believe in the existence of God if that conforms with his emotional nature. In other words, according to James, he has the right to decide the matter by recourse to his passions and emotions, discarding the basic principle of the ethics of belief.

However, the question that strikes us is the following: Why do we give the matter of religion this privilege and distinction so that we except it from the comprehensive ethical principle that guides the formation of beliefs and their contents? Do we allow these exceptions based on certain principles or arbitrarily and capriciously as James does? If we want to preserve the ethics of belief, we cannot allow to religion what we deny other subjects that require confirmation and belief.

For the moment we open the door to exceptions we can only close it with an act as arbitrary as the one that opened it. If we make an exception from the ethics of belief for belief in God, why do we not make the same exception for angels, devils, genies, imps, mermaids, the Greek gods, and all the other superstitions that people believed in and continue to vie to believe in? This permissive and lax position that James adopted about the ethics of belief and its principles forms a grave threat to the life of scientific research and the education and emancipation of minds. Moreover, if I am asked to accept some view and I believe it because I am persuaded of its truth, and then I discover I am deceived about it, I will go back on my belief as soon as I discover this deception. As for James, he asks me to believe in a proposition that he acknowledges has not yet been proved. I, therefore, find myself unable to accept such a proposition voluntarily as long as I possess full consciousness and my intellectual faculties. James' appeal to us to allow—as a matter of principle—our passions, emotions, and fancies to influence our judgments and considered opinions is dangerous. For whoever pursues scientific research is fully aware of the extent to which he has to be objective and how indifferent he must be vis-à-vis any latent passions or inclinations that may pull him to favor one position against another without a scientific basis. When a researcher is confronted with many possible solutions to a problem that he is working on, he knows how to suppress his personal and emotional inclinations towards one of these solutions in order to give way to cold facts and abstract logic to resolve the matter. When a researcher is excited to prove a particular hypothesis, he knows how to overcome this excitement with an intense desire not to fall into delusions that would lead him to falsely believe he has proved something he has not. The compatibility of an idea with our emotional nature cannot be an acceptable reason to believe in it, that is, if we want considered opinions not merely inherited ones. James defends himself in this way:

(1) We cannot suspend judgment on the issue of belief in God's existence forever because while we would avoid falling into error if he does not exist we would also miss out on great benefits if he does exist. James, in fact, misunderstands the problem, for the question is not about the worldly or eternal benefits that I could reap by believing in God and the similar losses that I might suffer from my lack of belief if he does exist. *[A 53]* The problem has no connection to the calculation of gains and losses or the logic of taking gambles and making bets, it is simply as follows: Is the issue of the existence of God a matter of truth or falsity, or is its truth as conceivable as its falsity and we do not have any evidence or proofs that would favor one of these options over the other? Our personal opinion about the existence of God should conform entirely with our answer to this question, not with the calculation of gains and losses.

(2) James says in defense of himself that the man who suspends judgment in the matter of the existence of God yields to his fear of falling into error and delusion while it is better he believes in His existence in accordance with his hope that his belief is true. However, James is in error, for our fear of falling into error is much more important than our hope of detecting a truth or our wish that our belief be true. For the number of errors that we might fall into is unlimited, while the truth is one. Since

the probabilities of falling into error are far greater than the probability of detecting the truth or the probability of finding oneself with the right belief, one is obliged to place strict and exacting rules on the search for knowledge, hoping to reduce the possibilities of error to the absolute minimum. Despite that, the number of such possibilities is frightening.

Contrary to James, then, it is much wiser for us to fear falling into error than to rush to submit to the hope of detecting true belief, especially before we have reduced the possibilities of error to the absolute minimum by means of scientific thinking and its familiar methodology. Even if the belief that we accepted on the basis of our emotions and inclinations is true by pure coincidence, it will lack value because attaining a true belief in this way is like the advantage of theft over honest toil. In other words, we have attained this true belief unlawfully and we cannot build general principles for attaining considered opinions on accidental foundations.

In the course of our criticism of James' views, we are obliged to mention that the thinker who does not believe in the existence of God or suspends judgment about this topic entirely might not do so as a consequence of his emotional nature, since his emotional nature might have inclined him to believe rather than to refuse to believe. He does this because the intellectual convictions that he has formed on clear scientific grounds do not allow him to believe in the existence of God without falling into self-contradiction and without sacrificing the coherence of his logic and thinking.

This does not imply that I want to abolish mankind's religious feelings from existence, but in my view it is necessary to distinguish between religion and religious feelings. Those feelings are crushed under the burden of petrified traditional religious doctrines and under the weight of frozen rites and rituals. We need to liberate this feeling from its prison in order for it to flourish and express itself through ways and means appropriate to the conditions and circumstances in which we live in the culture of the twentieth-century. For this reason, we must renounce the traditional idea alleging the existence of something like a special religious truth and to turn our concern toward religious feeling freed from these burdens and weights.

Likewise, it appears unnecessary to me for religious feelings to be associated with *[A 54]* supernatural beings, invisible presences, and strange powers, as has always been the case. This feeling is a quality that is able to color all our emotions, attitudes, thoughts, and higher goals in order to introduce into our view of the fluctuating and sundry events of life something of harmony, consistency, and security. In this sense, religious feelings are represented in the artist's view of beauty, the scientist's attitude toward searching for truth, the attitude of the activist towards the goals he is working to realize, or in the ordinary person's attitude to the performance of the daily duties of life.

Chapter Two

The Tragedy of Satan (*Iblis*)[1][2]

> *"I am the spirit that ever denies."*
>
> Goethe, Faust

Section One

Prologue

If we try to determine the basic feelings through which the three Semitic religions expressed man's relationship to God, we would discover that they are limited to three: love, fear, and hatred — love of God, fear of His power and punishment, and hatred of His enemy, Satan (*Iblis*). Religious thinkers treated these feelings in numerous books and lots of pages. Their

---

1 Translated from the Arabic by Dr. Mansour Ajami. The English translation of the Qur'an used in this chapter is that of Mohammed Marmaduke Pickthall, *The Meaning of the Glorious Qur'an*.

2 This essay was originally delivered as a lecture at the Arab Cultural Club, Beirut, Lebanon, December 10th, 1965. An abridged version appeared in the monthly journal *Hiwar*, Beirut (January, 1966). See also the journal of the Arab Cultural Club, *Al-Thaqafah al-ᶜArabiyyah*, Beirut (February, 1966.

views on Satan ranged from serious attempts to determine the position that he occupies in the order of the universe, his relationship to God, and the purpose of his existence, to mere profuse explanations of his deception of people and to teaching them well known invocations and incantations so that they can dismiss him and ward off his evil. There is no doubt that each one of us bears in his mind a particular image of Satan's character inherited as an indivisible part of his or her traditional culture and religious upbringing. I find it unnecessary *[A 56]* to expatiate on recalling this image of Satan in the popular mind because it is well known to all of us.

Satan was a favorite angel of God and was of great consequence in the order of the heavenly host until he disobeyed God's order and was expelled from paradise, incurring eternal damnation. Thus, Satan became the embodiment of everything evil, acquiring all the attributes that are incompatible with God. We note here that Satan's name indicates his essence, which is "*iblas*" — that is, total despair of God's mercy and of return to paradise (this according to some traditional Muslim interpretations of the meaning of *iblas*). We are all familiar with the proverb that signifies a total loss of hope: Like Satan's hope of return to paradise. The word Satan connotes scheming, temptation, suggestion of evil thought, instigation to rebellion, disobedience, and other hideous and abominable characteristics that the imagination of man has incorporated into a single character: Satan. In the course of time, man's imagination generously allotted to Satan great creative intellectual powers, innovative artistic capabilities, and the ability to perform supernatural and miraculous acts and deeds. Thus, Satan became next to God in terms of his powers, abilities, and achievements.

Imam Jamal al-Din ibn al-Jawzi wrote a book entitled *Talbis Iblis,* (*The Dissemblance of Satan*)[3] in which he recounted the ways that Satan employs to deceive people, leading them away from the right path. What is curious about this book is that not only does it depict the conventional image of Satan's character, but it also, inadvertently, confers on him innovative,

---

3   *Talbis Iblis*, ed. Muhammad Munir al-Dimashqi, (Cairo: Al-Nahdah Publishing House, 1928).

creative powers that elicit appreciation and admiration. A case in point is Ibn al-Jawzi's crediting to Satan the emergence of most great religious and philosophical movements in the history of Islamic civilization. He thus turns Satan into a great philosopher and a superb theologian. Ibn al-Jawzi claims that sophistry, materialism, naturalism, the theory of natures, the religions of the Far East, Christianity, scholastic theology, and the *Mu'tazilah* school were all the work of Satan and the result of his deception of thinkers and of *ulema* (religious scholars).[4] Likewise, Ibn al-Jawzi attributes the movements of the Kharijites and the Rafidites (*al-Rafida*, i.e., the Shi'a branch of Islam), asceticism and Sufism to Satan's deception of the imams (leaders) of these movements, including Abu Talib al-Makki and Imam al-Ghazali.[5] Of some philosophical ideas, Ibn al-Jawzi says, "Aristotle and his followers claimed that the earth was a star in the center of the celestial sphere and that there are people (*'awalim*), rivers and trees on each star, just as on Earth ... so consider what Satan has led those fools to believe, despite their claim to sound mind."[6] Moreover, Ibn al-Jawzi recounts the following about Satan's deception of grammarians and men of letters: "He deceived those people and preoccupied them with the important disciplines of grammar and language, which are individual duties (*fard 'ayn*) and diverted them from the necessary knowledge *[A 57]* of the acts of worship (*'ibadat*) and from what is worth knowing, such as morals and righteousness (*salah al-qulub*)."[7]

It can thus be inferred that the prevalent idea about Satan's capabilities is not limited primarily to leading people astray from the right path, but rather proceeds to include vast powers and great capabilities. If taken seriously, the powers attributed to Satan would make him responsible for the course of most events and for most philosophical, artistic, and political movements in the history of civilization.

The above quick review examined the popular traditional image of Satan and the powers attributed to him. That aside, the purpose of this

---

4   Ibid. 39-44, 65, 73, 82-83.
5   Ibid. 164-165.
6   Ibid. 45-47.
7   Ibid. 126.

study is to reconsider the story of Satan and to study his character, attitude, responsibilities and fate from a perspective different from the beliefs and ideas that have heretofore governed our conception of this creature. The primary sources to be examined are the Qur'anic verses that recount the story and biography of Satan, as well as works by Muslim thinkers who took interest in Satan, his character, his disobedience, his function and his end.

However, I would like to make it clear that this study is conducted within a specific mythic-religious framework, which ensues from man's mythical imagination and speculative faculties. I do not intend to treat the story of Satan within the purview of pure religious faith, or to talk about him as if he were a real existing being. Rather, I will approach him as a mythical character created by man's speculative faculties and amplified by man's fertile imagination. In dealing with the subject of Satan, I find myself face to face with an ancient, deep rooted mythic-religious tradition. What I most desire to achieve is to reconsider one of the primary characters to come down to us in this heritage, but always remaining within the confines of the primary data of mythological thinking, and without deviating from its basic postulates.

It is worth mentioning here that the popular preconceived notion of myth and its importance is somewhat removed from the real role that myths play in people's lives and the texture of cultures. We are accustomed, for example, to dismiss something as mere "legend or myth," to depreciate its importance, to banish it from mind, to deny it any practical reality and/ or objectivity and to show that it is mere illusion and fantasy. It is therefore necessary to digress a little and explain some important facts about the nature of myth and the significance of mythological thinking for man and society.

Philosophers have defined man as a rational being, an animal endowed with the faculty of speech and reason. If man is such, then he is also a "mythological" animal, for just as man is the only animal that is endowed with speech and reason, he is also the only animal that creates fables and legends and transforms them into [A 58] complex mythologies, and that then believes in them categorically as if they were real indubitable facts. Mythical thinking is thus an essential characteristic of man and an important aspect of his mental activity in the broad sense of the word. That is the reason why many researchers have directed their attention to the study of the mythical activity of man, for uncovering fundamental truths about him, and his society, capabilities, cultures, and civilizations.

By way of example, when you hear me speak of the "tragedy of Satan" in this lecture you undoubtedly go back in your minds to the old organic connection between tragedy and drama on the one hand and myth and mythical thinking on the other. Moreover, a reconsideration of this legendary character that we customarily call Satan will yield new dimensions and significant results as regards religion, art and philosophy. Researchers have spared no effort to explain the organic relationships and connections between mythical thinking and the religious, artistic, and philosophical dimensions of any of the great issues that mankind faces.

Mythology in itself has been and still is potentially a religion, potentially an art, and potentially a philosophy, because it contains in its flexible and indeterminate framework (a) the elements of comfort and solace that are necessary for every religion, (b) the elements of creative artistic expression necessary for human aesthetic responses to the stimuli that affect humans everywhere, and (c) a disposition to explain events and interpret existence, as well as to inquire about its origins and purpose. Additionally, myth has been and still is the medium through which mankind confronted its great and persistent problems, such problems as death, destiny, evil, and the origin, purpose, and meaning of things in general. For that reason, mythology has always been a creative cultural force and a rich source for religious thinking, philosophical contemplation, and artistic expression. For further elucidation, I shall quote a statement by the German philosopher Ernst Cassirer (1874-1945), who was one of the pioneering scholars to study the nature of myth. He showed its essential relationship to man's other intellectual, spiritual, and artistic activities. Cassirer defined the world of myth, the world to which I have confined myself in this lecture, in the following words:

The world of myth is a dramatic world – a world of actions, of forces, of conflicting powers. In every phenomenon of nature it sees the collision of these powers. Mythical perception is always impregnated with these emotional qualities. Whatever is seen or felt is surrounded by a special atmosphere – an atmosphere of joy or grief, of anguish, of excitement, of exultation or gloom. Here we cannot speak of "things" as a dead or indifferent stuff. All objects are benignant or malignant, friendly or inimical, familiar or uncanny, alluring and fascinating or repellent and threatening.[8] *[A 59]*

I must affirm at the end of this prefatory section of my essay that the mention of God, Satan, jinn, angels, and the heavenly host does not mean that these names refer to real but invisible beings. The structure of language by its nature necessitates that I write and speak in a certain manner that seemingly suggests the actual existence of these characters. This is merely linguistic illusion. If I were writing about Prince Hamlet, for example, none of you would believe that the name Hamlet referred to a real being outside the scope of the literary heritage from Shakespeare. Likewise, when we say "Hamlet killed his uncle," we do not believe that such an incident did actually occur in Denmark. Similarly, when we say "God expelled Satan from Paradise," we should not think that such an incident did occur in the history of the universe. Such utterances are meant symbolically and are not descriptions of actual events.

Section Two

The sources that we are consulting in this study on the story of Satan begin with a description of his lofty position in the heavenly host before he was expelled from Paradise. In his book *Taflis Iblis* (*The Failure of Satan*), Imam Izz al-Din al-Maqdisi addresses Satan thus:

> God in His omnipotence created you, showed you His wondrous creations, summoned you to His presence, clothed you with the

---

8   Ernst Cassirer, *An Essay on Man: An Introduction to a Philosophy of Human Culture* (New York: Doubleday & Co., 1953), 102-103.

robe of His unity, crowned you with His hallowed and praiseworthy crown, allowed you to move freely amongst His angels. These angels sought your light, enjoyed your presence, were guided by your knowledge, and followed your example. Hence, you still remained in the heavenly host, savoring the fullest cup and the sweetest speech. How often were you a teacher for the angels and a leader of the cherubim?[9]

Then there are the Qur'anic verses that relate what happened to Satan, how he disobeyed God, and how God cursed him until the Day of Judgment and expelled him from paradise:

And when thy Lord said unto the angels: Lo! I am about to place a viceroy in the earth, they said: Wilt Thou place therein one who will do harm therein and will shed blood, while we, we hymn Thy praise and sanctify Thee? He said: Surely I know that which ye know not. And He taught Adam all the names, and then showed them to the angels, saying: Inform me of the names of these, if ye are truthful. *[A 60]*

They said: Be glorified! We have no knowledge saving that which Thou hast taught us. Lo! Thou, only Thou, art the Knower, the Wise. He said: O Adam! Inform them of their names, and when he had informed them of their names, He said: Did I not tell you that I know the secret of the heavens and the earth? And I know that which ye disclose and which ye hide. And when We said unto the angels: Prostrate yourselves before Adam, they fell prostrate, all save Satan. He demurred through pride, and so became a disbeliever. (*Qur'an 2: 30-34*)

And (remember) when thy Lord said unto the angels: Lo! I am creating a mortal out of potter's clay of black mud altered. So, when I have made him and have breathed into him of My spirit, do ye fall down, prostrating yourselves unto him. So the angels fell prostrate, all of them together save Satan. He refused to be among the prostrate. He said: O Satan! What ails thee that thou art not among the prostrate? He said: Why should I prostrate myself unto a mortal

---

9   Izz al-Din al-Maqdisi, *Taflis Iblis* (Cairo: Matbaᶜat Madrasat Walidat Abbas al-Awwal,1906), 11.

whom Thou hast created out of potter's clay of black mud altered? He said: Then go thou forth from hence, for verily thou art outcast. And lo! The curse shall be upon thee till the Day of Judgment. He said: My Lord! Reprieve me till the day when they are raised. He said: Then lo! thou art of those reprieved till an appointed time. He said: My Lord! Because Thou has sent me astray, I verily shall adorn the path of error for them in the earth, and shall mislead them every one, save such of them as are Thy perfectly devoted slaves. (*Qur'an* 15: 28-40)

And We created you, then fashioned you, then told the angels: Fall ye prostrate before Adam! And they fell prostrate, all save Satan, who was not of those who make prostration. He said: What hindered thee that thou didst not fall prostrate when I bade thee? (Satan) said: I am better than him. Thou created me of fire while him Thou didst create of mud. He said: Then go down hence! It is not for thee to show pride here, so go forth! Lo! Thou art of those degraded. He said: Reprieve me till the day when they are raised (from the dead). He said: Lo! Thou art of those reprieved. He said: Now, because Thou hast sent me astray, verily I shall lurk in ambush for them on Thy Right Path. Then I shall come upon them from before them and from behind them and from their right hands and from their left hands, and Thou will not find most of them beholden (unto Thee). He said: Go forth from hence, degraded, banished. As for such of them as follow thee, surely I will fill hell with all of you. (*Qur'an* 7: 11-18)

The story of Satan, as recounted in these verses, is simple on the face of it. God ordered him to prostrate himself before Adam but he refused and suffered the consequences. However, to surpass this superficial view of the problem of Satan, we need to go back to an important idea advanced by some Muslim scholars: The distinction between divine order and divine will or desire. An order by its nature is either obeyed and executed or is disobeyed. The one given the order has the choice of obeying or disobeying. As for divine will, it is not subject to such considerations because it cannot, by its very nature, be refused. Anything that the divine will wants is of necessity existent. God willed the existence of a great many things but also ordered mankind to keep away from them. Similarly, He ordered man to perform certain things but also wanted man to fulfill things other than the ones He had ordered.[10] Thus, we can say that God ordered Satan to prostrate himself before *[A 61]* Adam but willed him to disobey His order. Had God willed Satan to fall prostrate, he would have done so immediately, since God's slave has no strength or power to disobey divine will. If we were to consider the matter from this perspective, we would be able to regard order and command as accidental, or contingent, in comparison with the eternity of divine will and the timelessness of God.

If we reconsider the Qur'anic verses that we have just cited, it becomes clear that God wanted the angels to "hymn His praise and sanctify Him." Al-Tabari states in his famous *Tafsir* that "praising and sanctifying" God constitute profession of the Oneness of God (*tawhid*), affirming His utter transcendence and denying to Him the attributes that the polytheists assign to Him.[11] In other words, *tawhid* (profession of the Oneness of God) is the foremost and absolute duty of angels to their Creator, and is thus the reason why the angels are totally immersed in fulfilling their duty to God with all their being and essence. As for the other duties imposed on the heavenly host, they are accidental and secondary in comparison with the absolute duty that derives from the divine will itself.

---

10 Al-Tabari, in his famous *Tafsir* of the Qur'an, related the following myth, which is of great significance to the subject of this essay: God sent Gabriel to Earth to fetch some clay. The Earth said, "God forbid that you should diminish me or disfigure me. So Gabriel did not take anything and returned to God, saying, "O God, the Earth sought your protection so I granted it to it. Then God sent Michael to do the same thing. The Earth sought God's protection and Michael granted it to Earth. Michael returned to God and reported the same answer as Gabriel's, whereupon God sent the Angel of Death and Earth sought God's protection, the same as she had done the previous two times. The Angel of Death said, "I too seek refuge in God that I should go back to him without executing his order. So the Angel of Death took some soil from different parts of the surface of the Earth — red, white, and black soil. That is the reason why the sons of Adam are so different. (*Tafsir al-Tabari*, vol. 1, ed. Mahmud Muhammad Shakir (Cairo: Dar al-Maᶜarif), 459)). This story represents the difference between will and command. God ordered both Gabriel and Michael to bring him some soil but God willed that the order be fulfilled by the Angel of Death. So God received what he had willed.

11 Ibid. 475.

After having demonstrated the difference between absolute duty toward God and the partial duty of obedience to the orders of God, it is now possible to distinguish the following points about Satan's refusal of God's order:

1) There is no doubt that Satan disobeyed the divine order when he refused to prostrate himself before Adam, but he was in total conformity with divine will and with his absolute duty toward his Creator.

2) Had Satan prostrated himself before Adam he would have departed from the profession of the Oneness of God and rebelled against his absolute duty toward God. God wanted the angels to sanctify Him and to hymn His praise. Thus, prostrating himself before Adam would have subjected Satan to the errors of the polytheists, who ascribe to Him attributes He is free from Falling prostrate before any other than God is absolutely impermissible, because such an act constitutes polytheism. In fact, Satan's choice raises a very important question: Does real obedience consist in obeying an order or in submission to God's will? Does righteousness lie in submission to absolute duty or to the secondary duties of obedience? If the answer to this question were simple and clear, tragedy would not have been a part of man's life, Satan would not have found himself in such a dilemma, and he would not have fallen between the claws of command and will. We infer from this that Satan's attitude represents absolute insistence on Oneness in its purest sense and manifestation. It is as though *[A 62]* Satan wanted to say, "A forehead that has fallen prostrate before the One God will not be humbled before any other existent creature."[12]

Al-Hallaj, the martyr of Sufism, expressed such an opinion in his book *Kitab al-Tawasin:*

> Moses met Satan at the steep incline of Mount Sinai and said to him: "What hindered thee that thou didst not fall prostrate?" Satan replied, "What hindered me was my profession of the One God. Had I prostrated myself (before Adam) I would have been like you. You

---

12 *Taflis Iblis*, 15.

were summoned once to 'gaze upon the mountain,' and you gazed. I was called one thousand times to prostrate myself, but I did not, for I believe in my profession of the Oneness of God."[13]

Satan justified his refusal to prostrate himself before Adam logically and clearly: "I am better than him. You created me of fire, while him Thou did create of mud." In addition, the Qur'anic verses just mentioned imply a latent justification of Satan's refusal: his foreknowledge that Adam and his progeny would create havoc and disaster and would shed blood on earth. Such was the common feeling of all the angels when they said to God, "Wilt Thou place therein one who will do harm therein and will shed blood, while we, we hymn Thy praise and sanctify Thee?" The angels, including Satan, were cognizant of the great sins and offenses that Adam and his progeny would perpetrate on earth. Thus, they found it to be an enormity that God should create those who would disobey Him and who would shed blood.

A close examination of Satan's first argument, which consists of a comparison between his essence, fire, and Adam's essence, clay, demonstrates that it was not as much haughtiness and vainglory as it was a re-invoking of a fundamental truth, which God had willed and brought into being. This truth is that the natures created by God are not all of the same degree of sublimity and perfection. Rather, He distinguished between them, not only with respect to their material and natural characteristics but also with regard to their worth and perfection. Accordingly, we can classify beings and kinds in a specific hierarchy of perfection which starts with Absolute Perfection itself, and descends gradually according to the degree of perfection that God had bestowed on each kind, until we draw near nothingness, the lowest limit that we stop at.

There is no doubt that fire, by nature and essence, occupies a higher and more sublime rank in this order than clay. In other words, Satan's comparison between his essence and that of Adam involves a specific

---

13 Al Hallaj, "Tasin al-Azal wa-'l-Iltibas" in *Kitab al-Tawasin,* ed. Louis Massignon (Paris: 1913).

philosophical viewpoint of the order of the universe and the classification of natures according to their degree of perfection. Satan's reply was thus correct, because the Creator had created things as they are regarding their degrees of perfection and sublimity, and His order to Satan to prostrate himself before Adam constitutes an obvious violation of this system and a departure from the hierarchy that God willed and brought into being.

If Satan's essence in the ladder of perfections was higher than Adam's, then fire can only lower itself to clay by following a course contrary to its nature, which is incompatible with the degree of perfection bestowed upon it by God. This will remain impossible until there is a radical change in the divine will, whereupon it changes the order of essences or natures from what they had been since He made them. *[A 63]* In other words, God ordered Satan to do one thing but willed him to perform another. We will, therefore, realize later that the command to lay prostrate was not an order of will but rather an order of trial.

It is curious to note in this regard that the change that occurred in Satan after his expulsion from paradise did not affect his essence, but rather his attributes and modes. His image was thus disfigured and he became damned and cursed. In his own special way, al-Hallaj illustrated this reality in the above-cited dialogue between Moses and Satan, whereby Satan explains to Moses that the change and disfigurement that befell him affected only his external and ephemeral conditions, but did not affect his permanent essence or his constant knowledge of the provisions of the divine will. Moses said to Satan: "You ignored the order." Satan replied: "That was a trial, not an order." Moses said: "He surely changed your image." Satan replied: "Moses, this is all deception. The circumstance is unstable; it changes, whereas the true knowledge is still the same. It has not changed. Only the persona has changed."[14]

As for the second argument that Satan presented to justify his refusal to lay prostrate before Adam, it was based on the angels' knowledge that Adam and his progeny would do harm unto the world and would shed

---

14 "Tasin al-Azal wa-'l-Iltibas"

blood. Therefore, how could Satan, who was immersed in the profession of Oneness, in God's praise and sanctification, the one who was the imam of angels (archangel), the preacher of the cherubim, how could one such as he fall prostrate before a creature who would do harm on earth and would shed blood? Al-Hallaj summarized this aspect of the subject as such:

> God said to Satan: "Do you not lay prostrate, O ignominious one?" Satan replied: "I love Thee and he who is in love is humble (*mahin*). You characterized me as ignominious, but I have read in A Revealed Book what this will bring upon me, O Thou Omnipotent One. How could I debase myself to Adam while you created me of fire and created him of clay? Clay and fire are irreconcilable opposites. I have served you longer, am of greater worth, am more knowledgeable, and am more perfect of age than Adam."[15]

We thus infer that the story of Satan as recounted in the Qur'anic verses is not as simple as we had imagined. It is not a story of conflict between good and evil, right and wrong. Satan fell between two millstones, the millstone of divine will and that of divine command. He had to make a choice that would determine his destiny, a choice between his absolute duty of professing the Oneness of God, of hymning His praise and sanctifying Him and the secondary duties of obedience that God had ordered him to fulfill. His ordeal was therefore replete with dramatic and tragic elements.

Before I proceed with unpacking the implications of this conception of Satan's ordeal, *[A 64]* I feel obliged to refute the assertions promoted by Abbas Mahmud al-Aqqad in his book, *Iblis*. Al-Aqqad attempts to defend the superficial traditional conception of Satan's character as merely a being who disobeyed God's order, and so God expelled him from paradise. As such, Al-Aqqad refuses to acknowledge Satan's ordeal, and upholds the necessity of Satan's prostration before Adam. Upon scrutiny, we find that Al-Aqqad's opinion is based on two arguments.

---

15   Ibid.

1) Angels had to lay prostrate before Adam because he was better than they. Adam was capable of doing good and evil, whereas angels could do good only. They are safeguarded against the temptation of evil and thus it is not attributable to them.[16]

2) Satan must prostrate himself before Adam because God had taught Adam all the names but had not taught them to the Angels, which makes Adam superior to them.[17]

I shall refute each argument separately.

It seems to me that al-Aqqad's claim that Adam was superior to the angels because he was subject to both good and evil, whereas they are safe from such temptations, is fundamentally false for the following reasons:

a) The story of Satan demonstrates that even the chiefs of the angels and those favored by God among them are not safe from the temptation of evil, or else Satan would not have disobeyed God and would not have met such a miserable fate. We therefore infer that angels are subject to good and evil. Like man, they are subject to the trials of evil and are required to do good, which negates Adam's superiority to angels and consequently eliminates the need to lay prostrate before him.

b) If we assume, hypothetically, with al-Aqqad that the angels are not subject to good and evil but rather always do good, due to their nature and essence, does that mean that Adam is better than they? Let us rephrase the question in more general terms: Which creatures are superior: Those who do good on occasion and do evil on other occasions, inflicting harm on earth and shedding blood, or those who do good only, constantly and forever?

The answer to this question is very clear and needs no discussion, based on the premise that our moral conception of the perfect will dictates that it is the will that constantly and effortlessly does good, because doing good has become part of its essence and intrinsic nature. As for the imperfect will, it is still struggling and striving to defeat the temptation of evil in an attempt to come close to the perfect will, which is its ideal.

---

16 Abbas Mahmud al-Aqqad, *Iblis* (Cairo: Dar Al-Hilal), 10, 11.
17 Ibid. 148.

If the angels, according to al-Aqqad's claim, are free from the temptation of evil, then God had undoubtedly bestowed upon them a perfect will that would make them far superior to Adam and his progeny. When God said to the angels, "Lo! I am about to place a viceroy in the earth," the angels demurred before such an enormity and answered: "Wilt Thou place therein one who will do harm therein and will shed blood?" Does al-Aqqad intend to make Adam's ability to do harm and shed blood a source of his superiority over the angels?

We now proceed to refute al-Aqqad's second argument, the claim that it is the angels' duty to fall prostrate before [A 65] Adam because God had taught him, not the angels, all the names. We have shown earlier that Satan was superior to Adam because of Satan's intrinsic nature and essence; his superiority was not due to contingent, ephemeral conditions such as those acquired by Adam when God taught him all the names. In other words, Adam's knowledge of all the names does not constitute one, or indeed any, of his distinguishing and essential characteristics.

There is no doubt that the angels could have learned all the names if God had wanted that. We therefore infer that Adam's knowledge of all the names was contingent, and was bestowed upon him by God to entice the angels to lay prostrate before him. Hence:

1) Adam is not superior to the angels, including Satan, neither because of his ability to do good and evil nor due to his knowledge of all the names.

2) Satan's essence is better than and superior to Adam's essence, because God created him from fire and created Adam from clay. God had not intended clay to be as high in the order of things as fire.

3) Al-Aqqad's claim that it was incumbent upon Satan to fall prostrate before Adam because Adam was superior to the angels is false and to be rejected.

Section Three

We return now to Satan's ordeal that resulted from the contradiction of command and will. Al-Hallaj expressed Satan's ordeal with splendid conciseness: "When Satan was told to lay prostrate before Adam, he addressed the Truthful (God): "Has the lofty honor of prostration only for You been lifted, so I prostrate myself for him? By ordering me to lay prostrate (before Adam), You have prevented me from doing so.""[18]

Imam al-Maqdisi defined the nature of the contradiction between divine order and divine will as follows:

> I have considered with certitude the circle of eternal happiness and eternal damnation. It turns on the line of the command and the centers of the will. Between them is indeterminate subtlety and lonely narrow space. The traveler in this strait has no companion for success. The giver of the order grants, but the will plunders. What is endowed by the giver of the order is plundered by the will. The order-giver says, "Do," but the will says, "Do not do."[19]

It appears that Imam al-Maqdisi had considerable understanding of the importance of the dramatic and tragic elements of Satan's ordeal; hence his emphasis on the element of contradiction faced by Satan and on his inability to find an appropriate exit from his ordeal. The choice that Satan had to make was critical for his destiny. His eternal happiness or misery depended on his choice. He could surrender to the requirements of the will and be consistent with his absolute duty, thereby attaining eventual happiness, *[A 66]* or he could slide into submission to God's order and to the secondary duties of obedience, thus failing the test and becoming forever miserable. In short, the order to lay prostrate placed Satan's being, life, and eternal happiness in the balance because "the giver of the order grants, but the will plunders," and "the order-giver says do, but the will says do not do."

In addition, al-Maqdisi's statement shows that those who undergo such an ordeal do not have a clear, bright path, nor are they given a chance to distinguish easily between a right choice and a wrong choice because of the indistinguishable "subtlety...of the two." Furthermore, those who are placed in such a predicament find themselves totally alone, unable to

---

18   *Kitab al-Tawasin*, Introduction, 11-12.
19   *Taflis Iblis*, 4.

benefit from the counsel or assistance of friend or companion. They have to make the choice alone and they must bear the consequences of their choice. The path that they were predestined to take is, as al-Maqdisi said, a "lonely narrow space."

In the following pages I shall try to determine the elements of tragedy in Satan's ordeal and to highlight its various aspects as precisely and clearly as the subject allows. I will therefore rely on two principal sources: the Greek drama of Sophocles and the story of Abraham in the Semitic religious tradition.

I need not dwell long on the story of Abraham. Abraham was ordered to slay his son Isaac (or Ishmael) and when he was about to execute the order, God ransomed him "with a tremendous victim (*Qur'an* 37: 107)."[20] I pause here for a moment to refer to a well-known study by Kierkegaard of the story of Abraham in his book *Fear and Trembling*. I have relied in this section of my study on the general outlines of Kierkegaard's interpretation of Abraham's trial. However, this should not preclude some basic differences between the opinions that I will present and Kierkegaard's special standpoint on the persona of Abraham. There is no doubt that the story of Abraham contains powerful tragic possibilities and many of the basic elements of tragedy. However, we cannot under any circumstances consider it a real tragedy because it has a happy, optimistic, and pleasing ending. The feeling left by the story of Abraham differs completely and qualitatively from the feeling left by the story of King Oedipus, for example.[21] *[A 67]*

---

20 A group of *mujtahidun* (legists) say that the son that Abraham was ordered to slay was Isaac, while others say it was Ishmael. Al-Tabari discussed the opinions and arguments of the two groups in his *Tafsir* and adopted the opinion of those who said it was Isaac. I shall follow al-Tabari's conclusion. *Tafsir al-Tabari*, old edition, Al-Matbaʿah al-Maymaniyyah (Egypt), Vol. 8 part 3, p. 49.

21 Kierkegaard considers Abraham's recovery of his son Isaac a special religious ending that elevates the story of Abraham above the level of tragedy in its known literary sense. For him, Abraham's persona has surpassed by leagues the tragic heroes found in world literature. In reality, the story of Abraham falls completely short of reaching the status of tragedy and his character remains well below that of the tragic hero for the reasons mentioned above.

There are many considerations that make Satan's ordeal a real tragedy, and I will point them out in sequence:

A tragedy often occurs at the time of major crises and violent events that upset the status quo, rock the foundations of current systems, shake the prevailing values so much so that those undergoing such trials feel that their former being and familiar mode of existence have been put to trial and that the moral, spiritual, and material components of their surrounding world are about to collapse. God had given Abraham "a gentle son." And when his son was old enough to walk with him, Abraham said, "O my dear son, I have seen in a dream that I must sacrifice thee…" (*Qur'an* 37: 101-102) Abraham was ordered to sacrifice his son as an offering to God. This order upset all measures and standards, broke down all values, blurred and confused all features and characteristics. The merciful compassionate father has to kill his son, with premeditation, calmness, and submission.

Satan was a teacher to the angels and a leader to the cherubim. He was, as al-Maqdisi observes, calm and peaceful, sound and virtuous, and while he was in the presence of witnesses, God brought Adam into being and ordered him to lay prostrate before Adam.[22] Thereupon the order of the heavenly host shook, and all standards and measures were toppled again. The forehead of Satan, which had only prostrated itself before the One had to prostrate itself before a human. The teacher who taught *tawhid* to angels had to disavow the earlier sanctification and glorification of God. Fire had to submit to clay. But Satan refused to prostrate himself before Adam, and was thus damned until the Day of Judgment. In other words, the story presents Satan's disavowal and his expulsion from paradise at the highest of his glory, then at the lowest point of his suffering and misery. In this respect, the story of Satan was much like the ancient Greek story that presents King Oedipus at the apex of his power and glory and then presents him wandering in the labyrinths of despair, suffering, and agony. Both Satan and King Oedipus became outcasts, disfigured and loathsome, after they tumbled

---

22 *Taflis Iblis*, 15.

to the abyss of suffering. Whoever had supported them became their adversary.

When we consider the drama *Antigone*, we discover that the heroine's tragic end was a consequence of the essential contradiction between what Antigone represents on the one hand and what Creon, the King of Thebes, represents on the other. Antigone was absolutely determined to bury her murdered brother, regardless of happenstance or cost. Her motive was her great love for her brother and her unshakeable belief in the need to bury the dead, as decreed by the gods. Antigone addresses her sister Ismene as follows:[23]

> Go thine own way; myself will bury him.
> How sweet to die in such employ, to rest,
> —Sister and brother linked in love's embrace—
> A sinless sinner, banned awhile on earth,
> But by the dead commended; *[A 68]* and with them
> I shall abide forever. As for thee,
> Scorn, if thou wilt, the eternal laws of Heaven.

King Creon, on the other hand, was motivated by a noble, patriotic emotion when he ordered punishment against the brother who bore arms against the city and was killed at its gates. He was also sincere in his attempt to uphold the rule of law and to restore order to the city of Thebes after the chaos that had swept it. It was therefore incumbent on him to be firm, to insist on the thorough execution of his orders and directives, and to threaten with extreme punishment whoever violated the law. All of these measures were natural and necessary in Thebes, a city that had suffered the calamities of war, disease, and chaos before Creon took the reins of government. The result was the tragic conflict between the temporal requirements and needs of the city, as represented in the character of Creon, and the divine requirements, as represented in the character of Antigone. In the end, everyone endured death, despair, and tragedy.

---

23 *Sophocles,* The Loeb Classical Library (Cambridge: Harvard University Press, 1977), 321.

When Creon asked Antigone, "And yet wert bold enough to break the law?" She answered:

> Yea, for these laws were not ordained of Zeus,
> And she who sits enthroned with gods below,
> Justice, enacted not these human laws.
> Nor did I deem that thou, a mortal man,
> Could by a breath annul and override
> The immutable unwritten laws of Heaven.
> They were not born today nor yesterday;
> They die not; and none knoweth whence they
> Sprang.
> I was not like, who feared no mortal's frown,
> To disobey these laws and so provoke
> The wrath of Heaven. I know that I must die,
> Even had thou not proclaimed it; and if death
> Is thereby hastened, I shall count it gain.[24]

If we were to consider the story of Abraham from such perspective, we would discover that it contains a contradiction similar to the one that Sophocles depicted in his play. There is no doubt that Abraham suffered tremendously as a result of the contradiction between his respect for the emotional requirements and moral obligations of paternity on the one hand and the imperative to submit to the divine order that decreed the slaying of his son Isaac on the other. Abraham loved his son more than he loved himself and he performed his paternal duties superbly well. But what could he do when his love for his son and his paternal duties were incompatible with the requirements of total obedience to God's order, and with his absolute religious duties to his God?

It must be admitted that Abraham's ordeal is charged with the elements of tragedy and its tensions to a larger degree than is Antigone's, because the basic contradiction in Sophocles' play is between temporal authority and the eternal orders of Heaven. Each side of this contradiction has its own independent origin. As for Abraham, the two sides of the contradiction revert ultimately to the same origin, God. When Antigone

---

24 Ibid. 349.

obeyed the orders of Heaven she disobeyed *[A 69]* the orders of temporal authority. But when Abraham submitted to God's order and placed the knife on his son's neck, he disobeyed the absolute moral norms that God had bestowed upon man: Rules that govern fathers' treatment of sons and vice versa. In other words, when Abraham obeyed his God from the religious standpoint, he was obliged to disobey him from the moral standpoint.

Satan's ordeal is not qualitatively different from the ordeal of either Antigone or Abraham. He had a direct divine order to prostrate himself before Adam and at the same time he was under the requirement of divine will that called for the profession of Oneness, sanctification, and praise of God and that prohibited prostration before anyone but the eternal God. Satan submitted to the requirements of divine will and thereby disobeyed the order to prostrate himself. He was thus expelled from paradise, damned and foreordained to absolute despair of returning to paradise. However, Satan's tragedy was bigger and more catastrophic than Abraham's ordeal, which turned out not to be a tragedy, because Abraham was able, in the end, to slay a ram in place of his son Isaac. The contradiction that Satan faced was not between the duties of religious obedience and those of moral obedience, but rather between the duties of obedience to the divine order only. Expressed otherwise, Satan confronted God in direct and compromising self-contradiction, thereby becoming a victim of this contradiction and of the stand that he, Satan, had chosen and assumed.

A careful examination of *Antigone* reveals more than a conventional heroine who represents all good, truth, and beauty, while her adversary represents the opposite of such qualities. Likewise, a subtle understanding of the story of Abraham in its humanistic dimensions cannot but reveal that his attempt to slay his son was not simply an abominable crime incompatible with the simplest axioms of humaneness and morality.

The same is true of the story of Satan. A careful examination of his ordeal and of his disobedience of the prostration order reveals more than an embodiment of rebellion, evil, and sin. Furthermore, if we consider matters from a different perspective, we will have no doubt that Satan was disobedient and a denier. Yet, we should not forget that his denial (*juhud*) was the most sublime form of sanctification of God and the grandest example of commitment to the reality of Oneness. Satan sinned when he argued with his God, but it was God who permitted him to argue, and who listened to him when he said: "I am better than him. Thou created me of fire, whilst him Thou didst create of clay." Here, Satan's tragic character is manifest as a mixture of innocence and sin, beauty and ugliness, right and wrong, good and evil. Satan possesses all these attributes, just as do the heroes of the great tragedies of literature. Satan had to reject prostration totally. Likewise, Orestes had to kill his mother and Hamlet to kill his uncle. Like Orestes and Hamlet, Satan had to suffer the resulting tribulation, pain, and despair. All of these heroes found themselves on the horns of a dilemma. They are at once in the right and are not right. Only those who are intrepid, robust, and of heroic mettle can endure such tragic tension.

For further elucidation, we should differentiate between two kinds of tragedy: The "tragedy of alienation" *[A 70]* and the "tragedy of fate." Here I am suggesting that Satan's ordeal clearly represents those two kinds of tragedy. Misfortune in the tragedy of alienation is the result of separation from a "fixed situation" that the hero had been associated with but then found himself dissociated from. The works of Milton, Dostoyevsky, Kafka, and Camus (in his book, *The Stranger*) are good examples of the tragedy of alienation. As for Satan's alienation and its tribulations, al-Hallaj describes it in the words of Satan as follows:

> He isolated me, left me alone, confused me, expelled me, lest I associate with the faithful; prevented me from those who are jealous on account of my jealousy. He transformed me on account of my confusion; confused me on account of my estrangement; made me *haram* (unlawful) on account of my companionship; disfigured me on account of my praise; excommunicated me on account of my abandonment; abandoned me on account of my disclosures (with Him), exposed me on account of my connection (to Him).[25]

---

25 "Tasin al-Azal wa-'l-Iltibas"

Imam al-Maqdisi described Satan's alienation and misery in these lines spoken by Satan:

> And to perfect my misery I asked to be reprieved (till the day of resurrection). So, I became the laughing stock of those in the Presence. I pine away when I hear those who invoke and repeat His name; I am rent when I see those giving thanks to Him. I run away from the shadow of one, and from the pure deeds of another. One burns me with his breath, while the other disables me with his strength. When the remorseful repents, he breaks my back and when the stray one returns he shortens my life. All that I built with the disobedient in a year is demolished by repentance in a year. I am in interminable woe, unalterable war and a sorrow that lasts long.[26]

Abu Hayyan al-Tawhidi's splendid description of alienation applies aptly to Satan's situation:

> O Ye! The stranger (*gharib*) is one whose sun of beauty has set; one who is estranged from his loved ones and from his censurers; one who speaks and acts in strange ways. The stranger is one whose description says: One ordeal after another, whose title indicates: One trial after another; and whose truth shows in him time and again. Oh, mercy on the stranger! His journey extends without arrival, his tribulation lasts without wrong, his hurt intensifies without fail, his suffering magnifies to no avail.[27]

Sophocles' *King Oedipus* and Shakespeare's *Romeo and Juliet* are considered to be among the best works on the tragedy of fate. Sophocles' play reveals how fate took its inevitable course, how all prophecies were realized, and how all efforts by Oedipus and Jocasta to escape their dark fate failed. An examination of Satan's ordeal from a similar perspective shows that he also was subject in all his deeds [A 71] to God's preordained fate just like any creature of God's kingdom, as stated in the following holy tradition:[28]

---

26 *Taflis Iblis*, 36f.

27 *al-Isharat al-Ilahiyyah*, ed. Abd al-Rahman Badawi (Cairo, 1950), 80-82.

28 This is *hadith qudsi*, a Muslim tradition in which God Himself speaks, as opposed to *hadith nabawi*, an ordinary prophetic tradition [trans. note].

> The pen was the first thing that God created. He said to it, "Write."
> The pen replied: "What do I write?" God said, "The fates of everything
> until the Hour of Resurrection. He who dies believing otherwise is
> not one of Mine."[29]

Al-Hallaj too expressed this truth in a very famous line of poetry about
Satan: "He dropped him, hands tied, into the open sea and said to him,
Beware! Beware! Do not get wet."

In other words, Satan was subject in his circumstance, choice,
expulsion, damnation and disfigurement to the ordinances of the Divine
Will and to the inescapable fate that He had decreed. He was compelled by
God's wisdom, as they say, and overwhelmed by God's will, as attested to by
God's words: "Lo! We have created everything with a fate." (*Qur'an* 54: 49)

Al-Hallaj wrote the following on Satan's submission to his fate as
divinely decreed:

> The Truthful, may He be praised, said to Satan, "The choice is mine, not
> yours." Satan answered, "All choices, and mine as well, are Yours. You,
> Creator, have made the choice for me. If You have forbidden me from
> prostrating myself [before Adam] it is because You are the All Invincible.
> If I failed to express myself, it is because you are the All-Hearing. If you
> want me to prostrate myself before him I am the obedient. Of all those
> I know, I know You; none knows You better than me. Do not blame me,
> for I am not to blame. Protect me, Lord; I am all alone.[30]

Not everyone who has been wronged by fate and crushed by predestined
decree is a hero. Nor is everyone who finds himself in a tragic ordeal like
those of Satan, Antigone, and Abraham a tragic character. It depends to
a large extent on the quality of one's reaction to one's ordeal and on the
nature of one's response to one's destiny. Antigone's sister, Ismene, for
example, was well aware of the conflict that led Antigone to her tragic
end. However, we cannot under any circumstances consider Ismene a tragic

---

29 Shaykh Muhammad al-Madani, *al-Ittihafat al-Saniyyah fi 'l-Ahadith 'l-Qudsiyyah*
     (Hyderabad: 1258 A. H.), 87.
30 "Tasin al-Azal wa-'l-Iltibas".

personality because her response to that conflict was negative and she totally surrendered to the flow of events. That is the reason why she counseled prudence, raised doubts, and expressed fears, which proves that hers was not the mettle of heroes. The same applies to the angels whose "mark of them is on their foreheads from the traces of prostration." (*Qur'an* 48: 29)

It would be interesting to make a comparison between Satan's attitude and that of Adam. Adam disobeyed God just as did Satan. If God had willed Adam not to disobey, Adam would not have disobeyed, nor would God have reproached him for his disobedience. Adam did not evince any positive reaction (to God's reproach) but rather said, "Our Lord! We have wronged ourselves. If Thou forgive us not and have not mercy on us, surely we are of the lost!" (*Qur'an* 7: 23)

As for the tragic hero who fought his destiny like King Oedipus did, he would not have said "I have wronged myself," because he knew well that it was his [A 72] ineluctable fate that had wronged him. Satan, on the other hand, responded positively to God's reproach, saying, "My Lord! Because Thou hast sent me astray, I verily shall adorn the path of error for them in the earth…," thereby denying that he had wronged himself or that he was responsible for his destiny and his end. Once again, al-Tawhidi's description of the stranger applies to Satan: "He has no excuse so he may be excused; he committed no offense so he may be pardoned; he committed no disgrace so he may be forgiven." [31]

Adam was afraid of admitting this truth when God reproached him, whereas Satan argued with God and attempted to defend his act and to justify his choice, although he was aware that there was no escape from the fate that God had preordained for him. As such, he was comparable to Oedipus and Jocasta when they attempted to escape their ominous destiny, even though they knew that their failure was expected and inevitable. Satan, however, remained positive, in attitude and deed, even after he was damned, as proven by his reaction: "Verily, I shall adorn the path of error for them in the earth and shall mislead them every one." (*Qur'an* 15: 39)

---

31 *al-Isharat al-Ilahiyyah*, p. 81.

The heroes of the great works of tragedy in world literature were thus made of the same mettle as Satan and their tragic personae were modeled after him. No wonder that such tragic characters were either in direct contact with Satan or that they had clear Satanic characteristics. It is no coincidence either that the great tragic characters are most often drawn from groups of eccentrics, saboteurs, rebels, infidels, deniers and murderers. It is for that reason that legal trials abound in famous tragedies. Examples of authors and such literary works are those of Aeschylus, Kafka, *The Brothers Karamazov*, and Camus' novel *The Stranger*. It is possible to consider the argument that took place between Satan and God in the Qur'an as a speedy court-martial in which Satan was given a chance to defend himself before God delivered a verdict that was already in force.

In investigating the nature of tragedy, it is difficult not to touch on the subject of the emotion of pride and the role that emotion plays in the life of tragic characters. Pride assumes special significance because of the opinion that attributes Satan's refusal to prostrate himself before Adam to the motives of pride and vainglory. The Truthful (God) said to Satan when He expelled him from paradise: "Then go down hence! It is not for thee to show pride here, so go forth! Lo! Thou art of those degraded." (*Qur'an* 7: 13)

In order to comprehend the true nature of Satan's pride, we must distinguish between pride in the sense of arrogance and "tragic pride," which characterizes the great tragic personae. That is not to say that the tragic hero cannot be arrogant. However, this reprehensible quality, arrogance, remains accidental and contingent in relation to his heroism and tragedy. Hubris and quixotic pride can only elicit pity and ridicule; tragic pride imposes a serious attitude toward the hero, and great admiration and appreciation for him, even if his attitude is contrary to our principles and attitudes. For that reason, pride has always been an important incentive that has motivated tragic characters, from King Oedipus to Ivan Karamazov. *[A 73]*

The essence of tragic pride is manifest in the hero's refusal to remain passive in the face of what he considers to be a challenge to his duty, status and dignity, even though he knows that such a challenge is part of his fate and that his pride will lead him to destruction, despair, and death. Oedipus, Antigone, and Satan came to this end. Adam, on the other hand, did not possess that kind of pride, and had he been predestined to become a tragic character he would not have proclaimed, "Our Lord! We have wronged ourselves. If Thou forgive us not and have not mercy on us, surely we are of the lost." From this we deduce that Satan's pride did not derive from empty arrogance, or from insolence toward God, but rather was a tragic pride that prompted him to seek refuge in God from the fate that God had determined for him.

Satan did not change his attitude toward God even after he was expelled from paradise and damned by God. He still acknowledged God's omnipotence and was afraid of Him and would accept no deity but Him, as is evident from the Qur'anic verses which say: "And the hypocrites are on the likeness of the devil when he tells man to disbelieve, then, when he disbelieves (Satan) saith, "Lo! I am quit of thee. Lo! I fear Allah, the Lord of the worlds." (*Qur'an* 59: 16) Also, on the evidence of Satan's answer when he made an oath before God: "Then, by Thy might, I surely will beguile them every one, save Thy single-minded slaves among them." (*Qur'an* 38: 83) Satan thus demonstrated that nothing was more precious to him than God's might, even after he was eternally damned. Moreover, Satan excluded God's devoted servants ("single-minded slaves") from his oath as if he were trying to prove his appreciation of God and his sincere loyalty to the Lord of the worlds, even after he was expelled and cursed. Not only was Satan an alien, but he was also an alien in his alienation, as al-Tawhidi stated.

In the conversation that he imagined between Moses and Satan, al-Hallaj describes Satan's attitude toward God after he received eternal damnation as follows:

Moses said to Satan, "Do you mention His name in praise (*dhikr*)?" Satan replied, "O, Moses, the thought does not invoke God's name. I am mentioned and He is mentioned, His mention is my mention and my mention is His mention, can the ones who mention exist except with one another? My service to Him is now purer, my time is freer and my praise is more distinct. In time past it was my good fortune to serve Him, but now I serve Him for His good fortune."[32]

Imam al-Maqdisi had an unconventional view of Satan's destiny and pride, influenced by Al-Hallaj's viewpoint.

> He (God) said to me, "Prostrate yourself before someone other than I." I said, "No one but You." He said, "I curse you." I said, "No harm done. If You draw me near You, then You are You." He said, "You do that in arrogance and vainglory." I said, "Lord! Whoever has known You for an instant in his lifetime, or has been with You for a moment throughout his life, or accompanied You in your love for a while, surely can be proud. Just imagine how much more proud would be one who spent his whole lifetime with You and who built monuments out of your love. How many times have I day and night professed your Oneness. How many times have I learned privately and publicly the lessons of your sanctity and praise? Traditions and signs witness for me, the abodes know my right and the night and day believe me. Where was Adam when I was the *imam* of the angels, the preacher to all the cherubim, and the leader of your close companions? I have worshipped *[A 74]* You since time immemorial, and You have willed for me since time immemorial. When the signs of your will appeared, the traces of worship disappeared. The legist (*mujtahid*) missed in his judgment. The master lost his high rank and the arrow of fate (death) unmistakably struck his heart. Whether I prostrate myself before Adam or not, worship You or not, it is inevitable that I return to preordained fate. You have created me of fire and it is inevitable that I return to fire. "Thereof We created you, and thereunto We return you." (*Qur'an* 20: 55)[33]

Section Four

In the previous pages, I treated the predicament of Satan on many levels. I began with the popular traditional viewpoint; then I described his ordeal

---

32 "Tasin al-Azal wa-'l-Iltibas"
33 *Taflis Iblis*, pp. 21-22.

and then I specified the tragic aspects of his character and attitude. There is no doubt that as we move from one of these three levels to the other, Satan's reality, as well as the numerous facets of his character, become more distinct and profound. This does not mean that our understanding of Satan's character on the tragic level will reveal his reality completely and in full. The reason is that his character is not as much the product of dramatic literary imagination as it is the offspring of pure religious imagination.

Our tragic view of Satan will, therefore, remain deficient, and will reveal only part of his truth. A treatment of Satan on a purely religious level would, however, complete our picture of him and would reveal his real and ultimate status in the order of creation. The main reason compelling me to make such a statement is that tragedy, in its definitive and absolute sense, cannot exist within the framework of the three Semitic religions.

It is impossible for religion to accept tragedy in its definitive form because divine providence encompasses the universe completely and leads it to the ultimate ends that God had chosen for it. That is why it is natural for religion to claim that it can surpass tragedy, no matter how afflicting it is, and that it can solve all the complexities involved in it, if not in this worldly life, then in the hereafter. The tragic view of events, for instance, requires that heroes suffer grave, absolutely irreparable losses, symbolized often by death or total despair. Heroes are also required to suffer undeserved and unwanted disaster and torture.

Religion, on the other hand, rejects such a tragic logic and maintains that the pious will someday be recompensed for the losses they suffer, just as God compensated Job for the disasters that had befallen him, and rewarded him for his long patience. Whereas losses suffered by evildoers are the just punishment they deserve because of their sins and evil deeds, as indicated by the Qur'anic verse: "And whoso doeth good an atom's weight will see it then, And whoso doeth ill an atom's weight will see it then." (*Qur'an* 99: 7, 8) Even the tragedy of death is, according to religion, only but a temporary loss *[A 75]* that signifies transition from the temporal world to the eternal abode. In other words, religion accepts tragedy only as a transitory, temporary phase. Subsequently, Satan's tragedy must be a temporary one and will someday come to an end.

After this reference to the limitations of the tragic view of Satan's character, I would like to pose the following question: Why was Satan ordered to prostrate himself before Adam? More precisely, why did God put him in this predicament? The answer is that God wanted to test and try Satan just as He did Job and Abraham and other pious men after them. The reference to Satan's trial is clear in what he said to his God: "My Lord! Because Thou hast sent me astray, I verily shall adorn the path of error for them in the earth," and "Now, because Thou hast sent me astray, verily I shall lurk in ambush for them on Thy Right Path." That is, Satan will lead people astray, tempt and test them just as God had sent him astray, tempted and tested him. Satan was an archangel and the orator of the cherubim. God wanted to test him, and so he ordered him to prostrate himself before Adam in order to determine his adherence to the essence of Oneness and his devotion to his mission of sanctification and glorification of God. Satan proved that he was willing to sacrifice everything for the sake of his profession of one God. Al-Hallaj says of Satan:

> Of all the angels, Satan was the most knowledgeable of prostration, the closest to what Is, the most exerting of efforts, the most honoring of vows, and the closest to the Worshiped One. The angels fell prostrate before Adam for the purpose of assisting him; Satan refused to prostrate himself before Adam because of the long time he had spent envisioning God.[34]

And just as God tested Abraham by asking him to sacrifice the most precious thing he had for His sake, God similarly tested Satan by asking him to sacrifice the dearest thing he had for the sake of his God and Beloved. One of the characteristics of a religious test is that it thrusts the one who is tested into a forbidding and unbearable predicament. Consequently, his reality is distinctly revealed, without distortion or falsification. The main idea that I would like to present here is that Satan had successfully passed

---

34 "Tasin al-Azal wa-'l-Iltibas"

the test that God had put to him. This truth becomes evident on the basis of the following considerations:

1. Abraham passed the test because he suspended his paternal duties and his human and familial commitments in order to obey divine orders and fulfill his duty to his God at whatever cost. We can similarly say that Satan passed the test because he suspended the partial duties of obedience in order to submit to divine will and adhere to his absolute duty of acknowledging the oneness and sanctity of God.

2. Just as the divine order transformed the slaying of Isaac from a mere vicious crime into a great sacrifice and an unparalleled gift, Satan's adherence to his absolute duty transformed his refusal to prostrate himself before Adam from mere disobedience to the most sublime form of sanctification a creature has ever given to God.

3. In fact, the divine order rendered Abraham's paternal duties and human commitments into trial-duties, obedience to which would have entailed Abraham's failing the test. *[A 76]* Similarly, Satan's partial duties became trial-duties in relation to the absolute duty. Had Satan submitted to them, he would have failed the test.

4. Abraham did not behave like an ordinary human being with regard to his paternal duties, but rather behaved in the manner of prophets and saints, thus revealing his reality through the trial. Likewise, Satan did not behave like the angels in the face of his partial duties toward God, but followed the conduct of saints, the pious, and intimates with God, thus revealing his truth in its full purity and pristine nature.

5. It is clear that divine trial is the cause of the affliction, agony, and despair that the tested one suffers. Abraham's strong desire to save Isaac and keep him was the cause of his agony and misery. Had it not been for this intense desire, his test would not have received much attention, because Abraham would have offered his God something only slightly precious, something whose loss would not have been a great disaster. So it was with Satan's trial. When God tried him, Satan had an intense desire to obey the order of prostration before Adam, and it was extremely painful for him to sacrifice such desire for the sake of adhering to the

truth of the oneness of God. Otherwise, Satan would have sacrificed something for which he originally had had very little desire. Both Satan and Abraham knew that God was testing them and was asking of them the most difficult and precious sacrifices of all. But no sacrifice was too difficult for them for the sake of God. For that reason, Satan refused to prostrate himself before Adam, and Abraham rejected all paternal and human relations.

When we treated Satan's predicament on the level of tragedy and compared it to the story of Abraham and to the play *Antigone*, we mentioned that Abraham's predicament failed to reach the level of tragedy because of that famous ram, and because of the impossibility of the existence of real tragedy in religion. We also mentioned that Antigone's predicament exceeds that of Abraham in importance because it represents a real tragedy. As for Satan's predicament, we considered it the ultimate tragedy because it gives expression to tragedy in its most explicit form, utmost limit, and most profound meaning.

However, when we study this subject on the level of religious trial, we are obliged to change this classification and replace it with a new one that is harmonious with the logic of religion and its stance vis-à-vis tragedy. If Satan's reality could have been manifested on the level of tragedy only, our chief concerns would have ended with the earlier classification.

The new classification places Antigone's predicament at the lowest rung of the ladder, because her trial imposed on her the choice between an order by temporal authority as against divine orders, each order originating from a different source. On the other hand, Abraham's trial was more potent and meaningful because it gave him a choice between a direct divine order and his paternal duties and human and moral commitments, which Abraham thought were sacred and sent down from Heaven. In other words, Abraham's choice was between two orders that emanated from the same source, God.

With regard to Satan's trial, it is the ultimate trial of trials, the most significant, and the most bitter, because it forced him to choose between the requirements of divine will on the one hand and the direct divine order on the other. That is to say, Satan did not have to choose between the temporal and the eternal as Antigone did, nor between the divine and the moral as Abraham *[A 77]* had to, but between the divine and the divine, between the eternal and the eternal. For that reason, Satan's trial was unbearable, his disaster immeasurable, and his despair indescribable.

One of the basic components of a successful religious trial is the total ignorance of the one who is being tried of the result of the trial and whether the issue of such a trial will be in his favor or not. Had Abraham suspected for a moment that he would be slaying a ram in place of his son Isaac, his predicament would not have been a trial but a farce. Had Job expected compensation for his patience through the disasters that God had inflicted upon him, thus enduring great distress in the hope of reaping the ease that would succeed it, his trial would have lost its meaning and substance and he would have failed the test. And had it ever occurred to Satan that his damnation was not eternal or that his ultimate end was not hell and a terrible fate, his predicament would have turned from a tragedy-laden trial to a farce. In other words, one condition of a successful trial is the undoubting, firm belief of the one who is being tried that his trial would have a tragic end. How great his joy will then be when he finds out that the trial has a happy ending, as happened to Abraham when he recovered his son and to Job when God gave him back all his wealth and children a hundredfold.

Since God rewarded Abraham and Job for their patience and adherence to their absolute duty toward Him, we can thus deduce that He will also reward Satan for his success in passing the test and for his sacrifice, and will compensate him for suffering a tragic loss and for enduring hardships, agony, and estrangement.

However, if this conclusion is correct, why did, then, God damn Satan until the Day of Judgment? The answer is simple: He damned him until the Day of Judgment because the trial itself required it. Had Satan believed that his damnation was temporary and that there was hope that he would return to paradise, his trial would have lost its meaning and substance.

This is so because his adherence to the reality of Oneness, despite his total despair of salvation, is the proof of his successful passing of the test. This is similar to Abraham's despair of saving his son Isaac. Placing the knife on his son's neck was solid proof of Abraham's passing of the test to which God had subjected him. In other words, the eternal damnation does not disclose Satan's real fate much as it forms an integral part of his trial.

As for Satan's real fate, it had to remain a secret concealed from him until it was time to divulge it, just as Isaac's fate remained a secret concealed from Abraham until it was proper time to disclose it. Furthermore, Satan could not be damned forever, especially after successfully passing the test, because such a situation would constitute a real and major tragedy in the universe. Religion's logic, as I have repeatedly mentioned, never allows that.

Just as our understanding of Satan's character on the level of tragedy does not explain his total reality, neither does the treatment of his character on the level of trial and affliction. We must bear in mind, though, that the level of trial draws us more explicitly and profoundly to his reality than any of the other above-mentioned levels. In order to comprehend the total reality of Satan and his actual place in the universe, we must define his direct and essential relationship with the Divine will. No matter how hard I looked, I could not find a better expression of Satan's relationship with the Divine will than that of Imam al-Maqdisi's, who said through Satan: *[A 78]*

> He created me as He willed. He brought me into being as He willed. He used me as He willed. He preordained for me what He willed, so I could not bear to will except what He willed. I never exceeded what He willed, nor have I done except what He willed. If He willed, He would restore me to what He willed and would guide me with what He willed. But thus He willed, and I was what He willed. Who then would be my support against fate, and would stand to protect me from destiny? But whatever pleases Him of me, I very gladly accept. Oh! What is one to do? One whose head is in the grip of Divine subjugation (*qahr*), his heart in the hand of Divine Decree, and his present state stems from the judgment of eternity (*qidam*). It is all over. The pen has dried.[35]

---

35 *Taflis Iblis*, 13.

In other words, Satan was made by divine will, the subject to its decrees, and the executor of its demands. When Satan chose refusal and rebellion, he only chose what God had chosen for him from the beginning. Satan was used by what God had willed for him, caught in the grip of His subjugation. As such, command and interdiction (*al-amr wa-'l-nahy*) are null and void as far as Satan is concerned, even though the pretext that was used to expel him was based on command and interdiction.

Further explaining the true position of Satan and God's purpose of expelling him, Imam al-Maqdisi continues to say on behalf of Satan:

> O Listener, do you think that I mismanaged? That I rejected predestination (*taqdir*)? That I was changed by the change? Nay! By His exalted might and His splendid omnipotence, I have not. But He has created the beautiful and the ugly (good and evil), the straight and the correct, combining the thing and its opposite in order to demonstrate His perfect omnipotence. And things are only known through their opposites. At first, He had me teach the virtues to angels in the heavenly host, and adorn the orbits with these virtues. I was the teacher of Oneness (*tawhid*). When the children in the school of knowledge read their lessons in Oneness and learned the alphabet-letters of His sanctifications and glorification, He transported me from heaven to earth to teach them the opposite of that, to adorn the vices and show them to them. Through me, the beautiful and the ugly (good and evil) were thus known, the straight and the correct were distinguished. I am in both heaven and earth, the master of knowing and teacher of teachers. I am of inimitable power and observer of the Presence of Wisdom. Who then is closer to His Presence (*hadrah*) than I? Who is more renowned in His mention than I? I have all the honor that He mentioned me, even though He damned me. I have all the pride that He reprieved me, even though He expelled me. By my knowledge of Him He denied me … Happiness disappeared because of separation. You think it is separation? If I had dropped in His estimation, I fell into the heart of the heart of Estimation.[36]

---

36 Ibid. 22-23.

Section Five

I shall devote this section of my study to finding an acceptable religious interpretation for some of the paradoxes that occurred in the previous sections of the essay and to answering some outstanding important questions. The following is a classification of the most important of these paradoxes and questions:

1. When I posed the question, why did God order Satan to prostrate himself before Adam? I answered it by saying that God wanted to test and try him as he tested and tried Abraham and Job after him. The new question that arises before us now is: Why does God test His angels and his people when He knows everything they divulge or conceal? Can we, for example, specify any of the divine attributes that calls upon God to test His people? Rather, to which one of these divine attributes should we ascribe such a tendency to test people?

2. When we distinguished, at the beginning of this essay, between Will and Command, we mentioned that God sometimes orders something while He would have willed to realize something else. I wonder, is there a religious explanation for this paradox in God's behavior?

3. We have also seen that Satan was caught in the grip of God's power, and was totally subject to the fate willed and decreed for him, like the rest of His creatures. Hence, the effect of divine command and interdiction is nullified as far as Satan is concerned. If this be true, why then did God expel Satan from paradise on the pretext of command and interdiction? In addition, God has since eternity predetermined who would go to heaven and who would go to hell. Religious proofs that support this statement are numerous. I shall cite, by way of example, only the following holy *hadith*: "God Almighty seized a handful and said: this goes to paradise with my blessing, and I care not. Then He seized another handful and said: this goes to hell, and I care not."[37] But despite all that, God revealed scriptures and sent messengers and charged them with commands and

---

37   *al-Ittihafat al-Saniyya fi 'l-Ahadith al-Qudsiyya*, 68.

interdictions and distinguished between the lawful and the unlawful. What is the benefit of all this for those who are compelled by His wisdom and who are manipulated by His preordained fate?

4. If God is the Creator of all things and the One who predetermines good and evil for His people, why then does He want people to believe that Satan is the cause of all evil and sin? And why does He want to burden Satan with the sins of those He had created evil and made to do evil? Can we explain this paradox by ascribing it to any of the well-known attributes of God?

I believe that the divine attribute that we are searching for to answer these questions is that of cunning (*makr*: plotting, scheming). Following are some Qur'anic verses that illustrate the nature of this attribute:

1. "And they (the disbelievers) schemed, and Allah schemed (against them): and Allah is the best of schemers." (*Qur'an* 3: 54)

2. "And when those who disbelieve plot against thee (O Muhammad) to wound thee fatally, or to kill thee or to drive thee forth; *[A 80]* they plot, but Allah also plots; and Allah is the best of plotters." (*Qur'an* 8: 30)

3. "And when We cause mankind to taste of mercy after some adversity which had afflicted them, behold! They have some plot against Our revelations. Say: Allah is swifter in plotting. Lo! Our messengers write down that which Ye plot." (*Qur'an* 10: 21)

We also find that some other verses ascribe to God a similar attribute, that of mocking, as in the following verse: "Allah (Himself) doth mock them, leaving them to wander blindly on in their contumacy." (*Qur'an* 2: 15) Some verses stated the same meaning without mentioning or specifying divine cunning, as in the following ones:

1. "And let not those who disbelieve imagine that the reins We give them bode well unto their souls. We only give them rein that they may grow in sinfulness. And theirs will be a shameful doom." (*Qur'an* 3: 178)

2. "And when We would destroy a township We send commandment to its folk who live at ease, and afterward they commit abomination therein, and so the Word (of doom) hath effect for it. (*Qur'an* 17: 16) In other words, it is destroyed.

3. "Lo! The hypocrites seek to beguile Allah, but it is Allah who beguiles them."(*Qur'an* 4: 142)

We deduce from al-Tabari's interpretation of the above-mentioned verses the following:

a) Cunning (*makr*) implies mocking and beguilement.[38]

b) Cunning implies disclosing something for someone and at the same time harboring something else for him: "God shows mankind judgments (*ahkam*) in this world contrary to what He has for them in the afterlife."[39]

c) God gives people their reins; that is, "He prolongs their life, happiness, and influence, so that when they have felt peaceful and secure He can suddenly doom them."[40]

d) When God said: "And when We would destroy a township We send commandment to its folk who live at ease, and afterward they commit abomination therein, and so the Word (of doom) hath effect for it," He had willed the destruction of the township. But lest God's people object to what He had willed, He resorted to cunning. Thus, He ordered the township folk, who lived at ease, to act sinfully and go astray so that it would appear to all that they had deserved such destruction, which is not the case.

In his famous book *Qut al-Qulub*, Abu Talib al-Makki explains the idea of divine cunning by tying it clearly to divine testing:

> He related to us on the authority of Abu Muhammad Sahl, said he: I perceived as if I had been ushered into paradise where I met three hundred prophets. I asked them: What was the most frightening thing you ever dreaded in life on earth? They said to me: An evil ending out of God's cunning, which is indescribable, indiscernible, and inscrutable. God's cunning is infinite, because His will and His judgments have no purpose. An example of that is the famous account about the Prophet and Gabriel who both wept out of fear of God. God suggested to them that they have no reason to cry *[A 81]* since he has secured them.

---

38 *Tafsir al-Tabari*, vol. 1, 301-302.
39 Ibid. 303.
40 Ibid. vol 7, 421-423.

They said to Him: But who is secure from Your cunning? Had they
not known that His cunning was infinite because his judgment has no
purpose they would not have said to Him: but who is secure from Your
cunning? Although He had said to them that He had secured them.
His reassuring words should have ended His cunning, and they should
have seen the end of His cunning, but they were afraid from the rest of
His cunning that was concealed from them. It was as though they were
afraid that His words: "I have secured you against my cunning" were
also a cunning move on His part. They were afraid that He was testing
them as He did with His companion Abraham, when the mangonel
catapulted him in midair and Abraham said: "Sufficient unto me is
God, my Lord." Gabriel intruded on him asking, do you need anything?
Abraham answered no, living up to his words, "Sufficient unto me is
God," and thereby confirming word with deed.[41]

We can state, after this quick review of the idea of divine cunning that the
favor that God had shown Satan was different from the fate, predicament,
and ending He had willed and harbored for him. That is to say, God
practiced His cunning against Satan by ordering him outwardly to prostrate
himself before Adam while inwardly willing him to disobey the order so
that He would have a pretext to do anything He wished to him, and carry
out the fate he had preordained for him. The order of trial, then, was only
an instrument of divine cunning whose objective was to execute the decrees
of divine will and justify them before His creatures. It will thus all look
acceptable to them and they will not have a pretext against Him for what
He has done to them.

As Abu Talib al-Makki has said, there is no purpose to His will and
to His decrees. Divine cunning intervenes to make things appear to people
different from what they actually are, i.e., to make the divine will seem as
if it had objectives, justifications, and reasons. Accordingly, God practiced
His cunning against the angels by making it appear to them as if Satan had
been expelled from paradise for a sound reason, disobedience. Had it not
been for this cunning arrangement, the angels would have regarded the

---

41 *Qut al-Qulub (Food for the Hearts)*, vol. 1, p. 229.

expulsion of their chief (Satan) a greater enormity than His saying: "Lo! I am about to place a viceroy in the earth."

Furthermore, it would have been difficult for them to bear with the decrees of divine will, or to face such decrees directly, without the intervention of that cunning and its justifications and explanations. That is why God expelled him from paradise on the pretext of command and interdiction, not on the grounds of just carrying out His will against him.

Similarly, it is better for people, from a practical point of view, to believe that Satan disobeyed His Lord's order and was for that reason expelled. For, if people were truly to believe that God had preordained Satan's miserable destiny since eternity, their minds would be unable comprehend the wisdom of such an act, and they would lose their minds and would cease to believe in His justice and mercy. I therefore believe that Imam al-Maqdisi was absolutely right when he wrote the following about Satan:

> If someone erred, people would say Satan made him fall into error. If somebody forgot something, people would say Satan made him forget. If somebody did something wrong, they would say this is Satan's doing. I am thus the bearer of sinners' offenses, and the bearer of the heavy burdens of the sinful.[42]

We have seen how Abu Talib al-Makki associated Abraham's trial with divine cunning, because when Abraham was about to fall into the fire, he completely entrusted himself to God by saying: "Sufficient unto me is God, my Lord." God wanted to test the depth of Abraham's trust in Him, so He schemed against him by sending *[A 82]* Gabriel to offer him help. That is to say, God sent Gabriel to entice Abraham to renounce his trust of God. But Abraham refused Gabriel's help, passed the test, and the fire thus became coolness and peace upon Abraham. Put differently, God had since eternity willed Abraham to be one of the people of Paradise and one of His pious prophets. He therefore tested him so that none of His creatures would raise objections against Him for the kind of fate and destiny that He had willed for Abraham.

---

42   *Taflis Iblis*, 36.

As for Satan, God had since eternity wanted him to be the teacher of Oneness of God in the heavenly host and the teacher of evil and sin on earth. That is why God tested Satan and schemed against him so that none of His creatures would have a pretext against the miserable destiny that He had willed for him.

Although God had since eternity decided who would be the people of Paradise and who would be the people of Hell, He nevertheless sent messengers, revealed Holy Scriptures, filled them with command and interdiction, and distinguished between *halal* and *haram*. He did that in order to make it clear to His people that their happiness and misery depended on their behavior and choices, on following His prophets and on adhering to His laws. As a result, they would have no objection to the fate that He had preordained for them. For, "Allah verily sends whom He will astray, and guides whom He will," and "He will not be questioned as to that which He doeth, but they will be questioned." (*Qur'an* 21: 23) This means that God's sending of messengers and Holy Scriptures and His distinguishing between *halal* and *haram* are no more than tools of His cunning in order to carry through the decrees He had already willed for people. This is similar to the situation of the township that God wanted to destroy, and so He ordered its affluent folk to lead a dissolute life and prolonged the good life of some people so they could further indulge in sin, then inflicting on them a terrible doom.

Although Satan was compelled by God's wisdom and was totally powerless and helpless vis-à-vis His Lord, God did not carry out His will against him and damn him until after He cunningly tested him by ordering him to lie prostrate before Adam. It thus appeared to everyone that Satan was responsible for his act and therefore deserved that punishment.

We have repeatedly contended that God was the creator of good and evil, as indicated by the following holy tradition: "God, may He be exalted, says: there is no deity besides me. I created good and preordained it. Blessed are those whom I created to do good, created good for them, and caused them to do good. I am God and there is no deity but I. I created evil and preordained it. Woe unto those whom I created to do evil, created evil for them, and caused them to do evil."[43]

It is due to His cunning that people believe the opposite of that and attribute faults and shameful deeds either to themselves, as Adam did when he said, "Our Lord! We have wronged ourselves," or to Satan's deception and temptation. It is also God's cunning that leads people to ascribe good, justice, and mercy to Him, as Adam did when he said, "If Thou forgive us not and have not mercy on us, surely we are of the lost!" In addition to that, it is proper for people, from a practical point of view, to generally believe that God has an enemy, the cursed Satan, the source of all evil, error, and sin. For if they were truly to believe that God was the source of all their disasters and afflictions, their minds would not be able to endure such a fact, and they would lose their minds and disbelieve in God and his blessings.

Imam al-Maqdisi wrote the following in the name *[A 83]* of Satan:

> And now, God has made me the reason for the existence of error, and the cause of betaking command and interdiction. In reality, there is no cause for His command, no consequence for His judgment, no reason for the distancing of His enemies and no relevance to the closeness of His saints. God Almighty is not in need of His creatures. He is self-existent. He is the caretaker of His people. The good deeds of the doers of good are of no use to Him, nor do the misdeeds of the evildoers harm Him. His command was carried out; His judgment was executed. His pen went dry with what exists in His Kingdom…
> If He willed, He would punish; and if He willed, He would pardon. He does not have to confirm His threats. He alone is the master of His threats. It is up to Him to punish for no reason or to make happy for no relation or gain.[44]

If Adam could ascribe fault to himself or to Satan who tempted him, and to ask his God for forgiveness and mercy in keeping with Jesus' counsel: "Give unto Caesar that which is Caesar's and unto God that which is God's," to whom should Satan ascribe his disobedience and refusal? Or as

---

43   *al-Ittihafat al-Saniyya fi 'l-Ahadith al-Qudsiyya*, 71.
44   *Taflis Iblis*, 38-39.

Satan himself said, "Since I am Adam's Satan, I wonder who my Satan is?"[45] Naturally, Satan ascribes his refusal to its real and ultimate source by saying, "Now, because Thou hast sent me astray," thus giving unto God that which is God's, and giving nothing unto Caesar, because Caesar owns absolutely nothing as far as Satan is concerned. And Caesar has no power or strength to have anything ascribed to him.

If we were to elaborate on a comparison between Adam's position and that of Satan, we would discover that if Satan was the first tragic hero in the universe, then Adam was the first opportunist. That is because Adam refused to take a definite position vis-à-vis the contradiction between the divine command and the divine will, prompted by a desire for salvation at any cost, as evidenced by the reply of his which we cited. If it turns out at the end of time that the divine command is correct and Adam is really responsible for his own disobedience, Adam would have confessed to his guilt and asked for God's pardon when he said, "Our Lord! We have wronged ourselves," thus keeping open the chance of salvation. At the same time, if the divine will turns out to be correct and Adam is not really responsible for his disobedience, He would have again saved himself by resigning himself to the will of God and trusting all to His mercy and forgiveness (like Abraham) in adding: "If Thou forgive us not and have not mercy on us, surely we are of the lost."

In other words, when Adam ascribed the action to himself and assumed responsibility for his disobedience by saying: "Our Lord! We have wronged ourselves," he acted as a free agent with free will and as such disavowed that God had preordained that injustice and willed it for him. But, when Adam added, "If Thou forgive us not and have not mercy on us, surely we are of the lost!" he acted as a predestinarian, clinging to Divine mercy, which is connected to Divine will, and as such disavowed responsibility for the injustice, because in this case God would have predetermined since eternity whether He was going to have mercy on Adam or to punish him. Meanwhile, the injustice would be God's pretext against Adam (in case he wanted to punish him in eternity) and Adam would have no objection

---

45 Ibid., 16.

against His Lord. Thus, Adam tried, out of precaution, to save himself through both free-agency and predestinarianism at one and the same time, since he was not certain which one would *[A 84]* ultimately turn out correct.

As for Satan, he took a definite position by saying: "Now, because Thou hast sent me astray," referring nothing to himself, but rather referring everything to its real source, the divine will. By so doing, Satan was a sincere predestinarian and did not try to take advantage of free will as Adam did for his own safety and salvation.

Some legists have refused to ascribe imperfection to divine will. They contend that Satan is the source of evil and the creator of sin (*ma'siyah*),[46] deeming God too exalted for creating evil and preordaining it for His people. This opinion (*ijtihad*) is more in conformity with philosophical theories that influenced Muslim thinkers than with the purely religious approach to the subject. Since we are now treating Satan's character and position in the universe on a purely religious level, we cannot adopt that opinion, especially since it attributes to Satan not only the ability to distort and to cause mischief, but also to create and originate. This is unacceptable from a religious point of view. If Satan had wanted to create sin, God would have been capable of preventing it. Since God did not prevent it, we can then deduce that the existence of sin is in conformity with His eternal will.

We have already cited Abu Talib al-Makki's statement that "the end is of God's cunning, which is indescribable, indiscernible, and inscrutable." This should remind us of the ultimate end that I forecast for Satan when I said that God will reward him for passing the divine test and will return him to Paradise when this universal drama nears its conclusion. The following are the reasons and considerations that have prompted me to conclude that Satan's end will be a happy and satisfactory one:

A. Satan's tenacious adherence to the reality of Oneness was unparalleled. Therefore, he cannot come to an end in Hell, in accordance with the holy *hadith* that states: "God, may He be exalted, said: I am God. There is no deity but I. Whoever acknowledges my Oneness shall enter

---

46 *Tafsir al-Tabari*, vol. 1, 477-488, 508

My bastion, and whoever enters my bastion shall be secure from My punishment."[47]

B. Satan passed God's test and patiently endured the disaster that befell him as a result. Therefore, his ultimate reward is guaranteed, as indicated by the holy *hadith* that states: "God, may He be exalted, said: If I test one of my believing creatures and he praises Me and patiently endures My affliction, he shall awaken as free of sin as when his mother gave birth to him. God will say to His scribes (*hafazah*): I have shackled this slave of Mine and tested him, so [you must] reward him as you used to before the test."[48]

Had it not been for this foreseen happy ending for Satan, his ending would have been a real and ultimate tragedy, which cannot be accepted by religion's logic, as we have already seen. Since the ultimate end is of God's cunning, He made Abraham and Job believe that the result of their test would be contrary to what it actually was and contrary to the result that God had wanted it to be. That is to say, the decrees that God had shown Abraham and Job at the beginning of the *[A 85]* test were different from the ones He had harbored for them regarding its ending.

This assumption applies to Satan, since God's cunning requires that Satan firmly believe that his end will not be anything but miserable and desperate. We thus deduce that Satan's damnation was not an expression of the real end which God had willed for him, but was divine cunning whose objective was to carry out the decrees of His will against him.

Let us suppose for the sake of the argument that I am right about what I said regarding the reality of Satan, his end, and his final destiny. What consequences does such a supposition entail with respect to our personal view of Satan?

First, I believe that we must drastically modify our traditional view of Satan and effect a crucial change in our conception of his character and position. Secondly, we must rehabilitate him to his true position: that of an

---

47 *al-Ittihafat al-Saniyya fi 'l-Ahadith al-Qudsiyya*, 4.
48 Ibid., 10.

angel who has wholeheartedly and in all sincerity devoted himself to the service of his God and who has carried out the decrees of His will with utmost care and precision. Lastly, we must desist from heaping abuse and insults on him, forgive him, seek forgiveness for him, and ask people to think well of him, after we have falsely and slanderously made him responsible for all faults and abominations.

I feel also that it is my duty to warn you that forgiving and rehabilitating Satan has significant consequences that are not obvious to everyone. Such a step obliges us to change many of our religious views and traditional beliefs about this worldly life and the hereafter. In order to give you a simple idea about the grave consequences that a pardon of Satan might entail, I shall quote a funny and beautiful story written by Tawfiq al-Hakim, "*Al-Shahid*" ("The Martyr").

Tawfiq al-Hakim relates in his story that Satan decided one day to turn to God in repentance and to refrain from wrongdoing so that he could dedicate himself to doing good and to following the right path. Satan went to the Rector of al-Azhar to repent at his hands and embrace The True Religion (Islam) with his guidance. The following dialogue ensued between Satan and the Rector of al-Azhar:

"Satan becoming a believer? This is great, but…"

"What? Is it not the right of people to embrace God's religion in droves? Is not the following verse in God's Holy Book: 'Then hymn the praises of thy Lord, and seek forgiveness of Him'? Here I am! I hymn God's praises and seek His forgiveness. I want to embrace His religion in all purity and sincerity. I want to become a Muslim, a good Muslim, and I want to be an example for those who follow the right path."

The Rector of al-Azhar began to ponder the consequences. If Satan were to become a Muslim, how would the Qur'an be recited? Could people still say: "I seek refuge in God from accursed Satan"? If this verse were to be abrogated, then it would follow that most verses of the Qur'an would have to be abrogated. Cursing Satan and warning people against his evil deeds, abominations, and temptation do occupy a sizable proportion *[A 86]* of God's Book. How could the Rector of al-Azhar accept Satan's embracing of Islam without damaging the whole structure of Islam? The Rector of al-Azhar raised his head, looked at Satan, and said, "You have come to me with something I have no power over. This is far beyond my authority and capability. I do not have what you seek. I am not the right authority in this matter."

"Then to whom should I go? Are you not the chiefs of The Religion? How then do I reach God? Is that not what those who want to draw near God do?"

The Rector of al-Azhar kept silent for a moment, scratched his beard, and said: "You have good intentions. There is no doubt about that! But despite all that, I must tell you frankly that my specialty is to lift high the word of Islam and to preserve the glory of al-Azhar. It is not my specialty to put my hand in yours."

In other words, the Rector of al-Azhar realized the necessity of Satan's existence for the promotion of religion and for preserving its institutions. Were Satan to disappear, religion's existence and continuity would be unnecessary and unjustifiable. And as Al-Hakim says in the same story: "How can Satan be erased without the extinction of all those images, myths, meanings, and themes that have saturated people's hearts and stimulated their imaginations? What would be the significance of the "Day of Judgment" if evil were erased from the face of the earth? Would the adherents of Satan who had followed him before his belief in Islam be punished? Or would their misdeeds be erased so long as Satan's repentance had been accepted?"

After Satan despaired of the Rector of al-Azhar, he went directly to Heaven and spoke with Gabriel. Satan asked Gabriel to intercede with God for him so he could obtain forgiveness and acceptance of his repentance. The following dialogue took place between Satan and Gabriel:

"Yes, indeed! But your disappearance from the earth would bring down pillars and shake walls, would obliterate features and confuse lineaments, would efface colors and destroy traits. Virtue has no meaning without the existence of vice… no meaning for right without wrong, for good without bad, or white without black, or light without darkness, or good without evil. Only through your darkness can people see God's light.

Your presence on earth is necessary so long as earth remains a place of descent for those sublime attributes that God has bestowed on his human creatures!"

"My existence is essential for the presence of good itself? My dark soul should remain dark so it can reflect God's light? I shall be content with my loathsome lot for the sake of preserving good and for the sake of God's purity. But would people's wrath still pursue me and damnation be stuck to my name despite the noble intentions and the good faith that reside in my heart?" *[A 87]*

"Yes! You must remain cursed until the end of time. If damnation were removed from you, then everything would collapse."

"I beg your forgiveness, O God! Why do I have to bear this onerous burden? Why was I given this frightful fate? Why don't You make me now one of Your simple angels so I can be allowed to love You and love Your light, and be rewarded for such love with compassion from You and praise from people? Here I am! My love for You is incomparable and *nonpareil*. My love for you requires this sacrifice which is not perceived by angels nor is known to people. My love for You compels me to accept wearing the cloak of disobedience against You and to appear as if I were rebelling against You. My love for You necessitates that I endure Your damnation and people's curse of me. It is a love You do not allow me even the honor of claiming, or the joy of associating with. A love, if concealed by ascetics, would fill their hearts with light. I conceal that love, but its light refuses to approach my heart."

"Satan wept, left Heaven in obedience and descended to earth in total submission. But a suppressed sigh burst out of his breast as he penetrated the sky; a sigh reechoed by the stars and celestial bodies. It was as though the stars and celestial bodies had banded together to utter that bleeding scream:

"I am a Martyr! ... I am a Martyr! ..."

Chapter Three

Reply to a Criticism

1

A critic published[1] a short critique of some of the ideas I presented in the lecture that I gave at the Arab Cultural Club on December 10, 1965

---

1   Some writers undertook "a reply" to my study of the character of Satan, and what they wrote was published in the journal *Al-Thaqafat al-'Arabiyyah* [*Arab Culture*] magazine (Beirut, February 1966). The reader will find my reply above in two sections, as it was published in the same issue of the journal *Arab Culture*, after some minor alterations. It is worth noting that the critics were traditional and reactionary intellectuals and thus they overlook that my study of the character of Satan in the Qur'an was nothing but an attempt to reconsider a well-defined problem out of the Arab cultural heritage on a new and contemporary basis and by means of current ideas and concepts (like tragedy, alienation, and the tragic hero arising from despair) in order to give it a meaning in relation to contemporary culture that differed from the literal meaning to be accepted or rejected as a whole. The rejuvenation of culture only takes place by connecting it to the living and to the issues and problems that people presently encounter, feel, think about, suffer, and express in their contemporary art, literature, and culture, and in their efforts to constantly and continually reassess what is called heritage. We enrich our Arab culture when we try to connect the traditional story of Satan, for example, to Greek literature and contemporary world literature and with some aspects of the Arab tradition itself like the Sufi tradition. What I wrote in this matter is only an attempt and I hope it has attained some success at this level.

under the title "The Tragedy of Satan" in the *Sunday Supplement to Al-Nahar* (December 19, 1965) and in one of the daily newspapers, *Al-Ahrar* (December 19, 1965). *[A 89]*

First: I wish to thank the critic for frankly acknowledging that he had neither heard nor read the lecture in question and that his critique relied on very brief excerpts of the lecture that appeared in some daily newspapers. Despite that acknowledgment, he claimed in the course of his critique of the ideas in my lecture that they "were drivel without any scientific or intellectual value," just as he claimed that I relied in my argument on "weak and shallow principles and on a biased and unscientific study." Here I must ask the critic how the spirit of science that he extols allows him to fire off such comprehensive judgments of a text that he did not read carefully and did not study with care. Is he relying on strong and deep principles and does he demonstrate scientific gravity and a critical spirit when his critique relies only on the very brief summaries in daily newspapers?

Second: I wish to explain to the critic that his distinguishing between two types of divine commands (the obligatory and the legislative) is not at all incompatible with what I said in my lecture, for I made the same distinction under a slightly different name. What he calls the "obligatory order" I call in my lecture an "order of the will," and for what he called the "legislative order" I used the technical term "order" alone, a widespread usage among those who discuss these subjects.

Third: the critic responds to my statement that God commanded Satan to prostrate himself (a legislative order according to his terminology) but willed him to disobey by saying: "Satan was free to prostrate or not prostrate himself before Adam without any force or compulsion." However, this response is entirely false for the following reasons:

1) Because it means that Satan is the agent of his disobedience and thus the original source of evil in the world, and thus attributes to him not only the power to deform or corrupt but the power to create and shape. However, since Muslims believe that "fate and divine decree for good or evil are from Almighty God alone," that view is inacceptable from a purely religious perspective.

2) If Satan had wanted to create disobedience by refusing to prostrate himself, God would be able to prevent that refusal, since Satan can only do what is compatible with God's eternal will.

3) Either God had willed and determined disobedience for Satan or he did not: there is no other option. For the other option would imply that Satan carried out his will (in his choosing of refusal and thus creating disobedience) in a way that violates the will of God. This, however, is not possible from a purely religious perspective. The only option is the first one, the one that denies that Satan could freely choose disobedience, which refutes the critic's opinion concerning the freedom of Satan. In other words, God made Satan according to His will, and used him according to His will, and if He wanted to guide him along the straight path and in choosing the truth then He could do so, since He guides who He chooses and leads astray who He chooses. He is accountable to no one but holds all others accountable, according to the logic of Islam. [A 90]

Fourth: The critic claims that the prostration of Satan to Adam "is a prostration of respect and not one of worship." It appears to me that the critic is confusing the meaning of respect and the meanings and implications of prostration. While prostration certainly includes respect it also exceeds it to a great degree, passing into exaltation, adoration, and submission until respect almost fades away. Prostration constitutes an external sign and bodily expression of the true existing relation between Creator and creature in Islam. It signifies that the worshipper has delivered himself entirely and absolutely to his Lord and submitted totally to his will. Thus, prostration expresses an entirely different state in type and quality from respect, no matter how lofty and sublime the latter is.

In addition to that, there are many movements and rituals included in the external expressions of worship, but only the act of prostration expresses the final and total submission of the worshiper to the will of his Lord. Accordingly, the Muslim begins his prayers standing on his feet and then gradually raises the expression of self-effacement before his Creator by shifting from standing to bowing to kneeling to prostration several times. In other words, his prayers reach their apex when he falls prostrate in front of God and His presence. This is why I said in my lecture that prostration is only permissible to the Divine Essence. My proof is the Qur'anic verse that states: "Only those believe in Our revelations who, when they are reminded of them, fall down prostrate and hymn the praise of their Lord, and they are not scornful." (*Qur'an* 32:15) This verse makes an airtight connection between "glorifying God" and "prostration" since prostration is the furthest a human body can go as an external expression of sanctifying God when he remembers verses in the *Qur'an*. As it also forms the external expression of the internal glorification of God that the believer is immersed in when he hears the verses of the Qur'an. Al-Tabari states that "the glorification of God" is "professing the Oneness of God and the purifying and stripping from Him of what the polytheists added."[2] Therefore prostrating oneself to someone other than God is the external sign and bodily expression of deviating from the glorification of God and departing from the Oneness of God, and having fallen for the polytheistic attributions to the Eternal Essence. In other words, and contra the critic, prostration is part of the essence of worship and the Oneness of God.

Fifth: The critic wonders in the course of his critique if the angels had deviated from the Oneness of God in their prostration of themselves to Adam and had become polytheists. In order to reply to this important question I find myself forced to refer to the three levels that I used in my lecture to consider the character of Satan: The level of tragedy, the level of trial, and the purely religious level that reveals the direct relationship of Satan to the will of God. Only if I limit myself to the tragic view of the character of Satan would I answer yes to the question of the critic and say that the angels became polytheists by prostrating themselves to Adam. However, the tragic view is a partial view of this matter, for reasons that I made clear in the text of the lecture and which I have no time to repeat here. If I answered the same question *[A 91]* by means of the logic of religious trial, I would say that the angels did not deviate necessarily from

---

2   *Tafsir al-Tabari*, vol. 1, ed. Mahmud Muhammad Shakir (Cairo: Dar al-Maᶜarif), 475.

the truth of monotheism (just as the refusal of Satan is nothing but the greatest sanctification a creature has ever offered to the Divine Essence) since their prostration to Adam was an inseparable part of the trial with which God tested Satan. For the religious trial submits the candidate to the test of bearing the unbearable, and if the angels had not prostrated themselves to Adam (performing the details of the trial just as God willed it) then the trial of Satan would have lost its point and meaning, for he would not have had to bear the unbearable. Thus the prostration of the angels before Adam pushed the trial to its furthest extent, pushing Satan into the absolute solitude in which he was obliged to bear it alone without his friends and intimates among the angels. If we shift to the purely religious level in treating the same question I would also say that the angels did not necessarily deviate from the truth of the Oneness of God in their prostration to Adam since they were compelled by God's wisdom and submitted in their prostration and conditions to the decisions of His will and the command of His irresistible judgment. The angels prostrated themselves compelled by His will and Satan refused to prostrate himself compelled by His will, thus making of him the cause of error and defect and of command and interdiction.

> In reality, there is no cause for His command, no consequence for His judgment, no reason for the distancing of His enemies and no relevance to the closeness of His saints. God Almighty is not in need of His creatures. He is self-existent. He is the caretaker of His people. The good deeds of the doers of good are of no use to Him, nor do the misdeeds of the evildoers harm Him. His command was carried out; His judgment was executed. His pen went dry with what exists in His Kingdom... If He willed, He would punish; and if He willed, He would pardon. He does not have to confirm His threats. He alone is the master of His threats. It is up to Him to punish for no reason or to make happy for no relation or gain.[3]

---

3   Izz al-Din al-Maqdisi, *Taflis Iblis* (Cairo: Matbaᶜat Madrasat Walidat Abbas al-Awwal,1906), 38-39.

2

I still believe that my previous reply to the critic is a convincing and sufficient answer to the original allegations he made against some of the main ideas appearing in my lecture "The Tragedy of Satan." Therefore, I shall devote the following pages to comment on the most important points that the critic made in his extended reply. I will begin with some general remarks.

a) It is truly regrettable that the critic so stubbornly refuses to examine the complete text of my lecture and that he takes pride that the lengthy pages he writes in criticism of my lecture rely only on excerpts from the daily newspapers and a short reply that I published in the weekly Sunday Supplement to Al-Nahar. The critic repeats in the course of his critique more than once that he can dispense with reading the whole text of the lecture that he attacks. However, if this is true, then he should dispense with writing about it also. I (and my attentive readers) can dispense with examining what he wrote as a consequence of the incomplete and distorted idea that he has formed of my lecture. I do not know what he thinks he can gain from this obduracy and stubbornness in refusing to examine the published text about which he writes so many pages. Does he believe that *[A 92]* this narrow-minded negative position will convince the fair-minded reader of the truth of his claim, undermine the strength of my argument, and render it trivial? I leave the answer to the readers themselves.

b) It is also very painful that the critic descends in his discussion to the level of insults, accusations, and open threats, sometimes violent. All of this is exhibited in his mention of the poet Bashar Ibn Burd and his death by flogging after he was charged with atheism because of what he said about Satan. The critic seems unaware that we are living in the second half of the twentieth century and in a country that guarantees freedom of opinion, belief, and expression without any fear, oppression, or revenge. I will add that the critic has done me an honor when he compares my name and work with a great poet like Bashar Ibn Burd. Let it be his honor to side with and defend those who flogged him.

c) The critic charges that I satisfied myself with my own explanations of the verses of the Qur'an that tell the story of Satan instead of seeking out the traditional religious authorities to corroborate my views. The falseness of this charge will be obvious to everyone who reads my lecture completely and sees for themselves that I relied on the interpretations of Al-Tabari to explain the meanings of those verses. I scrupulously recorded the pages from which I cited these explanations. The following is a non-exhaustive list of the important religious sources I consulted: *Talbis Iblis* (*The Dissemblance of Satan*) by Ibn Al-Jawzi, *Taflis Iblis* (*The Failure of Satan*) by Imam Izz al-Din al-Maqdisi, *Kitab Al-Tawasin* by Al-Hallaj, *Qout Al-Qoulub* (*Food for the Hearts*) by Abu Talib Al-Makki, and the holy hadith compiled by Shaykh Muhammad Al-Madani in his book *Al-Ittihafat al-Saniyyah fi 'l-Ahadith 'l-Qudsiyyah.*

d) I believe that one of the sources of conflict between the critic and I might be that he does not take seriously what I said in the beginning of my lecture on the framework within which I treat the character and biography of Satan. I commenced my lecture by saying that I would treat the story of Satan within the framework of mythological thinking and that I will not talk about him as a real existing being. I wanted to treat his character as researchers treat the mythological characters appearing to us in the myths of the Greeks, Sumerians, Semites, and other peoples, and to determine the relationship of these characters to literature, art, religion, philosophy, and thought in general. Since the critic was not aware of this aspect of my topic, he overlooked it entirely and regarded my lecture, instead, as a contribution to "Scholastic Theology" or "Divinity Studies." The critic should not have been surprised if he found some contradictions in the life, character, and actions of Satan since mythology rarely submits to the demands of the law of non-contradiction.

Let us now return to the distinction that the critic emphasizes between divine obligatory order and the divine legislative order (or between an order of the will and a mere order, according to the terminology that I used in my lecture). The critic writes the following about this topic: "The doctor said in his lecture that any order is, by its nature, either obeyed *[A 93]* and performed or disobeyed, and that everything related with the Divine Will occurs by necessity..." If the critic wants to know the exact truth of what I said then he must go back to the text of the published lecture where I wrote the following: "An order by its nature is either obeyed and executed or is disobeyed. The one given the order has the choice of obeying or disobeying. As for divine will, it is not subject to such considerations because it cannot, by its very nature, be refused. Anything that the divine will wants is of necessity existent." There is no confusion between orders of will and mere orders in this statement, but they are sharply and clearly distinguished. It turns out, then, that the objection the critic raises in this matter in order to ridicule my position is null and void from the start and the charge that he directs at me in this matter is refuted since it relies on a faulty reading of what I said and confuses the meanings in those lines. If the critic had read the text of my lecture instead of resting his critique on what newspaper reporters said about it then he would not have committed such a simple but grave error, and he would not have attributed to me statements and meanings that I did not state or mean, which would have spared the reader from having to follow the fruitless argument that he began on this point, and the first offender is the worst of the two. On the basis of this error he claims that I consider the order to prostrate oneself before Adam an obligatory command. However, in truth, I affirmed the exact opposite of this when I wrote that the order to prostrate oneself was not an order of the will but was an order of trial. Just as I wrote: "Had God willed Satan to fall prostrate, he would have done so immediately, since God's slave has no strength or power to disobey divine will." That means that if the command to prostration was an obligatory order (an order of the will) then Satan would have fallen prostrate immediately. The meaning of this statement does not differ from what the critic claims when he says "If the order to prostrate oneself were an obligatory order then God could bend the back of Satan and make him prostrate himself to Adam by force." I add to this that the critic acknowledges "that Satan not prostrating himself happened with the knowledge and will of God." This, despite the order to prostrate himself: Does not this series of statements imply that God ordered him to prostrate himself but that he did not want him to prostrate himself? How does this claim differ from my statement (which the critic described as false) that God ordered Satan to prostrate himself but that he wanted him to disobey that order?

As to whether Satan is free not to prostrate himself, the critic seeks refuge in the well-known theory of *Kasb*[4] (acquisition) to allow him to integrate the two absolutely contradictory perspectives and to make it possible to say that God is the cause of disobedience and obedience (guidance) but that it is up to Satan to *acquire* disobedience, and thus he is evil, or obedience, and thus he is good (choosing good). The contradiction between these two perspectives appears clearly when the critic says "Satan not prostrating himself happened with the knowledge and will of God," and "this does not mean that God intervened in the will of Satan when he acquired disobedience." I believe that everyone who carefully scrutinizes these statements will find them self-contradictory since if Satan's disobedience occurred with the will of God then how can we say that the will of God did not intervene in the causing of the acquisition of this disobedience? I do not know how the critic can swallow this clear contradiction. No matter how much he tries to efface it by resorting to theoretical tricks and quasi-realistic examples he will not succeed in making the inconsistencies internally consistent. *[A 94]* In any case, God had either wanted Satan to acquire disobedience or He did not, there is no third possibility. If He did not want him to acquire disobedience then Satan acquired it despite the Divine Will, and executed his design without the design of God, but this is impossible (from the religious perspective, naturally). If the first option is correct, then God wanted him to acquire disobedience and the choice of Satan was pre-ordained. Therefore, Satan lacked freedom of choice in acquiring disobedience (or anything).

I would like to take this opportunity to state frankly to the critic (and the reader) that I believe that the theory of acquisition is an empty theory. It is a type of intellectual acrobatics and scholastic trickery (with reference to scholastic theology) that some seek refuge in to erase the contours of the

---

4   According to the *Encyclopedia Britannica*, kasb is "a doctrine in Islām adopted by the theologian al-Ashʿarī (d. 935) as a mean between predestination and free will. According to al-Ashʿarī, all actions, good and evil, are originated by God, but they are "acquired" (*maksūb*, whence *kasb*) by men. [trans. note]

decisive choice that the thinker must make between the two contradictory positions: compulsion or choice, predestination or free will, the slave creating his acts or God creating the acts of his slave. In other words, the theory of acquisition is nothing but an attempt to cover up the conflict between these two theories of the will and to escape at any price from the difficult religious impasse that forces someone with honesty and integrity to clearly and explicitly choose one of the two sides of the contradiction. The advocates of acquisition cover up this fact and minimize its significance, arguing that God is the creator of the acts of his slaves and that, by a strange wonder, the slave is still the one who chooses, is responsible, and is liable to reward and punishment. We ought to face this religious dilemma with frankness and acknowledge that each point of view has its reasons and a basis in the Qur'an, for hiding this fact under the theoretical fog of acquisition, which tries in vain to find a mediating point, lacks intellectual integrity.

As for what would have been the meaning and implications of Satan's prostration to Adam, I cited a number of arguments in my previous reply defending my view that prostration is the most extreme external expression of sanctifying and worshipping God possible for the human body. Nevertheless, the critic did not discuss or reply to these arguments but satisfied himself with repeating his view that Satan's prostration to Adam would have been a prostration of greeting and respect only. His evidence for this view was the following text from the *Tafsir* of al-Zamakhshari: "Prostration to Almighty God is an expression of worship but to others is a sign of respect, as the angels prostrated themselves to Adam and Joseph's father and brothers prostrated themselves to him."

I believe that the interpretation of Satan's prostration to Adam as a kind of greeting and honoring is arbitrary since there is nothing in the Qur'anic verses that narrate this event that suggests that we must understand prostration here differently than its obvious and well-known meaning among Muslims, where it is associated with worshipping and sanctifying. If the Qur'anic verses fail to point out how this prostration is distinct (as the critic acknowledges) then we should understand prostration by its prevailing meaning among Muslims.

What is, then, the prevailing meaning? To answer this I asked myself what are the ideas, conceptions, and meanings that arise *[A 95]* directly and spontaneously in the mind of the average Muslim when the topic of prostration is broached in front of him? After some investigation, I found that prostration is directly associated in his mind with sanctification, worship, self-effacement in front of God, and delivering himself over to Him. The last thing that strikes the Muslim is an association between prostration and greeting and honoring. What is the spontaneous reaction of the average Muslim when he hears that someone has prostrated himself to someone else in order to greet or honor him? He would find it shocking and audacious, and would declaim "God save me from the cursed devil!" Then he would ask if this person is a Muslim or a heretic or polytheist. Even if he were informed that he was a heretic, he would clap his hands together and say "there is no power or strength but in God."

If this is the spontaneous reaction to prostration among Muslims, then is it not capricious to introduce a novel interpretation that makes it merely greeting and honoring? Do Muslims honor people by prostrating themselves to them? I will infer, then, that al-Zamakhshari's suggestion that the prostration of Satan would only have been to greet and honor begs the question.

Since the obvious and spontaneous meaning of prostration makes the order to prostrate oneself before Adam a giant problem in the heart of the religion, some interpreters take refuge in a simple and easy solution, that is, to exempt Satan's prostration from the prevailing meaning of prostration among Muslims. However, this exemption lacks rational justification. There are peoples who considered prostration a way to greet or honor their kings and their powerful ones: The Qur'an talks about some of these ancient peoples. However, their customs and morals are not a template for the morals and customs of Muslims (and for God, religion is Islam). Moreover, most of the peoples who considered prostration a way to greet their kings also considered them to be gods, or at least sharing in the divine. Although the father and brothers of Joseph prostrated themselves to him in order to greet and honor him, in Islam prostration is associated only with sanctification and worship of God, and therefore Muslims do not honor anyone by prostrating themselves to him and do not greet their kings and their powerful ones by means of prostration.

The critic said that my employing three levels to treat the story of Satan shows that I am uncomfortable with my answer to his question about the position of the angels who prostrated themselves to Adam. It appears that the critic thinks on only one level on all occasions and thus did not comprehend the meaning and implications of my words. In other words, he has yet to realize that the results and facts that the researcher reaches in the first stage and that appear, in this stage, true and self-sufficient, will appear to him differently after their revision in the light of the results and facts reached at the end of the study. The first results will then appear partial and will not be complete until after they are incorporated with the facts of greater generality that emerge in following stages to form a solid, tightly-woven, cohesive system. Moreover, the problems that are still pending and the questions that remain unanswered in early stages of the study are explained when the researcher reaches the end of his study. If the critic were aware of the necessity of revising the beginning *[A 96]* in the light of the end, and if he had realized the facts about the nature of scientific-dialectical thinking, the nature of its continuous progress, and the relation of its parts with each other, he would not have directed such accusations at me. Therefore, I say to him that I gave him a clear and frank answer to his question about the position of the angels who prostrated themselves to Adam. I repeat that the angels did not necessarily practice polytheism since they prostrated themselves to perform the will of God, and if He wanted them to practice polytheism then they would practice polytheism and be heretics, and if He wanted them tortured on the Day of Judgment then they would undergo torture, and if He wanted them to be saved then they would be saved: "It is up to Him to punish for no reason or to make happy for no relation or gain."[5] Just as Satan would prostrate himself to submit to the will of God. They were ordered to prostrate themselves so that God could hold his slaves in thrall with command and interdiction rather than by divine decree and fate.

---

5   *Taflis Iblis*, 39.

Chapter Four

The Miracle of the Apparition of the Virgin and the Eradication of the Traces of Aggression[1]

"The recurrence of the Apparition of the Virgin indicates to us that the miracle will continue until Jerusalem is restored to the Arabs and liberated from Zionist terrorism..."[2]

Those who followed the commentaries of Mohammed Hassanein Heikal about the state of the Arabs after their defeat in June 1967 remember that the famous pundit said more than once that completely eradicating the traces of aggression without recourse to warfare or military power would require a miracle. But, he added, our age was not the age of miracles, for the time of miracles had passed and expired. However, circumstances wished to make a liar of Heikal since in May, 1968 *Al-Ahram* informed us of an announcement from His Holiness Pope Kyrillos *[A 98]* the Sixth in which he proclaimed and affirmed the veracity of the Apparition of the Virgin in the Coptic Orthodox Church in the suburb of Zeitoun, and it carried on its front page a picture that it called a photograph of the Virgin or Her Apparition.

---

1   This study was first published in *Dirasat 'Arabiyyah [Arab Studies]* (Beirut) July, 1968.
2   Dr. Ra'ouf Obeid, Professor of Criminal Law at the University of Ain Shams, the author of the first "scientific study of the fact of the appearance of the Virgin Mary in the church dedicated to her name in Zeitoun." *Al-Anwar* (Beirut) May 12, 1968, 2.

The Pope broadcast this news during a well-attended press conference swarming with all the Egyptian newspapers and media. In accordance with the customs of this type of familiar press conference (which are always busy with the distribution of photographs of the matter it wishes to announce and publicize), Bishop Samuel, one of the bishops participating in the press conference, announced the following: "One of the photography studios in the suburb of Zeitoun had been able to take a photograph of the Virgin Mary during one of the nights that she had appeared," exhibiting the photograph to both the press reporters and the television cameras (*Al-Ahram*, May 5, 1968, 2). He also stated, "The Apparition of the Virgin is at its fullest against a snow-white cloud or as a form of light preceded by the release of spiritual forms like doves (*Al-Ahram*, 1). On the following day, *Al-Anwar* newspaper in Beirut appeared with a giant headline in red ink: "The lens records the miracle of the Apparition of the Virgin in Cairo." It also published two similar photographs of what it considered to be holy light that formed the Apparition of the Virgin above the dome of the church (*Al-Anwar*, May 6, 1968). After this, almost the entire Egyptian press plunged into this astonishing religious delusion, adopting and promoting this "great national cause" and exerting itself to search for "decisive scientific proofs" of the occurrence of the miracle by searching out scholars and university professors to testify that that Apparition of the Virgin is something indubitable and real, and by accumulating witnesses, documents, and medical reports as evidence that the cause that the press and media had seized upon was confirmed objective fact. The press explained in full clarity that the Apparition of the Virgin had great implications related to politics, society, resistance, and tourism for the Arab population of Egypt and in regards to the restoration of the lands occupied after the 5th of June. All of these great and exhausting efforts seemed like an attempt to conceal doubts and hide the question marks hovering around the miraculous Apparition, as if the promoters of the miracle were saying to the people: "Please just believe us."

Naturally, this religious hysteria had ramifications in Lebanon, and *Al-Anwar* took charge of its marketing and promotion. It informed us of the news about the rigorous scientific study that confirmed "that the Apparition of the Virgin in Cairo is genuine." However, the major researches and "sciences" that the study relied on, according to *Al-Anwar* itself, were the following: conjurings, photographs of the spirits of the dead, the materialization of spirits through mediums, etc. ...*Al-Anwar* did not fail to publish the photographs of the material spirits that the mediums had summoned—disturbing their repose—with assurance that all of it was scientific and beyond doubt (*Al-Anwar*, May 12, 1968, 12). The only element that this "scientific study" missed, in addition to the conjured spirits, is the famous Zar ceremonies,[3] *[A 99]* which would have completed the picture of the leave of absence that the Arab mind had taken in this newspaper and the extent of its absorption in superstition, spiritualism, hoaxes, and perilous deceit. Perilous for several reasons: 1) it speaks in the name of science and reason and through the press and media, which have wide influence on the Arab masses; 2) it appears at a stage in which the Arabs face the greatest danger; and 3) it appears on the pages of a newspaper like *Al-Ahram*, which is known for its composure, calm, and caution concerning controversial subjects and contentious phenomena.

What is dangerous in this startling religious display in the Arab media is not that the great majority of the people hold traditional beliefs concerning the genuineness of miracles and the Apparition of the Virgin, and how She can appear whenever she wishes. Stories and tales about the occurrence of miracles that violate the laws of nature and that heal the people of their pains and sufferings are as old as mankind itself. They can be found in every religion, and religious books are full of such stories and legends. There is hardly a village in the world that is free of such stories and tales, which the people circulate as the absolute truth concerning the wonders performed by their holy men, the miracles of the saints, and strange, extraordinary events, especially when a village boasts of a religious shrine, sacred tomb, holy man, sheikh, saint, or magician.

---

3   A practice, common in southern Egypt, of curing mental illnesses through contact with the possessing spirit that causes them. Although it is part of Egyptian culture, it is prohibited in Islam. [trans. note]

All of these occurrences are familiar, elemental, and significant. It is the task of socialist regimes and scientific progress to uproot them and replace them with education and scientific culture. Equally familiar is that occasionally the belief in the occurrence of an extraordinary spiritual miracle at some place in the country moves wide segments of the people spontaneously and impulsively. After this movement reaches its peak, it weakens and dwindles until it disappears and matters return to their regular daily course. However, what is dangerous in the miracle of the Apparition of the Virgin is that the movement of the people, initially prompted by their inherited traditional beliefs, did not take a spontaneous course, whereby the believers make a pilgrimage to the church in question and some are healed, some die, and some believe, and then the matter ends in a completely natural way, as it is supposed to do. In Egypt, the course events took was entirely the opposite. The state institutions—its newspapers, media, and ministries—adopted the story of the Apparition of the Virgin, embracing and promoting it, and even drawing from it desired implications concerning politics, the resistance, and tourism, as I mentioned, transforming it into a religious hysteria that swept a large part of the population.

The great departure in this behavior and in this "serious" discussion of conjuring, the photographing of spiritual specters, and the tying of the liberation of Jerusalem and perseverance in confronting the enemy with the Apparition of the Virgin is that all of this was promoted by the media of a state that considers itself a revolutionary socialist state that places its media capacities in the service of the people with the goal of educating it and raising its scientific and intellectual level, not with the goal of misleading it by inciting it through a maze of religious hallucinations, *[A 100]* by embellishing its legends, and by giving them the appearance of scientific fact.

It would be no great matter if the press behind this intense wave of religious madness belonged to a reactionary country wishing to conceal its intellectual and material impotence to confront the challenges of the current struggle under the screen of religiosity and tie victory and defeat to powers transcending human abilities.

However, the true calamity is that the press that has thrown its support to this mission is supervised and steered by the Arab Socialist Union. The same can be said of the other newspapers enjoying the protection of the "Arab Progressive Liberationist Movement." They also could not refrain from spreading religious hysteria and promoting it with all available means. Everything that we have heard after the defeat about modern science, technology, and scientific methodology in thinking, planning, and self-preparation, and about rationality and balance in our words, declarations, and behavior, only took a moment to go up in smoke under the intense influence of this religious hysteria. It is truly regrettable that not a single intellectual, socialist, thinker, layman, literary critic, writer, or journalist in the Arab world has raised his or her voice to respond to these wild claims and to call those Arabs who were struck by this madness to rationality, balance, and refraining from manipulating the religious feelings of the masses. Who of them has refused to ride the current of madness along with the alleged scholars and professors who stand tall to support (with all boldness and daring, naturally) the official point of view concerning the Apparition of the Virgin? Distracting the Arab masses with stories about invisible beings, supernatural phenomena, and miracles in the second half of twentieth century, and especially in this period of the greatest urgency, will never destine us to success in solving our pressing worldly issues or help us to achieve our vital national rights, whether or not the Virgin is angry because of the loss of Jerusalem.

Allow me to make some basic remarks about what is called the miracle of the Apparition of the Virgin. I will base my discussion on some statements and commentaries that have been published about this miracle, officially or semi-officially, in order to reveal a number of crucial facts embedded in these statements and in order to provide evidence for what I said at the beginning of this chapter. In other words, upon my close examination of the materials that have been published about the Apparition of the Virgin, it became clear to me that they were packed with contradictions, falsifications, historical errors, ridiculous disparities, and immature primitive mythical thinking.

It also became clear to me that the materials had been steered in a certain direction to drag in conclusions and considerations having to do with politics, tourism, the media, and official policy, all of which have a direct connection to the terrible situation prevailing immediately after the defeat. I wish to expose the fabrications and demagoguery embedded in what was said and published on the Apparition of the Virgin in Cairo, hoping to make a humble contribution to calling back the Arab mind again to balance, rationality, and objectivity in how it views this religious delusion and to distance itself from the waves of religious commotion and foolish demagogy *[A 101]* that waste Arab time and efforts.[4]

(1) Al-Ahram published in its edition of May 5, 1968 a photograph of the Church of the Virgin in the suburb of Zeitoun in which a spot of intense white light that resembled an elongated balloon distended at the top appeared over one of its domes. The newspaper mentioned that the glowing spot in the picture was a photographic record of the specter of the Virgin and Her holy light as she appeared to the people. *Al-Ahram* gave a tone of seriousness to the photograph when it appended the following caption: "The photography department at *Al-Ahram* that undertook the printing of the photograph on the original film established that there was no trace of montage on the film."

On the following day, the Beirut newspaper *Al-Anwar* published the same photograph with the following comment: "The first photograph of the miracle of the Apparition of the Virgin."

The first point I wish to make about this photograph and the claims raised about it is that the religious and journalistic authorities responsible for the promotion of the story of the Apparition of the Virgin do not agree about the importance of the circulated photograph, or its authenticity or suitability as proof of the occurrence of the alleged miracle. For, while *Al-Anwar* considered it absolute proof of the occurrence of the miracle,

---

4 The texts I will discuss are published in the following newspapers: *Al-Ahram*, May 5, 1968, *Al-Anwar*, May 6 and 12, 1968, and *Watani* (a Coptic Egyptian weekly newspaper published by the Egyptian Illustrated Newspaper Company), May 5, 1968.

the Coptic religious newspaper _Watani_ declared on its first page that the photograph taken during the Apparition of the Virgin had been offered to it several times with strong and repeated pressure to publish it, "but that we declined because we were sure it did not represent reality and we are careful to publish only truths that we have verified."

This is the position of _Watani_, literally. The moral of this story is that this humble religious weekly newspaper was more balanced, cautious, and composed about the photograph than _Al-Ahram_, which is the revered newspaper unsurpassed by any other Arab newspaper in regards to fame, composure, caution, and distance from hyperbole and exaggeration. In other words, it appears that those who possessed the greatest vested interest in the story of the Virgin do not agree in the first place about the extent of the credibility of this photograph and whether it was tangible proof of the occurrence of the miracle. Or must we give greater credibility to the newspaper with the widest circulation because it has the widest circulation?

It appears to me that the claims about the possibility of recording the Apparition of the Virgin on regular film and by means of common photographic lenses, forms, in reality, the greatest possible excess in thinking and the most unbridled primitive flight of the imagination, unprecedented by any non-Arab among those who are devoted to the Virgin and believe in the possibility of her Apparition and her miracles, from a purely traditional religious perspective. _[A 102]_

There are stories about the Virgin appearing in various places around the world like France, Portugal, Jerusalem, and Lebanon. However, none of the competent religious authorities ever claimed before today the ability to photograph pure spiritual manifestations by recording the holy divine light upon film, and then developing, printing, and presenting it on television or in the newspapers. The purely traditional religious view considers the Apparition of the Virgin to be a sort of pure spiritual energy, as the Coptic clerics indicated in their statement published in _Al-Ahram_. In other words, the Apparition resembles a divine light that cannot be perceived by the material senses but can only be attested to by the heart, conscience, and insight. Or it is like the light that Al-Ghazali said God cast into his breast after a long period of questioning. Any idea that suggests that this light or this spiritual energy has the nature of matter or material light rays that the senses can capture and that lenses can reflect and record on film (to be developed and printed) is nothing but blasphemy (from a religious perspective, naturally). Such an idea returns us to those Islamic sects or their analogues in the history of Christianity that went all the way in likening the divine person to physical events, to the point of attributing corporeality to him, that is, the belief that the divine existence can be characterized as a real material existence located in space. Those promoting the photograph of the Apparition of the Virgin fell into an appalling religious error without knowing it since anything that lacks material existence cannot be recorded by the senses, captured by lenses, or printed on film.

The real miracle here, then, does not lie in the Apparition of the Virgin itself, since the hearts of the naive and the believers were already convinced of it (and still are), but rather it lies in the strange success that the craft of photography achieved in the suburb of Zeitoun, where lenses were able to capture an immaterial and absolutely spiritual energy on a piece of matter (film) by means of material equipment like a camera! The miracle is the easy passage from the material world to the spiritual world, transforming the spiritual into the material, and transmuting the material to the spiritual—compelling matter to accept completely, ordinarily, routinely, and naturally pure spiritual phenomena. Therefore, I suggest to those in charge to erect a memorial shrine for the photographer who performed this miracle and to raise a giant statue to him so that conjurers and spiritual mediums from all over the world have an object of pilgrimage. As I suggest to them the preservation of the film, camera, and other equipment used in this miracle in order to conserve the energy, holy light, and divine blessing that descended on them. Believers would flock from all over the world to seek their blessings.

I want to make two suggestions to those who are still troubled by the photograph and in need of an explanation: On a clear night, go up on your roof, taking your camera and film. Expose the film by opening the lens for different time intervals. Proceed with this experiment using various lenses and film types, etc. After developing the film (or films), you will find in the photographs spots of light whose shapes, lines, and compositions are odd and strange. And if you possess a wild imagination you will "see" whatever you wish in those photographs, just as happens to those who study shifting clouds and see in them *[A 103]* the shapes and pictures they wish to see. The atmosphere of the earth is full of cosmic rays (invisible to the naked eye), electric charges, and electromagnetic disturbances, etc. All of them leave their traces on sensitive materials like photographic film. Assuming that the photographs that *Al-Ahram* published were real, it was not necessary for the Virgin to descend down from the heavens to explain the large spots of light that appeared on the film after it was developed. Even a thinker from the Middle Ages would search for a natural explanation for the appearance of the spots on the photograph before dragging in the Virgin Mary, divine light, angels, the heavens, and celestial vaults to explain their existence and appearance. Close examination of the photograph that *Al-Ahram* (and then *Al-Anwar*) published would make clear that the spot of bright light (the specter of the Virgin, as is claimed) located above the dome of the church in the photograph is entirely in focus, while the figures of the dome and church blur, that is, they are entirely out of focus. According to the basic laws of light, when two objects stand at the same distance from the lens (here the specter and the dome of the church), if the first is in focus then the second should be in focus. Any violation would contradict the laws of nature pertaining to light and is thus impossible. Therefore, I do not believe that the published photograph is genuine or corresponds with reality. There must be some crucial flaw that specialists could uncover and explain. The only other possibility is that, in short, that the art of photography has performed a miracle, as I mentioned earlier.

(2) The kind of atmosphere that surrounded the Virgin's appearance deserve attention and consideration as to this striking religious phenomenon. *Watani* newspaper gave this atmosphere a precise description, stating that when the Virgin appeared:

> Some of the women gathered in the streets remembered this view
> as familiar to them from the photographs circulating of the Virgin
> Mary and shouted "This is our lady, the Virgin Mary!" At the same

time, voices were raised from the crowd declaring "You are blessed, oh Virgin!" Everyone began to rejoice and exalt. A thrilling and captivating sight, and a religious scene that roused the beat of chants, prayers, and supplications. One shed tears of joy, another prayed, a third prostrated himself, and a fourth requested Mary's healing intercession. Ululations were heard, saluting Her, the Mother of Light (*Watani*, May 5, 1968, 2).

It cannot escape the careful reader that this narrative is nothing but a classic description of the phenomenon of collective hysteria that sweeps these sorts of crowds of people. The newspaper continues its description of the throbbing, pulsating, feverish atmosphere that governed the crowd of witnesses, saying:

> Applause increased, and the shouting, rejoicing, and exulting intensified until it pierced the highest heavens ("oh Virgin...oh Virgin"). The crowd recited, chanted, and prayed all night until the break of dawn. Old men found themselves speeding along, *[A 104]* old women stepped lightly, and the pregnant scampered as if a spiritual power had given strength to their limbs. More than forty thousand people gathered in the streets surrounding the church from sunset until the break of dawn (*Watani*, 2).

Who among us (however poised and impartial) will fail "to see the Virgin" or not imagine that he saw the Virgin when he finds himself in such a feverish atmosphere and in the depths of this rejoicing, exultation, screaming, and wailing that pierces the highest heavens? Who would be so bold to say –in this furious environment—that he had not seen anything or that what he saw above the dome of the church did not resemble the Virgin but something else? What would be his fate at the hands of the God-fearing believers as they rejoiced and exulted? According to what *Watani* wrote, there were some skeptical, impartial elements mixed in among the great crowds: "Elements infiltrated the crowds, prompted by motives and intentions far from just innocent viewing, almost tainting the purity of the miracle and preventing the revelation of her image in its radiance and as we would wish for those coming from abroad to see her (*Watani*, 3)."

After being alerted to their presence, the Ministry of Tourism and other authorities decided the fate of those skeptical infiltrators. *Watani* reported that "the Ministry of Tourism is expected to cooperate with administrative bodies and others in order to organize street traffic around the church and monitor corrupt elements that infiltrate the crowd in a repellent way in order to defile the beauty of the image of the Virgin (*Watani*, 3)."The same newspaper indicated, in another passage, "the endeavor of the secret police and Arab Socialist Union" to protect the miracle from fabrications, lies, and falsehoods (*Watani*, 5).

The media and the press attempted to create the impression on the readers that everyone in the enormous crowd was unanimous in how they saw the specter of the Virgin. For example, one of the churchmen described the Apparition of the Virgin as follows:

> The light was not shed on a single person or group of people. Rather, it appeared like the sun when it rises on everyone (*Watani*, 3).

Nevertheless, close examination of what was published about the topic reveals other statements that contradict these words and indicate the opposite. The clerics had tried to rationalize the lack of unanimity and explain it with their special logic and in their special manner. However, we will be guided about the lack of unanimity by the conflicting statements of the religious officials, as the following text makes clear:

> One priest, whose opinion is shared by many clerics, *[A 105]* stated that not everyone had the same vision nor did that vision have the same degree of clarity, but rather that spiritual fertility, religious transparency, and depth of faith influenced greatly the vision of the Virgin Mary. For it was observed among the throng that some saw a clear image while some saw only a light and some, perhaps, did not see anything. On April 9, 1968, twin brothers were present: to one she appeared completely while the other did not see anything but a weak ray of light. It was also observed that the Virgin Mary appears with total clarity and in an entirely pure form to children, because of their share of purity and transparency, and because they are still remote from the filthiness of this earthly life. Even those who were not granted the vision were able observe a religious festival where spiritual songs were chanted and prayers made. Everyone was affected by holy feelings

> and almost everyone indulged in the hope of seeing her at another moment. And although they remained standing the whole night, from dusk until the break of dawn, they did not feel exhausted and went home with hearts full of rest, contentment, and faith (*Watani*, 2).

These words make clear that the apparition of light was limited to some groups and individuals and that it "did not appear like the sun that rises on everyone." As for those who did not witness the Virgin, their efforts were not in vain because they had participated in an enormous religious festival and were affected by all sorts of emotions and feelings while they shared in this feverish atmosphere. The same words make clear that the participants in the festival, in practical terms, saw what they wanted to see because of the projection of their agitated psychological conditions on the external world and its appearances. A neutral observer, therefore, should not be expected to see anything. From this stems the special reference to children and their almost exceptional capacity to see the specter of the Virgin in total clarity, since we know well the extent of the receptivity of children to be swiftly affected by the atmosphere surrounding them, their dazzling ability to project the pictures from their imaginations and psychological states on the outside world, the unlimited fertility of their imaginations, and their capacity to behave as if the contents of their imaginations are the real facts around them.

These statements, made by those with an essential vested interest in the story of the miracle, unmistakably contradict other statements they made and with what was said by the newspapers and media promoting "the Apparition of the Virgin" and how it "appeared to all," followed by everyone rejoicing and exulting in what they saw, as we find in the following text:

> The Virgin Mary appeared in her heavenly light more clearly and more radiantly and at that time everyone confirmed that the girl before them was undoubtedly the Virgin Mary (*Watani*, 2).

One reason to accept this manner of thinking about the dubious circumstances surrounding the occurrence of the miracle of the Apparition is the story the newspapers published about a citizen by the name of

Marcelle who claimed that the Virgin visited her at home and then "foam" appeared on the mouth of her son. When his mouth was wiped with a handkerchief, the handkerchief was left with the print of a palm with a cross in its center (*Al-Ahram*, 3). *[A 106]*

> On the following day, the Pope proclaimed the story to be an absolute fabrication, while backing the rest of the other stories....However, the investigative committee that the Pope formed had accepted this story such as it was, considering it a kind of faith (*Al-Ahram*, 3).

Al-Ahram continued to detail the events in the story of Marcelle, the Pope, and the Virgin. The official speaker of the Coptic Church said in the above-mentioned press conference that additional investigation revealed that the story of the handkerchief was a fabrication:

> The committee re-investigated the story of Mrs. Marcelle, and gaps became apparent, among them that she stated that the window of the room opened suddenly and with such violence that it almost shattered, as if a storm had started. However, the apparition of the Virgin does not arrive like a destructive storm but as a gentle breeze. Similarly, Her apparition—as spirit or specter—does not require the opening of a window. The blood present on the handkerchief was not real, for such blood only appears during the performance of an exorcism. In spite of all this, the Pope did not confirm it to be a fabrication, but warned the faithful from believing everything that people say... Currently, laboratory research is being conducted on the handkerchief to learn the truth (*Al-Ahram*, 3).

Note the contradictions between the statements, for first we are informed that the Pope proclaimed the story of the handkerchief to be an absolute fabrication and then we are told that the Pope did not declare it to be a fabrication but was awaiting the results of the laboratory tests on the handkerchief! Is the Arab mind afflicted with insanity or what?

Watani related the story of the handkerchief in a way that differed in some details from what *Al-Ahram* had published. It reported that the Virgin pressed her hand on the handkerchief and the mark of the cross appeared in the center of the hand (*Watani*, 5). Then it commented on the story of Marcelle in the following way:

> The truth about the handkerchief is that Mr. Adel Taher, the Representative of the Ministry of Tourism, dispatched Professor William Farid, the Director of Public Affairs in Tourism, to investigate what was said about it. Professor Farid affirmed that it was not at all true. The secret police and the Arab Socialist Union also took an interest in the issue. The falsehood of the story of the handkerchief became apparent to them…She also lied about how the Virgin appeared to her. For the Virgin neither opens windows nor enters during storms, but penetrates walls and partitions and arrives in tranquility and peace, just as she did in France, Portugal, and Jerusalem, and recently at the church in the suburb of Zeitoun (*Watani*, 5).

We had not been previously advised that representatives of the Ministry of Tourism, the secret police, and officials in the Arab Socialist Union were specialists *[A 107]* in examining miracles or extraordinary wonders and in distinguishing the genuine from the fabricated. We would like to express our thanks to the Virgin because She revealed to us this odd expertise and spiritual knowledge that these men enjoy on account of their official positions and responsibilities. As for why we must assume that the Virgin does not open windows, this is a secret not yet revealed by those evaluating the issues of the miracle, its explanations, and its ideology.

(3) We mentioned that the people's faith in the occurrence of miracles, wonders, and extraordinary incidents is widespread and well-known, just as we mentioned that what truly incites astonishment in regards to the story of the Apparition of the Virgin in Cairo is that a progressive state advocating liberation has adopted and promoted this story through its press, institutions, ministries, and officials. Is this appropriate for a country that considers itself walking along the path of socialism, industrialization, and the adoption of scientific methodology for organizing and planning, and for confronting the challenges of the enemy and overcoming of the crisis left behind by the defeat of June 1967? The following is an example of the media promotion of the miracle:

On the next morning, the crowds had dispersed and the news had traveled like lightning among the residents of Cairo and then across the whole country. The news was carried by Eastern and Western news agencies and disseminated by Western newspapers and magazines and a variety of broadcasters and television stations abroad (*Watani*, 2).

The official embrace of the religious mania that swept this enormous number of people showed itself in many ways, some of which we have mentioned. However, the matter did not stop here but passed from the manifestation of religious hysteria to drawing conclusions concerning tourism and politics in the context of the state of the Arabs after the defeat. An example of what I mean is from *Watani*, where it reports some news about the consequences of the miracle for tourism:

Mr. Sha'rawi Juma'a, Minister of the Interior, took an interest in the miracle of the Apparition of the Virgin at the church in Zeitoun. He held a meeting, which was attended by Mr. Sa'ad Zayed, Governor of Cairo, and led a discussion about organizing traffic in the environs of the Church and cleansing it from everything at odds with its spiritual standing, since it would become a global holy shrine...(*Watani*, 1).

The Ministry of Tourism issued an important and detailed report about the Apparition of the Virgin and dispatched it to all the world capitals...The news about the vivid and recurring Apparition of the Virgin in the church claimed international importance in all the capitals of Europe and the Middle East. Foreign embassies in Cairo sent important reports on the Apparition of the Virgin back to their countries...(*Watani*, 2).

Professor Adel Taher, Representative of the Ministry of Tourism, had delegated to Mr. Willam Farid, Director of Information at the Ministry, to follow the Apparition of the Virgin at the church and to pass on to him Her news, and he traveled there a number of times and wrote a report about what he saw (*Watani*, 3). *[A 108]*

During the press conference that we have referred to many times, one of the journalists raised the following question: "Are there plans to transform the suburb of Zeitoun into a tourism center?" Bishop Samuel (the official spokesman) replied: "This announcement is a good start for this center, for it is an acknowledgement that this place has become a holy place. All the necessary plans will be prepared to establish holy shrines and monuments there (*Al-Ahram*, 3).

We need not dive too deeply into these reports to recognize that those assessing the miracle yearned to transform the suburb of Zeitoun into a tourism center at any cost, for that desire is obvious and goes far beyond what is necessary or appropriate.

The political implications inherent in this momentous religious manifestation are found in several excerpts from what was written about the Apparition of the Virgin and its connection to the "elimination of the traces of the aggression" and the liberation of the occupied Arab lands. *Al-Ahram* gave prominence to the following headline on its second page: "The Apparition of the Virgin indicates that God will be on our side and that the heavens have not abandoned us." That is, after everything that has happened, the Arabs are still asked, from the bottom of their hearts, to implore the heavens for victory and beg for it from God instead of being asked to depend entirely on themselves and their fighting spirit and determination without any consolation, sympathy, or hope for outside help, whether from the heavens or the United Nations (as if there were a difference). The following justification for the Apparition of the Virgin in Egypt at this time emerged in that well-attended press conference:

> We say that saints and martyrs appear to the faithful in times of stress in order to support and encourage them. Therefore the Virgin arrived to support the Egyptian people, who are faithful and blessed according to the text of the Holy Bible, in the misfortune or crisis that they are passing through now and to make them aware that God has not forgotten His promise to them that they are His blessed people…and to call the Egyptian people to cling to its faith and beliefs in this time in which appeals to atheism, the voices of blasphemy, and the clamor to flee from God and faith are widespread…We have yet to forget that man who was sent into space and returned to say that he searched for God in the heavens but did not find Him (*Al-Ahram*, 3)!

It is clear from this statement and the machinations hidden behind it that the Virgin did not appear in order to appeal to the Arabs in Egypt to hold fast to their revolution, deepen their commitment to socialism, and push forward along the progressive, fighting path in order to respond to the Israeli challenge. She came instead to ask them to persevere in clinging to their inherited obsolete beliefs and the obscurantist ideology holding sway over their minds. In other words, She wants them to face the future by retreating to the rear instead of rushing forward, and this is as clear as the insinuation and suspicion directed towards the Soviet Union and its astronauts.

What remains is to inquire about the saints who appeared to the Cuban and *[A 109]* Vietnamese peoples in the time of stress. Did this apparition have any relation to the enormous victories that the two peoples achieved against the colonialist aggression, or did these peoples draw their ideals from heroes, leaving the saints, supernatural beings, and religious martyrs to the side, in order to succeed in their world and triumph in their battles?

The following statement of Bishop Grigorius in the aforementioned press conference is another example of how political implications were derived from the story of the Apparition of the Virgin:

> It is good news and a heavenly sign that God is with us and will not abandon us…We have been hearing since last June that God has abandoned us, for if not, then why the setback?…However, this public appearance in front of thousands means that God is with us, that He will stand at our side, and that all should feel this crisis is only an anomaly and that the heavens are still on our side…Just as this Apparition perhaps means that the Virgin Mary is not pleased with what the Jews violated and are violating in the Holy Lands in the city of Jerusalem…What took place there grieves her as she is the protector of the Holy Lands, and thus she has come to announce to mankind her anger and grief and call for the purifying of Jerusalem from those who defile it (*Al-Ahram*, 3).

Is the Virgin obliged to descend from heaven so that the Arabs realize that the liberation of Jerusalem and all the occupied lands is an urgent national necessity? Or have we forgotten that that the issue of liberation is axiomatic and thus does not require heavenly support, a miraculous interpretation, or a reminder from the Virgin Mary?

In regards to the political implications, Father Ayrout explained that the miraculous Apparition of the Virgin had always been associated, since old times, with certain messages that She revealed or dictated to those to whom She appeared. Then Father Ayrout identified the message of the Virgin in this Apparition, saying: "Here she wanted to compensate those whom the aggression prevented from visiting the Holy Land and Jerusalem" (*Al-Ahram*, 2). *Watani* added:

> Some of the clergy gave Her Apparition a number of meanings: The Virgin Mary appeared to the Egyptian people to compensate the Egyptian pilgrims for their being deprived of visiting Jerusalem after the aggression had closed the doors in their faces. The Heavenly Light appeared to them because they were deprived of the glorious light of the resurrection and needed a consolation that would calm and cheer their souls (*Watani*, 2).

I wonder whether the Arabs today need consolation, calm, and talk that cheers them up or criticism, rebuff, anxiety, and everything that would inflame them in order to confront the occupation and the deadly challenges that they face.

Finally, in the same press conference, Grigorius, the Bishop of Higher Education and Scientific Research (indeed!), stated:

> Perhaps this Apparition is a good portent and a heavenly sign from God that He is *[A 110]* with us and will stand behind us in order to raise morale among the people, for the crisis is an anomaly and will soon end. Indeed, the Virgin —after the Jews have seized the holy places in Jerusalem—is dismayed by what has happened there, and thus this Apparition is a sign from the heavens that God is not pleased by what is happening in Jerusalem and that He will grant us victory (*Watani*, 2).

In contrast to the preceding statement, it should be clear to all Arabs that the crisis brought on by the defeat is not an anomaly at all, but a fundamental, fateful crisis that threatens Arab existence in its entirety. The Arabs must prepare themselves to confront it, not by considering it an anomalous crisis but rather by considering it a problem that will persist, crest, threaten, challenge, and obliterate. Any other conception of the crisis that serves to diminish its danger and potency is nothing but a deception, delusion, and empty blandishment. In contrast to everything that Bishop Grigorius said, neither miracles nor the Apparition of the Virgin nor blessings descending on the people of Egypt will truly raise the morale of the Arabs and restore their trust in the current leadership, for the only way to achieve this result (I almost said "this miracle") is to move swiftly on the clear path to victory without any confusion about the invading enemy.

(4) I can frankly say that the intellectual, cultural, and scientific level of the clergy in the Egyptian Coptic Church is exceedingly low and incapable of being described as composed, cautious, and intellectually responsible in how it handled and administered these issues. This fact has become clear to me after close examination of the statements and pronouncements that filled the newspapers on the occasion of the Apparition of the Virgin. A few examples will suffice:

(a) There was a well-attended national meeting held in the Church of Al-Mu'alaqa in old Cairo. Among the attendees were Pope Kyrillos the Sixth and a number of the clergy, including their Excellencies Bishop Samuel and Bishop Grigorius, the Bishop for Higher Education and Scientific Research. Mr. Abdul Majid Farid, the General Secretary of the Arab Socialist Union in Cairo, was also present. Bishop Samuel delivered a talk in which he emphasized "an established scientific and historical fact," that during Fatimid rule the Al-Mokattam mountain [a range of hills east of Cairo, *trans. note*] was in a different place than where it stands today. For the Caliph had asked one of the patriarchs of the Coptic Church to move it from its old place to where it is now, and the patriarch naturally obeyed the Caliph's order and performed it immediately and in a miraculous and wonderous manner. The following is the exact text of what Bishop Samuel stated about the miracle of moving Al-Mokattam in a semi-official speech before, among others, the representative of the Arab Socialist Union:

"The miracle of moving Al-Mokattam mountain was performed by one of the holy patriarchs after one of the Jewish ministers of Caliph al-Mu'izz li Din Allah suggested to him that he ask the Coptic patriarch *[A 111]* to move the mountain, then sitting in the heart of Cairo, a suggestion he made in order to provoke ethnic discord. He cited as a pretext for his request a verse that was often repeated by the Coptic clergy: 'If you have faith as a grain of mustard seed, you will tell this mountain, "Move from here to there," and it will move.'[5] The Caliph invited the patriarch and discussed the verse with him, and then demanded that he move Al-Mokattam. The patriarch absorbed himself in prayer and then went, with a group of his people, to the elevations of the mountain and prayed fervently. The mountain was moved, a miracle that was recorded in the books of history, and the evil intent of the Jewish minister was transformed to good, divine providence diverting his wicked intentions to provoke ethnic discord." His Excellency Bishop Samuel commented on this miracle by saying that the Jews have always striven to create discord and divisions and to provoke odious ethnic hatred, both then and now. However, adhering to faith and spiritual values, as exemplified by the National Charter and the March 30th Manifesto,[6] guarantees the annihilation of these attempts (*Watani*, p. 4).

We suggest to the honorable patriarch, on this occasion, that he pick up Al-Mokattam and drop it as quickly as possible directly over the Israeli war room during a meeting of the enemy's chief of staff. This might be of some use and benefit to the Arab cause, in general, and to the elimination of the traces of the aggression, in particular.

(b) One of those attending the press conference asked the clerical body a clever and important question:

Those who have seen the Virgin at the church in Zeitoun say that she resembles exactly the pictures they have seen in so many Christian churches and homes...However, we know that artists derived inspiration for this picture from their imaginations, and thus it is not

---

5   Matthew 17:20.
6   Two political documents of Nasserist Egypt. The first was issued before the 1967 defeat (1962), the second after it (1968).

accurate. Therefore, what the people say may not be accurate either (*Al-Ahram*, 2).

The response was the following:

> It is true that artists derived most of their inspiration for the picture of the Virgin Mary in circulation today from their imaginations... However, despite this, all of them, without exception, derived inspiration from the real features of the face of the Virgin, or added these in...For these real features are present in the picture that Saint Luke drew of Her...[which] still exists in Jerusalem today... This implies that the pictures of the Virgin existing today *[A 112]* are accurate and that Her features have been transferred from the original picture that Saint Luke drew of Her more than 1900 years ago (*Al-Ahram*, 2).

It should first be noted that the story changes between the beginning and the end of this response. The Bishop begins by stating that "artists derived most of their inspiration for the picture of the Virgin Mary in circulation today from their imaginations," and ends by stating the opposite, that "the pictures of the Virgin existing today are accurate and that Her features have been transferred from the original picture." Second, when I reviewed the reliable scientific sources, I found that nothing that the Bishop said about the pictures of the Virgin has any basis in truth, solid historical evidence, or rigorous scientific argument, and that it does not add up to anything more than religious legends and stories woven by the imagination. I consulted the work of Dr. Philip Schaff, *History of the Christian Church*, in eight volumes,[7] and it is clear from this authority (volume II, starting on page 281) that everything said about the existence of an original picture of the Virgin by the hand of Saint Luke is false. If Saint Luke had really drawn the Virgin, then this picture has disintegrated or ceased to be: there is not a trace of it left today in the study of the history of the Christian Church and the science of archaeology. The same authority states that the first drawings or

---

7   Philip Schaff, *History of the Christian Church* (Michigan: Wm. B. Erdman's Publishing Co.).

pictures of the Virgin do not date back as far as the first century but only the third century after the birth of Christ. In the best case, and with a low probability, they date back to the second century after His birth. I do not believe that the existence of such an important, prized picture in Jerusalem, as the Bishop claims, could have passed unnoticed by the archaeologists, historians of religion, and those studying the history of the church. If this fantastic story about the existence of the original picture of the Virgin had any truth, then we would find a mention of it or a reference to the existence of the alleged original picture in the more standard and common sources concerned with history and religion.

I ought to mention in regards to this topic a well-known matter, that in Europe the pictures and statues of the Virgin Mary have the features of European women; in Mexico, they have the exact features of Mexican women; and in Africa, the Virgin resembles African women, having black features.

In other words, every group sees the Virgin Mary in its own image. There is no harm in that, for depicting the Virgin is only a religious symbol that does not presuppose any claim on historical reality. Those, then, who thought they witnessed the Virgin above the dome of the church in Zeitoun in Cairo witnessed, in reality, the image of the Virgin that they had become accustomed to see previously in their religious upbringing and social environment. Even if we assume, for the sake of argument, that the familiar picture of the Virgin actually resembled the features of Mary, the Mother of Christ, this does not imply that the crowds swarming around the church of Zeitoun witnessed the Virgin herself, but rather implies that the crowds projected the image of the Virgin Mary that they carry in their imagination onto the outside world and its events.

(c) During the press conference, one of the archbishops stated: "No one disagrees about the holiness of the Virgin Mary...for She is the Holy Mother who became pregnant and gave birth by the spirit of God, without human seed, and everyone believes in Her holiness to the same degree..."(*Al-Ahram*, 3). *[A 113]*

It appears to me that the real point of this statement is to suggest that the miracle of the Apparition of the Virgin does not only concern Christians but also the entire Muslim population of Egypt because of the special status that the Virgin occupies in Islam. Another newspaper suggested this aloud in these words: "Her Apparition was not limited to the Christians or a single sect but encompassed all creeds, sects, and religions equally" (*Watani*, 2).

This is just bland, general language whose point is to flatter and conciliate. The truth is that differences about the status of the Virgin and her holiness exist between the Christians themselves, as is the case with Protestants, and they also exist between Christians and Muslims, since Christians consider Her to be the Mother of God, as is well-known, and this is the heart of blasphemy for Muslims. There is no intellectual or religious integrity in pretending to ignore all these differences and disparities in matters of religious belief since they are extremely essential and significant to believers. It is astonishing that in all that has been said and written about the Apparition of the Virgin She has never been referred to, even once, as the "Mother of God," which is the most significant description She carries among Christians, and the source of Her high and holy status and Her ability to intercede on their behalf. In reality, that the Virgin is the Mother of God is a fundamental theme in the Coptic creed since the Coptic Church says that Jesus Christ has one nature, a divine nature, and the Copts stick to this belief against Christians who believe in two natures, saying that Christ is human and divine at the same time, and against Nestorians, who emphasize His human nature. Because of the insistence of the Coptic Church on the divine nature of Christ, the Virgin Mary enjoys an extreme religious significance for them, for she is the Mother of God in the full meaning of the term, and not just the Mother of His human aspect. She is His mother in His incarnated divinity, full and complete. I believe that the Coptic clergy was neither faithful to its creed and its basic religious position nor honest with itself, its church, and its spiritual heritage when it omitted that She was the Mother of God in what it wrote and said about the miracle. For the clergy described the Virgin with a variety of descriptions and traditional characteristics but it bargained, concluded a truce, and relinquished the characterization that meant the most to its creed by ignoring that She is the Mother of God. The loss of integrity in such a fashion is sufficient by itself to stain everything that the Coptic Church said about the miracle of the Apparition of the Virgin and other issues.

(d) One of the archbishops participating in the press conference said the following about the scientific explanation of the Apparition of the Virgin:

> From a scientific perspective, it has been established that every human being has an "ether" that cannot be erased from existence and that can be materialized at any time in the form of ethereal atoms taking the shape of a human being…For example, science is able to photograph dozens of men and women who died hundreds of years ago. If this requires complicated electronic equipment and machines for ordinary people, *[A 114]* I do not believe that the same is required for saints and martyrs…but that faith is sufficient (*Al-Ahram*, 3).

It is not necessary for one to be an expert natural scientist or a specialist in electronics and "etherology" to show that this is empty chatter and more disgraceful and dangerous than superstitions and gibberish. For it speaks in the name of science, in a language that appears serious, out of the mouth of a senior religious official, and on the pages of a newspaper like *Al-Ahram*. It is a shame on the Arab intellect in the second half of the twentieth century that this empty talk about "human ether that cannot be erased from existence and that can be materialized at any time" and this folly about "photographing men and women who have been dead for hundreds of years" can be repeated. And all in the name of science, during an official press conference, under the patronage of a progressive state, in a socialist country, and after a terrible defeat that was partly due to the miserable level of scientific knowledge in every corner of the Arab world.

Since we were able, through faith, saints, and religious martyrs to achieve what others cannot without recourse to modern science and complicated electronic equipment and machines, then all we need to do is to leave these machines and equipment to Moshe Dayan and his people and turn to our saints, martyrs, and spiritual and invisible beings to achieve what they achieved! Is this the kind of cultural and popular guidance that the Arab people needs after the defeat?

While much has been said about miraculous healings and their occurring on the occasion of the Apparition of the Virgin, their scientific explanation is simple and well-known. For we all know that a large group of the kinds of disabilities that people suffer from, like some types of blindness, deafness, paralysis, etc. are not due to any kind of organic defect in the human body but arise from affective, emotional, and psychological factors, and these types of disabilities are called "psychosomatic." When the promoters of miraculous cures say that someone has been struck by a malady that medicine is unable to cure, this statement means nothing more than that the doctors have yet to find any organic or physiological defect in the organs of the patient that would lead to the emergence of this malady or attack, or the like. However, this does not exclude the possibility that the malady is psychological and inorganic but still capable of having a direct and deleterious effect on human physiology. Records of psychological treatment are full of examples of maladies and illnesses that "medicine was unable to cure" but that psychologists were able to treat and cure. I will mention here that violent emotional convulsions often accompany or briefly precede this process of healing.

Let us, for example, imagine a man whose hand is paralyzed for reasons that medicine is unable to determine. In other words, the cause is inorganic. Instead of sending him to be treated by a specialist, let us suggest to him that he go to the site of miracles, where wonders of healing are performed for many in a rapturous atmosphere charged with intense emotions to the greatest extent possible. In such a context, it is not difficult to imagine how his mind could generate a powerful, passionate agitation or emotional shock *[A 115]* that could amount to a breathing space for the buried psychological problem that he suffers from and that lies behind the paralyzed hand. He achieves in this way what he would have achieved under the supervision of a medical specialist, the paralysis passing away or showing indications of unexpected improvement.

These episodes of healing cannot be attributed to miracles or the supernatural in the least whether they occur in a hospital under the care of a psychologist, in the presence of a priest or sorcerer who claims to have healing powers, at a religious shrine, or among groups of believers awaiting the Apparition of the Virgin. In any case, many scientific studies have been written in foreign languages to explain this type of healing and the reader is able to consult some of them. I mentioned the issue of unexpected healing briefly to indicate that so-called miracles of healing are not supernatural events that science is unable to explain, as some believe and as those who evaluated the miracle of the Virgin in Cairo have stated. In other words, when the cause is known the wonder fades and the scientific truth appears to those who are interested in scientific truth.

Last but not least, the Arabs have reaped the painful consequences of this religious hysteria publicized and promoted by the press and media. The United Press released the following news from Cairo:

> Today, the heads of the Coptic Church in Cairo denied "rumors" about another Apparition of the Virgin after 15 people were trampled to death last night when a great mass rushed to the suburb of Shoubra after a rumor was repeated about a new Apparition there. Most of the dead were children between the ages of nine and eleven, in addition to two elderly persons. The police stated that at least 30 people were injured and the authorities undertook the closing of the church, etc. (*Al-Nahar*, May 21, 1968).

The results of this frenzied religious stage play was a tragedy whose victims are gone in vain, a group of innocent children and guileless, good-natured citizens, whose blood will only be redeemed by the tears of mothers and fathers and the sorrow of friends. I extend my best wishes in this awful tragedy to the supporters of the Virgin, miracles, tourism, and spiritual consolation for the loss of Jerusalem, my tributes to the producers of such plays, my praise to its promoters in the media and ministries, and my thanks to both the Coptic Church for its recent denial of the Apparition of the Virgin and to the authorities for closing the church just too late, that is, after what happened had happened, those who died had died, those who were injured were injured, and these children were trampled to death.

Chapter Five

Deception in
Contemporary Western Christian Thought

A collection of the lectures that were given at the American University of Beirut in 1967 on the topic *God and Man in Contemporary Christian Thought* has been published as one of a series of American University of Beirut Centennial Publications.[1] This book gathers the views and analyses of a considerable number of Christian clergy and thinkers who came from Western Europe and the United States to participate in that series of lectures on the occasion of the American University celebrating its centennial. A number of Arab Christians also participated in the symposium by giving lectures about the state of Christian thought in the region. However, I will direct this review towards the opinions of foreign thinkers in order to give the reader a critical conception of the general state of contemporary Christian thought in the West.

The first aspect of these lectures that attracts notice is that they focus, directly and indirectly, around one major problem, the relation of the Church (the Christian religion) to a modern world that is immersed

---

1   Charles Malik, ed., *God and Man in Contemporary Christian Thought* (Beirut: American University of Beirut Centennial Publications, 1969). The major part of this review was published as a criticism of the symposium in the supplement of *Al-Nahar* weekly magazine on June 4, 1967.

in secularism, a-religiosity, an immersion that covers *[A 117]* almost every aspect of its activity. The best example of this focus is the inaugural address that Dr. W.A. Visser't Hooft[2] gave under the title "The Contemporary Church."

Dr. Visser't Hooft began his address with a short description of the state of the Church in the Middle Ages and its comprehensive role in organizing all aspects of individual and social life. That was the age of an integrated Christian society. He then briefly examined the disintegration of the unity of the Christian world into a variety of Christian communities and different churches, especially after the Lutheran Reformation. What increased the intensity of this descent towards fragmentation and disintegration was the bloody struggle between Christianity as represented by its churches, on the one hand, and the nascent natural sciences and movements calling for individualism, humanism, and the interests of the rising middle class, on the other hand. Then the speaker reminded the audience of Nietzsche's famous call "God is dead" and briefly discussed the views of some of the famous critics of Christianity in the nineteenth century, among them Karl Marx and the French philosopher Auguste Comte. He then turned his attention to the revival that Western Christian religious thought had witnessed in the recent past and which is still resurgent to this day, especially among Protestant religious thinkers.

The first impression I formed of Dr. Visser't Hooft's address was that the representatives of Christianity in the contemporary Western world still feel themselves to be on the defensive in the face of the secular powers that have swept their societies with such force and violence. Dr. Visser't Hooft's speech showed, it is true, the existence of a peaceful settlement between Christianity and the forces it had battled against so bitterly for many centuries. The basis of this settlement is the (almost total) surrender on the part of Christian institutions of everything belonging to Caesar, keeping only what remains. Visser't Hooft views this settlement as a great triumph for the Church because it freed it from "entanglement with non-church

---

2   Then Secretary General of the World Council of Churches.

forces or powers."[3] As he considers it a great liberation for the Church that made it possible for it to seize new opportunities as "a Church which has no other ambition than to witness to its Gospel and to serve the world in word and deed."[4]

It seems to me that the leaders of Christian thought in the West are not really at ease with this settlement that they have reached with the secular forces that have fought them for all these years, and thus we always find them engrossed in drawn-out intellectual attempts to justify their existence (to themselves and others) by asserting the necessity of their message and maneuvering to determine a place for themselves in a world that is immersed in secularism in regards to its culture, production, life, and values.

The representatives of contemporary Christian thought acknowledge this fact and convey their realization that the contemporary world is able to survive and live quite easily without them and their institutions. In reality, Christian thinkers find something embarrassing in this acknowledgement and that is that the modern world is able to muster systems and theories appropriate for the life of contemporary society and man without taking into consideration the Christian message *[A 118]* and its doctrines and institutions. The best of those who expressed this fact was the young German Protestant theologian Bonhoeffer (whom the Nazis executed), whose name was repeated often during the symposium. He said, "It has become clear that everything (in a secular society) is carried out without God, and just as competently as before." In other words, whenever the course of history in secular societies shifts under pressure and stress beyond the control of the Church and its authority, Christian theologians strive again to define a place, however small, for themselves and their institutions, claiming that it is the place that they ought to occupy in this secular environment that proceeds in its way with the barest regard for them.

I have mentioned that the contemporary theologians appear to bless the peaceful settlement in question and work hard to convince themselves

---

3   "The Contemporary Church," 3.
4   "The Contemporary Church," 2.

(as well as others) that the losses suffered by the Church (Christianity) in being stripped of their fortresses and strongholds are, in fact, a liberation of the Church from worldly entanglements that are none of its business and which constitute an impediment to its real spiritual message.

However, although these theologians affect sincerity, their words betray their regret concerning the rise of secular forces and how they rolled over the Christian religious forces that ruled over minds, spirits, and societies for many centuries. In fact, they regret and are rather disappointed by the loss of this integrated Christian world where there was no distinction made between church, society, and state, and where people like them—clerics, legal scholars, judges, and thinkers—controlled the course of events and the path of history. In other words, despite what they state today about how the victory of the secular forces was like a liberation for the Church and the Christian religion from matters that did not concern them, I suspect that they really would have preferred it if these secular forces had failed to triumph and the Church had failed to have been "liberated" in the way that it actually happened: by force, against its will, and in the face of its fierce resistance to those same movements that they tell us today led to the "liberation" of the Christian religion!

All this becomes evident to whomever closely examines the meaning of the expressions that Dr. Visser't Hooft uses in describing some of the achievements made by the secularist movement in the West: "the turning away from the old certainties," (i.e., Christian beliefs), "the concentration of all attention and energy on man himself," the "so-called coming of age of man as an autonomous being [from traditional spiritual forces] and the resultant blurring of the image of God."[5] These expressions emerge in the context of a discourse in which the Christian theologian appears to praise these great secular achievements because they liberated the Church from a conception of religion that dates back to the Middle Ages and is not in harmony with the modern life that materialized after the Renaissance, the Scientific Revolution, and the Industrial Revolution. However, close

---

5   "The Contemporary Church," 3.

examination of the meaning of these expressions also exposes hidden feelings of regret on the part of these theologians towards *[A 119]* these events, and suggests another view, according to which the duty of the Church is to restore what secularism had undermined and to rehabilitate in some way the Christian beliefs that are no longer in focus because of the concentration of man on himself and his worldly state before everything else and because of his achievement of the kind of autonomy indicated by the lecturer.

In other words, I suspect that Christian theologians hold two incompatible views of the prevailing secular condition that surrounds them: the first, the overt view, blesses this condition and the second, the concealed view, wishes that it had not happened, at least not in the way that it did. As evidence, I must mention that a number of modern Christian thinkers, especially in Protestant circles, describe the state to which Christianity has arrived in the West as a "regression" (in particular, Bonhoeffer), and whoever places this process of regression in its historical context knows that it occurred as a result of a fierce battle on all fronts between the rising forces of secularism and the religious forces that had enjoyed almost total control, not as a result of a voluntary surrender on the part of Christianity of everything worldly out of a wish to preserve its original spiritual message. Anyone investigating these matters surmises that describing this great Christian waning as "regression" reveals something of the suppressed feelings that these theologians harbor towards the secular movement before which they regress. Indeed, the regression that they speak about is of the kind that anyone whom it befalls regrets it, tries to wriggle free of it and its consequences in some way, and attempts to restore some of the grounds lost as a result of force. This is the truth of their feelings towards the regression in question despite their spurious attempts to explain it away as for the benefit of Christianity and as working to liberate the Church, etc.

We can summarize the essence of Dr. Visser't Hooft's ideas as an attempt to justify the situation that Christianity finds itself in today, bestow on it legitimacy, and regard it as highly consistent with how Christianity should behave towards society, state, and man in this age, that is, that it be liberated from the traditional worldly entanglements of which it is now free, as if this was God's will from the beginning. This retrospective look allows Christian thinkers whose views are well represented by Visser't Hooft to strive to justify the present state by attempting to persuade us that what the Church was compelled to relinquish after bloody struggles did not belong to it in the first place and thus the Church did not lose but won the struggle since it only relinquished what was not its own.

In this manner, every religious thinker, in any age, can hang the cloak of divine legitimacy over the present state of his religion in comparison with that religion when it dominated its time. However, there is a question that must be answered in relation to this blatant rationalizing logic: Can the contemporary Christian be required to believe, for example, that the ardent, sincere, faithful Christian souls who defied death to defend the strongholds of the Christian Church and its authority, thought, and heritage against the hostile secular powers fell in vain, *[A 120]* and that their heroism was only an obstruction to the liberating of the Church from its worldly entanglements, and a defense of possessions that did not belong to the Church in the first place and were really outside its realm of concern?

Dr. Visser't Hooft paused in his speech at Nietzsche's famous cry "God is dead," and after declaring that he agreed with the words of Nietzsche in a particular respect he claimed that the great critics of Christianity, such as Auguste Comte, Karl Marx, and Nietzsche himself, had done Christianity an unrivaled service in assisting it in liberating itself from its traditional worldly entanglements that had nothing to do with religion. In fact, the speaker went even further in his proposing that these critics were secret allies of a revived Christianity which was now freed from anything that did not touch the essence of its message. Dr. Visser't Hooft concluded that the God whose death Nietzsche had announced was not, in fact, the living Christian God who was incarnated in Jesus and revealed in him but was rather the god whose existence the philosophers and earlier theologians derived from their metaphysical contemplations and rational proofs. The god who died was the abstract god invented by the philosophers and earlier theologians and, in the view of the speaker, this false god had only undermined genuine faith in the living God who still lives.

There is no more facile way for the religious thinker to save himself from the embarrassment that befalls him when he faces Nietzsche and his famous cry than by informing us that the God whom Marx and Comte attack and whose death Nietzsche announces is not the real living God to whom Christians pray but a different god who, while resembling the genuine God, is really an invention of man's thoughts and imagination. According to this rationalizing logic, if God dies a thousand times, the theological thinker is able to save his position by merely persisting in saying that the god who has died is not the God to whom Christians pray! The theologian places himself and his idea outside the scope of any criticism or challenge because he is always able to claim that everything that has been said in the history of thought in criticism of the Christian conception of God only applies to a false god, not to the real Christian God! However, the testimony of history differs from the testimony of Visser't Hooft's rationalizing logic.

For example, the God about whom Thomas Aquinas filled pages and pages with metaphysical contemplations and rational proofs of His existence is, according to Aquinas, the living Christian God who was incarnated in the Messiah and to whom all Christians pray and whose name all Christians praise, not the god invented by philosophers, who is nothing more than an empty intellectual abstraction. Does not Aquinas represent an important religious heritage that asserted that the God whose existence is derived by thinkers and philosophers from rational proofs is the same God in whom all Christians believe, no matter how naïve, simple, and illiterate they are?

If we follow the sequence of his thinking, it is clear that Nietzsche announced the death of this God and not some other god. However, ever since the views of Nietzsche became an integral part of the secular culture of the twentieth century, *[A 121]* forcing Christian theologians to confront Nietzsche directly, they seek refuge in the tricks of rationalizing logic in order to perform the magical act of transforming the German philosopher into a secret ally of Christianity and to drain the meaning of his utterance about the death of God of all meaning and sense, making him appear as if he was talking about a god dead from the beginning. For his famous sentence is transformed into a tautology that does not say anything more than that the dead god died! Why should we be bothered by such hollow verbal and logical games that transform Nietzsche's ringing cry, which disturbed and continues to disturb the world until today, into an empty and redundant phrase? If Nietzsche is right, then Christianity is in error. If Christianity is right, then Nietzsche is in error. This is indisputable and a discerning person ought to face it with frankness and integrity. Every attempt on the part of Visser't Hooft at deception by stating that both are right—Nietzsche in regards to the god of the philosophers and the Church in regards to the God revealed in Jesus Christ—is nothing but a verbal theological game that tries to mediate in vain between the two irreconcilable parties. This is exactly what Christians are supposed to have learned from Søren Kierkegaard in his persistent attacks on and exposure of the Hegelian attempts at "mediation" that flourished in his time.

Finally, I should revisit Visser't Hooft's assertion that "there will be a place for a Church which has no other ambition than to witness to its Gospel and to serve the world in word and deed."[6] This is fine as long as we do not forget that the ambition that the speaker envisions for Christianity did not emerge for internal reasons or from the Church itself but rather from its inability to resist overwhelming conditions and circumstances that do not and will not allow the Church to form a greater ambition. In Nietzsche's words: "Of all evil I deem you capable: therefore I want good from you. Verily, I have often laughed at the weaklings who thought themselves good because they had no claws."[7]

I will now turn to the lecture of Father Dvornik, in which I identified some intellectual features resembling those I touched on in commenting

---

6   "The Contemporary Church," 2.
7   Friedrich Nietzsche, "On Those Who Are Sublime" in *Thus Spoke Zarathustra*, translated by Walter Kaufmann.

on the previous lecture. Father Dvornik dedicated his study to the Great Schism between the Eastern and Western Churches. What first draws attention in this study is the author's attempt to minimize the importance of this schism and attribute it to a mere disagreement about political theories that were, on the one hand, advocated by the West, or, on the other hand, prevalent in the East. As a consequence, Father Dvornik views this dangerous schism within Christianity as a trivial "mistake" that resulted from a misunderstanding about some political opinions and views between the two quarreling parties.

Is it not naïve to explain an enormous historical event in the course of Western civilization like the Great Schism by attributing it to disagreements about how to interpret the political theories prevalent in the East and West? Since when did nations split, kingdoms fall, and Churches crumble *[A 122]* as a result of theoretical disagreements about political theories? Are there not weighty worldly issues, major vital interests, and absolute commitments for both sides that trump in importance and gravity Byzantine disagreements and arguments about political theories, whether in the East or West, for explaining this schism in the body of the Church? I have no doubt that the heroism, fanaticism, sacrifice, self-dedication, and cruelty exhibited by both sides as they defended their positions and interests cannot be explained by a mere disagreement about political theories but must be attributed to the sorts of serious factors and considerations that have a greater effect and influence on hearts and minds. Father Dvornik appears to want to write his own history of the Great Schism, viewing it as a "mistake" whose source was a misunderstanding about trivial matters, like arguments about political theories that were popular at the time, with the aim of serving present goals connected with the unity of the Christian churches. However, this view of the Great Schism does not reveal respect or deference to the wisdom, intelligence, sincerity, or piety of those who rushed into the battle that would divide the two Churches with all their strength, thinking, on many occasions, that the battle was between truth and falsehood (not due to a historical error) and that their eternal happiness and everlasting salvation depended on its outcome.

Is it not possible, we must wonder, to advance the goals of Christian unity without taking a mythological view of the history of the Great Schism and rendering it a means to achieve some contemporary goals? Is it not possible to repair the rift between the two churches in our day without characterizing a momentous historical event as a trivial "mistake" resulting from a misunderstanding? What is the meaning of judging a great historical event as a "great mistake?" Do our words bear any serious meaning when we look back and say that a particular period in history constitutes a "mistake" that should not have been or should not have occurred?

Of course, these judgments included in Father Dvornik's study do not really mean anything but that acknowledging today the reality of the schism and confronting it as a historical fact will not advance particular goals and thus we must minimize its historical significance and importance. The optimal way to achieve that is to assert that the schism was a "mistake" that resulted from a misunderstanding, and a trivial one at that, concerning a disagreement about some Eastern and Western political theories. If every thinker who is interested in similar issues imitated the example of Father Dvornik, then history would be effortlessly transformed into a long series of trivial "mistakes" that should not have happened. I trust serious historians will not emulate Father Dvornik when conducting their future research.

I turn now to commenting on the speech that Father Hans Küng gave under the title "The Church and Sincerity." Father Küng commenced his speech by discussing the idea of "sincerity" and the role it plays in all the various aspects of life in the twentieth century. I must note *[A 123]* that I was deeply disappointed in how Father Küng set out to use the notion of sincerity at the beginning, for he smothered its clarity in vagueness, obscurity, and generality. For example, he uses the notion of sincerity to comprehend many ethical attributes like truthfulness, genuineness, fairness, frankness, loyalty, nobility, integrity, and dignity, equating it with each of them. He makes no attempt to distinguish between the meanings of these attributes (although there are some connections) but merges them all within the scope of "sincerity," which allows him to conclude that sincerity is the chief characteristic of twentieth-century productions in the fields of literature, music, architecture, engineering, industry, philosophy, ethics, etc., until the twentieth-century becomes indisputably the century of sincerity.

I have no idea what he wants us to infer from this description of the twentieth century. However, according to how I understand the notion of sincerity, I cannot help but resist strongly Father Küng's conception of this century as indisputably the era of sincerity. Anyone who considers sincerity to be the best way to characterize the life of this century must enjoy an enormous helping of optimism and an extraordinary power to overlook the ugly and abhorrent sides of life, culture, and civilization in the contemporary world. I do not know how much sincerity or integrity there is in such optimism and obliviousness of the facts of contemporary life and the realities of the twentieth century.

I was attentive to the words of Father Küng about the "sincerity" that radiates into every corner of the life of the twentieth century until I realized that his real motive was to advise the Catholic Church to be sincere with itself since it finds itself today in an age of sincerity, lest the Church diverge from the chief trend of the age or lose its connection with its essential life. More simply, Father Küng is trying to urge and pressure the Church to implement a program of internal reform that would bring it into harmony with the exigencies of contemporary life and its prevailing traits in the twentieth century.

I think that Father Küng would have been much more sincere (towards himself and others) and much less prolix if he had just gone directly to the heart of the matter and told us frankly that his Church needs extensive and radical reform in both its doctrinal and organizational matters in order to make it relevant to the conditions of life in the twentieth century. Instead he resorts to coating this view from the inside and the outside with a shiny substance he sometimes calls "sincerity" and other times "adapting to the century of sincerity" and keeping abreast of it. For the sake of intellectual integrity, I must be frank: If Father Küng is unable to speak publicly about his views and opinions on these matters with total frankness and integrity because he occupies an official position in the Catholic Church, and if he is convinced of these thoughts to the degree that seeps to the surface in his speech, then sincerity would require him to pronounce his position from outside the Church and make clear his criticism of it and its condition with full frankness, integrity, and sincerity without *[A 124]* speaking obscurely and providing rationalizations. Only at that time will Father Küng be able to aim his criticism directly towards the Catholic Church and tell it that it is more like a fossil than an institution in harmony with the conditions of contemporary life, capable of interacting with its values and understanding its problems.

Father Küng's program for reforming the Church from the inside implies, in practice, the razing of the Catholic theological heritage of Aquinas to its foundations and total liberation from it. As I have learned from some colleagues and through talking with Father Küng, his reform program includes revolutionary steps that he did not wish to address in his public speech but reserves for private discussions only, such as liberation from the Marian doctrine and the belief in the infallibility of the Pope (which is limited to certain doctrinal matters), and trading the Catholic Church's traditional view of itself as the only true church in the complete and absolute sense of the term for a view of the Church as being no more than "the Mother Church" among many other churches. If these reforms were to take place in the Church, they would undoubtedly amount to a new victory for the secular forces that control the life of the twentieth century by erasing some of the remaining traces of the Middle Ages and the echoes of the residual feudal mentality within the Church. However, I also have no doubt that theologians like Father Küng will handle this matter in their special way by transforming the Church's surrender of some of its residual heritage from its golden eras into a new victory that will help remove obstacles that stand in the way of the emergence of its real message and so on: the rationalizing logic that we recognize from earlier pages.

There is no doubt that a sincere theologian like Father Küng finds himself in a difficult and embarrassing position when he tries to reform the Church by appealing to it to renounce its fundamental doctrines and the intellectual and dogmatic heritage that forms the cornerstone of its existence. The source of embarrassment is that it is not rational for Father

Küng to believe in the Marian Doctrine, Papal Infallibility, or Thomist theology since he wants to purify the Church from them on the grounds that they are leftovers from past eras and are incompatible with our conditions of living and thinking in the twentieth century. However, the question that intrudes on us is whether a Catholic is able to repudiate these beliefs without departing from his faith and disclaiming the current teachings of the Church? His own sincerity should oblige Father Küng to confront this perilous question with total frankness, but this is what he entirely fails to do in his lecture on "Sincerity and the Church." If Father Küng wishes to be a Catholic in his own special way until the day the Church reforms itself, then I have no objection to that, on the condition that he declares this with sincerity and integrity, especially since he chose to speak about the role of sincerity in the religious life of man within this secular century.

There is another subject that "sincerity" obliges us to confront clearly: What reasons can Father Küng give for demanding that the Church surrender the Marian Doctrine, Papal Infallibility, Thomist theology, *[A 125]* and its traditional view of itself as indisputably the true Church? Is it because these doctrines are in conflict with the judgments of reason and human experience and are not compatible with the conditions of life in the nuclear age and the knowledge gained by man in the age of the exploration of space? Are these Catholic doctrines that Father Küng wishes to jettison more in conflict with reason, experience, and the judgments of the twentieth century than the rest of the Christian doctrines, for example, Christ's Incarnation, Resurrection, and miracles? Sincerity and intellectual integrity oblige us to either renounce all these doctrines or accept them all despite their shortcomings.

Someone might say that Father Küng calls on the Church to free itself from these doctrines but not from others because the former have no basis in the true Christian message or in the Holy Bible. This is what Protestants have claimed (and died as martyrs for) and continue to claim until today and this is exactly what the Church has fought fiercely and aggressively for generations. Will the Catholic Church finally accept the Protestant position and admit that part of its sacred core doctrines and the theology of Aquinas have no basis at all in the Christian message and the Holy Bible? Once again we are confronted with that amazing logic of rationalization that we are already familiar with, this logic that looks back to announce that certain periods of history are nothing but a "mistake" that, in this case, led to a misunderstanding of the true Christian message and its Bible, in order to realize particular present goals. Just as Father Küng fails to face these major issues and important questions with clarity and sincerity, so he fails to explain to us to what degree the Church is able to surrender its sacred traditional beliefs, according to his program of reform, before it loses the distinct nature and special character that distinguish it from everything else in the world.

Sincerity, its seems to me, calls on us to acknowledge what Father Küng fails to speak clearly about, that the Church finds itself in a difficult position in the contemporary world, that it can either remain as it is in regards to essence and principles and so become a relic in the museums of Western culture or enter a process of change and transformation of its conventions that will lead to a complete transformation of its previous identity. As for the Protestant optimism that this process of transformation ought to be good for the Church, it is entirely unjustified.

Another aspect that drew my attention in Father Küng's lecture about "Sincerity and the Church" is the total silence about some vital matters that absorb the thoughts of contemporary man in the present time. In the midst of his insistence on the importance of sincerity for the Church in the twentieth century, Father Küng went as far as to criticize the traditional attire that Catholic clergy and nuns wear, and pronounced that the continuation of this custom did not reveal "sincerity" to the spirit of contemporary life and the reality of the twentieth century. Yet his insistence on the importance of sincerity for the Church did not lead him to discuss the position of the Church on the issue of birth control, the war in Vietnam, or divorce in the Church. Does Father Küng believe that the current position of the Church on these important matters *[A 126]* is characterized by sincerity towards the reality of the twentieth century and the truth of life in the age of nuclear power and the exploration of outer space? I am not saying that the Church is not engrossed in the study and review of these issues. Yet I will say that sincerity should oblige Father Küng to propose the position that the Church needs to adopt on these issues in order to exhibit sincerity towards the reality of our time, according to his opinion and arguments. Instead Father Küng wastes time in discussing trivial matters as in his criticism of clerical attire. In the hands of Father Küng, sincerity is transformed into a malleable tool for purifying the Church from some doctrinal features that the lecturing Father objects to from the point of view of twentieth-century man and that stand in the way of a rapprochement between the Christian churches. I cannot help but wonder about how sincere Father Küng's treatment of the subject of sincerity actually is?

I also learned from this symposium that the enthusiasm that we have observed and heard for the subject of Christian integration demonstrates that the Church realizes the truth of its deteriorating condition and precarious position in a world that is ruled by stable secular forces, and that it strives for rapprochement and unity because there is power in unity and perhaps an opportunity to regain something of the place of importance that it had previously occupied in the life of Western society. It is not rational to view the motives behind this Christian rapprochement as an outpouring of innocent brotherly emotions or pure Christian love that suddenly swept the fragmented Christian world after centuries of severe hostility and deep animosity. Dr. Visser't Hooft acknowledged that when he stated in his lecture: "It has become clear that ecumenism is not an opportunity going with the stream, but a battle against powers of darkness."[8] He did not, however, make clear to us who these "powers of darkness" are and who embodies them today.

Finally, I should state that the views of the modern theologians that I criticized could have been more convincing if Christianity were able to realize the higher ideal that Nietzsche proposed in the following lines:

> And perhaps the great day will come when people, distinguished by
> wars and victories and by the highest development of a military order
> and intelligence, and accustomed to make the heaviest sacrifices for

---

8   "The Contemporary Church," 8.

these things, will exclaim of its own free will, "We break the sword," and will smash its entire military establishment down to its lowest foundations. Rendering oneself unarmed when one had been the best-armed, out of a height of feeling—that is the means to real peace, which must always rest on a peace of mind.[9]

However, this great day was lost to the Christian church, escaping it long ago when it was stripped of its weapons against its will by forces that belong essentially to the secular movement that established what we call the modern world, shaped its scientific culture, and erected its industrial civilization.

---

9   Friedrich Nietzsche, "Wanderer and his Shadow" in *Human, All Too Human*, translated by Walter Kaufmann.

Chapter Six

Introduction to the Scientific-Materialist Conception of the Universe and its Development

1

It is widely recognized that most of the civilizations and cultures that gained prominence in the course of history and had an enduring influence possessed, in different historical ages, a general and comprehensive view of the nature of the universe, man, and life in general. Most of the time, this comprehensive view found expression either in mythology and epic, religion in a wide sense, broad philosophical speculation, or through a mix of these means and factors.

Expression of this comprehensive view in a particular culture might take place officially or consciously, in the words of philosophers, major thinkers, or canonical religious books, or it might take place in a spontaneous, unconscious way through its poets, artists, or leaders in general. For the sake of brevity, I will call the collection of comprehensive views about the nature of the universe that prevail in a particular era "the world picture" of that era (or of that civilization or any definite historical period in the life of mankind).

The study of the prevailing world picture in a particular age or at a particular stage of civilization reveals to us the totality of the most general views that permeate the thinking of that age and of its modes of work and production. In other words, it reveals to us a whole set of views and opinions, at a very high level of acceptance, generality, and comprehensiveness, that the age takes for granted intuitively and unconsciously about the origins of mankind and its fate, about knowledge, society, ethics, work, the production *[A 128]* of wealth, and so on.

Naturally, the contents of the world picture of a certain age are related to human life in society and strongly reflect a) the specific nature of the existing social relations, b) the means of production of wealth, and c) the degree of progress attained by the instruments of the production of that wealth. They are also dialectically related to a) the particular kind of science prevalent in that age, b) the degree of progress attained by that science, and c) the conception that that age has about the method which permits man to acquire reliable knowledge about all the important aspects of life and what affects them.

In other words, the views of a certain age about knowledge, scientific inquiry, and scientific method are influenced by the nature (kind) of the world picture characterizing that age. Similarly, the sciences prevalent in a certain age influence, in their turn, the formation and definition of the world picture produced by that age. For example, remember that the mythological world picture that dominated ancient Greek civilization attributed "life" to nature and thought that a spirit or anima permeates all of the nature's parts and motions. Thus we find that most of the Greek philosophical explanations of the phenomena of nature come in the form of certain specific ideas like "the natural motions of things," "final causes," and the "yearning of the world for the ideal," along with the other familiar ideas associated with this major tendency in Greek philosophy.

On the other hand, we can point to the important role of proofs based on the idea of "the infinite series"[1] in Greek metaphysical speculations in

---

1   As in Aristotle's proof of the existence of the First Mover, for example.

general (i.e. in the philosophical world picture bequeathed to us by the great Greek philosophers), and we can attribute this role to the successes that some sciences were able to accomplish in that age. I mean here specifically the Pythagorean proof that the square root of the number 2 is an irrational number. For this famous mathematical discovery is based on a proof that depends on the idea of the "infinite series" of quantities. Furthermore, the influence of the mathematical sciences in general and Euclidean geometry in particular on the formation of philosophical world pictures through the ages is well known enough not to require further elaboration.

Here, I will give an example of the reciprocal influence between the comprehensive world picture of a certain age, on the one hand, and the prevailing conception of knowledge and science in that age, on the other. When St. Augustine, with his spirit full of the new Christian world picture, encountered the failure in which the Greek rationalistic speculations had ended, he could not restrain himself from shouting with great enthusiasm: "Christ is the rock of our physics, our ethics, and our logic."

2

After these brief introductory remarks, I must explain that the goal of this *[A 129]* essay is the investigation of the world picture that modern man began to formulate in the beginning of the 17th century, and whose scientific thinking dominated all branches and levels of knowledge for a period of three centuries. The most important event that led to the prominence of this new world picture is doubtlessly the scientific revolution. It is hard to exaggerate the significance of this event in the life of mankind and subsequent history compared to all the events that followed it. A great scholar said the following about the significance and importance of the scientific revolution:

> That revolution…outshines everything since the rise of Christianity and reduces the Renaissance and Reformation to the rank of mere episodes, mere internal displacements, within the system of medieval

Christendom. Since it changed the character of men's habitual mental operations even in the conduct of the non-material sciences, while transforming the whole diagram of the physical universe and the very texture of human life itself, it looms so large as the real origin both of the modern world and of the modern mentality that our customary periodization of European history has become an anachronism and an encumbrance.[2]

The enormous progress that the Scientific Revolution achieved led to the prominence of a new world picture whose elements gained in coherence with the passing of time and the succession of great scientific discoveries (theoretical and practical) until Isaac Newton gave it an almost complete formulation. It became the custom to call the new world picture "mechanistic materialism" or "static materialism." As will become clear to us in the rest of the essay, mechanistic materialism uprooted in principle the previous world picture and came to dominate all types and aspects of scientific thought.

I will shift now to the explanation of the pillars of mechanistic materialism, as derived from Newton's book, *Mathematical Principles of Natural Philosophy*.

1. Absolute Space

Newton stated in his definition of the nature of absolute space the following:

> Absolute space, in its own nature, without relation to anything external, *[A 130]* remains always similar and immovable. Relative space is some movable dimension or measure of the absolute spaces; which our senses determine by its position to bodies.[3]

Newton conceived space as an infinite vessel with a finite quantity of matter in each of its regions. In other words, absolute space is the total, comprehensive container of all bodies in the universe, and therefore we are able to specify the

---

2   Herbert Butterfield, *The Origins of Modern Science* (London: MacMillan, 1951) vii, viii.
3   Isaac Newton, *The Mathematical Principles of Natural Philosophy* (Berkeley: University of California Press), 6.

position of any of these bodies by merely specifying its point (or collection of points) in absolute space. As for the relative spaces that we ascertain by the senses, they are relative and apparent, generated by means of the effect of bodies on the sense organs. The basic qualities that Newton bestowed on absolute space can be summarized in the following manner:

a) Absolute space is, by its nature, eternal and necessary (not created or accidental), and is prior in existence to the bodies located in it. Even if the matter distributed in its regions were to perish entirely, it would remain unchanged and unaltered. In other words, absolute space is, by its nature, entirely independent of the bodies it contains and their qualities.

b) Absolute space is composed of dimensionless points (strictly speaking, geometrical points). Absolute space is infinite because its points are entirely homogenous. These points can only be distinguished by means of the distinct bodies located in that space.

c) Absolute space is three-dimensional and Euclidean in character: the shortest distance between two of its points is a geometrical straight line.

We cannot conceive of the characteristics of space in any other way because it would lead to a clear logical contradiction (according to this theory). Geometry is the exact a priori science that describes the nature of absolute space and provides us with the necessary, established facts about it and its characteristics.

2. Absolute Time

Newton stated the following in his definition of the nature of absolute time:

> Absolute, true, and mathematical time, of itself, and from its own nature, flows equably without relation to anything external, and by another name is called duration: relative, apparent, and common time, is some sensible and external (whether accurate or unequaled) measure of duration by the means of motion, which is commonly used instead of true time; such as an hour, a day, a month, *[A 131]* a year...All motions may be accelerated and retarded, but the flowing of absolute time is not liable to any change. The duration or perseverance

of the existence of things remains the same, whether the motions are swift or slow, or none at all: and therefore this duration ought to be distinguished from what are only sensible measures thereof; and from which we deduce it, by means of the astronomical equation.[4]

Newton's theory of absolute time can be summarized as follows:

1) Newton distinguishes between the following:
    a) Absolute mathematical time;
    b) Relative, apparent time—the familiar time that determines the system of relationships among events;
    c) Psychological time—our private psychological perception of the passage of time.

2) Absolute time is the total comprehensive vessel that contains all events across the universe and enables the determination of the date of the occurrence of any event by specifying the temporal moment in which it occurred.

3) Absolute time is prior in existence, both ontologically and logically, to the occurrence of events, and it is, in its nature, eternal and necessary, remaining the same no matter what occurs in it. In other words, absolute time is entirely independent of the events that occur within it. It would be entirely unaffected if its contents entirely disappeared, remaining the same without any change or alteration, like the vessel that remains the same when its contents disappear. On the other hand, events can only be conceived along with the temporal vessel that contains them and in which they occur.

4) Absolute time is infinite because its successive moments are entirely homogenous. Homogenous moments of time can only be distinguished by means of the distinct events that occur at them, and that by means of the temporal relations that the moments define between these events.

5) According to Newton, the flow of time takes place at a constant steady rate and that it is necessarily and entirely independent of the laws that govern motion in time and space. Thus he states the following:

---

4   Ibid. 6.

> The order of the parts of time is immutable…. Suppose those parts to be moved out of their places, and they will be moved (if the expression may be allowed) out of themselves.[5] *[A 132]*

In other words, the idea of changing the rate of the flow of the moments of time from what it is is self-contradictory.

6) Newtonian time has four chief characteristics:

    a) Flow at an absolutely constant rate.

    b) Immediacy or instantaneity: According to Newton, time is composed of durationless and fleeting moments or instants at which events occur. Absolute immediacy or instantaneity is a real fact of the world.

    c) Succession: The moments of Newtonian time are arranged in an infinite series of uni-directional succession. The succession of events in a specified number of moments constitutes an absolute reality in the world that is not influenced by the measures used, no matter what their type or form, to measure time.

    d) Simultaneity: the simultaneity of events is an absolute reality in the world. It can be determined and measured with strict precision. Thus we conceive one temporal moment existing in many places. Newton says on this matter:

> Every particle of space is always, and every indivisible moment of duration is everywhere.[6]

3. Matter

All the things in the world are composed of individual atoms of matter, simple parts that cannot be divided into simpler parts. Each of these atoms is located at a particular point in absolute space and occurs at a moment of absolute time. These simple material bodies are characterized

---

5   Ibid. 8.
6   Ibid. 8.

solely by their primary mathematical qualities (size, mass, velocity, inertia, etc.). Sensible properties (color, scent, taste, touch, etc.) are not among the primary qualities of atoms of matter but rather are generated from the effect of the motion of bodies on the sense organs of living creatures. The sensible properties that we bestow, by force of habit, on the world around us as if they were its real independent qualities are, in reality, psychological and relative to the self that perceives and is affected by the motion of material bodies.

The lessons of chemistry tell us that among the physical qualities of water is that it is colorless, odorless, and tasteless. Nevertheless, water as we are familiar with it in our daily life and in our direct experience always has some color, smell, *[A 133]* and taste. The familiar explanation of the dissimilarity between what the lessons of chemistry teach, on the one hand, and what direct experience observes, on the other hand, stems from the theory of static materialism concerning the nature and characteristics of a simple atom of matter. In other words, the material molecules that compose water have no color, taste, or smell. However, these molecules have a particular effect on the sense organs (in the context of the surrounding conditions and circumstances) that generates in us perceptions of a particular color, taste, and smell that we then ascribe to water just as we ascribe warmth to woolen clothing (figuratively and metaphorically) although the warmth is in us and not in the clothing that we call warm.

4. Motion

Atoms of matter are subject to constant and continuous motion according to determinate laws that can be given a strict mathematical formulation. These are the familiar laws of motion, such as the law of inertia. The one kind of change or alteration that can befall individual atoms is a change of their positions in absolute space according to the laws of motion. In other words, all of the motions and transformations in the world, however great or complicated, are in the final analysis nothing more than mechanistic changes in the locations of atoms of matter. The atoms are merely arranged mechanistically in particular formations. After these formations dissolve, they are rearranged in different formations, and so on. The individual atom in itself is not subject to any kind of internal transformation (for example, growth) or organic change, and thus this theory is called "static materialism." Since the one motion that individual atoms are subject to is mere mechanistic displacement, the theory is also called "mechanistic materialism."

Among the basic pillars on which Newton built static materialism is the distinction between the absolute and relative motion of bodies (atoms). I will strive to clarify this idea by using one of the basic laws of motion. The law of inertia refers to the constant velocity of a body x that does not fall under the influence of an external force so that it traverses equal distances in equal times. This condition only applies if we conceive the existence of x alone in an infinite spatial vessel, for the co-existence of another body would influence it, as we know from the universal law of gravitation. Let us assume that x exists by itself in time and space. Then we are able to comprehend the meaning of the absolute motion of x on the basis of the segment of absolute time that it requires to cross a particular distance of absolute space.

The theory of mechanistic materialism achieved a brilliant success, unprecedented in the history of the sciences, because it offered unequivocal scientific answers and exact mathematical solutions to all *[A 134]* traditional problems and issues concerning the motion of celestial bodies and the prediction of their orbits and positions. The theory's ideas, methodologies, and approaches to research and explanation dominated all serious attempts to analyze natural phenomena—whatever their kind—and explain them scientifically. In other words, all the sciences followed the lead of mechanistic materialism in explaining the phenomena they studied until the "scientific explanation" of any phenomenon came to mean comprehending it according to the "mechanistic paradigm," starting with the basic units and how these units affect one another according to mechanistic laws alone. This orientation, which governed the sciences for a long time, was the subject of the following comments by the famous English scientist Lord Kelvin at the end of the 19th century:

I am never content until I have constructed a mechanistic model of the subject I am studying. If I succeed in making one, I understand; otherwise I do not.[7]

I wish to cite here several examples concerning the extension of the ideas and methodologies of mechanistic materialism to the remainder of the sciences and research in order to make clear how it dominated scientific thinking in general after it was launched in the areas of physics, astronomy, and the science of motion. As a first example, there is the theory of Thomas Hobbes concerning human society and its origin, and his explanation of the necessity of political authority along with the justification of its existence.[8] Hobbes followed the methodology of mechanistic materialism in analyzing the phenomenon, commencing his explanation with the simplest possible elements and then reconstructing it on the basis of the mechanistic interaction between the simple parts according to particular causal laws. The simple elements that comprise Hobbesian society are the individual human beings who are moved by the instinct for survival and the law of self-preservation independently of any other considerations or active forces. Man in his "natural state," in other words, before he enters organized social life, is an individual atom colliding with counterpart isolated human atoms, influencing and being influenced in a mechanistic (or quasi-mechanistic) manner. The results of these collisions and reciprocal influences among human atoms produces organized human life under the supervision of a political authority that blunts the sharpness of these constant collisions and curbs the pain and distress they cause. In other words, the human atoms are arranged in particular formations that are tied together by contractual bonds that take immediate effect when the parties enter into the bond. This is the essence of life in human society.

In the realm of economic activities, the simple unit is "economic man" (as Adam Smith named him), who *[A 135]* is relentlessly on the move and

---

7   Mary B. Hesse, *Science and the Human Imagination* (London: SCM Press Ltd, 1954), 60.
8   Hobbes adopted the methodologies and explanations of mechanistic materialism directly from the writings of Galileo.

in an automatic fashion in order to increase his profits and reduce his losses as much as possible. A society's general economic activity is composed of all the reciprocal effects between "human economic atoms" according to their mechanistic motions, and this within the scope of the free market with its fixed characteristics and laws. The idea of a free market that contains "economic atoms" moving in accordance with its fixed characteristics resembles strongly the idea of an absolute empty space that contains all the motions that befall material atoms according to the fixed characteristics of space. We find the same tendency governing the study of morality in utilitarian theories. "Moral man" is in his nature disposed to maximize his quantity of happiness and minimize his quantity of pain and misery. The result of the interaction of these "selfish moral atoms" is the generation of moral life in society, and the specification of its standards of virtue and right. The famous classical thinker Jeremy Bentham tried to accomplish the latter goal in his philosophy of morals and legislation.[9]

Mechanistic materialism next spread to the study of life and gave it a new true scientific basis. The scientist T. H. Huxley made the following comments about the mechanistic view of the science of animal physiology:

> Animal physiology is the knowledge of the functions and activities of animals. It regards animal bodies as machines impelled by certain forces, and performing an amount of work which can be expressed in terms of the ordinary forces of nature. The final object of physiology is to deduce the facts of morphology, on the one hand, and those of distribution on the other, from the laws of the molecular forces of matter.[10]

We cannot help but mention here the theory of Darwin, who occupies the same rank in the biological sciences that Newton occupies in the physical sciences. He is the Newton of biology because he was able to explain the origin, evolution, and division of species, and how living beings adapted to their environment, without reference to traditional explanations that focus

---

9   Jeremy Bentham, *Principles of Morals and Legislation*, (London: Henry Frowde, 1789).
10   T.H. Huxley, *Science Gossip* (1867), 74.

on final causes and metaphysical ideas about the system of nature and its need for a creator and organizer, but rather employing purely mechanistic laws. With the appearance of Freud, the mechanistic materialist orientation took control of psychology and produced new explanations of psychological phenomena. We need only mention that the Freudian explanation derives the complicated personality of man from basic elements and then explains this personality, with all its inclinations and different aspects, on the basis of purely mechanistic interactions *[A 136]* among these elements, or more precisely, the strictly mechanistic interaction between the *id* and the *super-ego*. This is the interaction that forms the human personality to a great extent, including both healthy, sick, and destructive dispositions. Whitehead cited a verse from Alfred Tennyson in order to summarize in a sentence the meaning of the world picture of mechanistic materialism:

"The stars," she whispers, "blindly run.[11]"

3

Although mechanistic materialism ruled almost completely over modern scientific thinking for about three centuries, this does not imply that it did not confront great criticism, disparagement, and defiance from a variety of groups of thinkers and critics. The first wave of criticism that this mechanistic world picture faced came from the right. It claimed that it was materialist, godless, and pessimistic in relation to mankind and its final fate, and it reproached it for designating space and time as absolute, an epithet that belonged to God alone. The most important representative of this right-wing tendency to criticize and reject materialism was the English philosopher Bishop Berkeley, who tried to replace it with a spiritual, idealist world picture that considered all the sensible qualities, in the final analysis, to be almost literally ideas in the mind of God. While on this topic, we should

---

11 "In Memoriam," section III.

also mention that the German philosopher Leibniz became involved in a famous argument with Newton and his followers in which he attacked the principles of static materialism from a purely spiritual, idealist perspective.

This orientation towards rejecting materialism rose to prominence with a group of British poets and artists who belonged to the Romantic Movement.[12] These poets rose against the purely mechanistic view of the universe because they claimed that it eliminated all meaning and purpose from existence and made nature blind as to the course of its events. They also found fault in how it abstracted from nature, as it is in itself and in truth, all the qualities that charmed the eye and seduced the senses (color, taste, scent, etc.)—the qualities that we usually consider to be the adornment of things and the source of their beauty and charm. Indeed, all these qualities are subjective and relative to the perceiving self, and have no reality in the truth of simple material bodies. Poets and artists objected to mechanistic materialism because it *[A 137]* stole from nature a very important part of the qualities that everyone enjoyed in his daily life and that the artist savored wherever he turned. However, the right-wing criticism of mechanistic materialism did not meet ready ears outside the circle of a band of men of letters, clerics, and philosophers with a decided idealist orientation. It lacked any effect on the natural and human sciences, and on the stark and increasing tendency to adopt the materialist ideas, methodologies, and approaches that had proved so successful in explaining phenomena.

However, mechanistic materialism's greatest challenge came from the left, under the name of dialectical materialism. This critique appeared in the works of Marx and Engels and the group of thinkers belonging to this revolutionary school of thought. Dialectical materialism's critique of static materialism can be summarized in the following points:

1) Since the old materialism offered a static conception of the simple primary material units from which things are composed, it remains unable to

---

12 See chapter five of Alfred North Whitehead's book, *Science and the Modern World*, where he discusses the reaction mechanistic materialism generated among the English Romantic poets.

offer realistic and correct explanations of the dynamic aspects of the world, and especially unable to explain certain phenomena like organic growth, macro changes in history, and economic and social transformations. Dialectical materialism rejects, moreover, the idea of an individual atom that is not subject, in itself, to any kind of change, development, or growth, and replaces it with a dynamic concept of matter whose essence and core is continuous development rather than change being a quality external and contingent to the static atom in itself, as in the old conception. Dialectical materialism rejects the conception of matter as simple indivisible atoms where each one has an exactly defined place at every instant of absolute time. It also rejects the complementary conception that holds that all the atoms of matter distributed in absolute space form at any temporal moment a static reality whose past, present, and future cannot be distinguished by means of their original qualities because the passage of time does not affect them at all. Alfred North Whitehead, too, directed a similar critique at static materialism in the first quarter of the twentieth century, calling it the "fallacy of simple location." In other words, dialectical materialism insists that the passage of time does not always leave the nature of matter as it was, for the reality of matter is constant process, where there is continuous transformation, growth, and development. Engels formulated his critique of mechanistic materialism in the following words:

> The old natural philosophy [the physics of static materialism, *author's note*], in spite of its real value and the many fruitful seeds it contained, was manifestly unable to satisfy us. The old natural philosophy...erred because it did not concede to nature *[A 138]* any development in time, any "succession," but only "co-existence."[13]

A long time after Engels wrote this, the English philosopher Whitehead made the same critique of static materialism, saying:

> Furthermore, this fact that the material is indifferent to the division of time leads to the conclusion that the lapse of time is an accident, rather than the essence, of the material.... Thus the transition of time

---

13   Friedrich Engels, "Introduction to the Second Edition" in *Anti-Duhring*, 12-14.

> has nothing to do with the character of the material....The aboriginal stuff, or material, from which a materialistic philosophy starts, is incapable of evolution. [14]

Based on this realistic, dynamic view of the universe, dialectical materialism emphasizes the fact of essential organic ties between everything that exists in the world, in contrast to how the old theory imposes "isolation" on each atom of matter on the basis of the idea of simple location. The following is a straightforward explanation of the view of dialectical materialism on this topic:

> Contrary to metaphysics, the dialectic does not consider nature as a state of rest, frozenness, stagnation, and stability. Rather, it considers it as a state of constant motion, change, and uninterrupted renewal and development. In nature, there is always something generating and developing, and something disintegrating and perishing. That is why we wish [to establish] the dialectical method, so that one would not be satisfied with viewing events from the perspective of their relations to one another and from the perspective of their mutual adaptation to one another, but also from the perspective of their motion, change, development, appearance, and disappearance. [15]

When dialectical materialism emphasizes that motion (process) is the essence of material reality, it does not mean by motion mechanistic change in the positions of material masses in space. Engels makes this issue clear in his criticism of mechanistic materialism, saying:

> But this mechanistic motion does not exhaust motion as a whole. Motion is not merely change of place, in fields higher than mechanics it is also change of quality. [16]

In other words, motion, according to this conception, is not externally and contingently related to *[A 139]* the nature of matter, but it is real

---

14   See Whitehead's *Science and the Modern World*, 50-51, 109-110.
15   Gustav A. Wetter, *Dialectical Materialism* (London: Routledge Kegan Paul, 1958), 314-315.
16   Friedrich Engels, *Dialectics of Nature* (Moscow: Foreign Language Publishing House, 1954), 334.

development and cumulative historical growth that constantly generates a higher and more advanced form of beings in nature, that is, higher and more advanced in terms of the refinement of their structure and degree of their complexity. Lenin spoke about the importance of process in this kind of conception of materialist reality in a pithy but significant phrase:

> Whether we say the world is moving matter, or that the world is material motion, makes no difference whatever.

Whitehead had subsequently suggested the same idea in his critique of mechanistic materialism when he said that *development* in static materialism was nothing but a word used to describe a change of external relations (spatiality) between parts of matter. However, this drains the process of development and growth of their cumulative historical contents, and of its serious meaning and realistic sense.[17]

2) Among the important reproaches that dialectical materialism makes of static materialism is a tendency to abstraction that leads it to confuse totally static mental abstractions and sensible, dynamic, corporeal reality. The old materialistic theory constructs a number of abstract conceptions (like an atom of matter in its simple location) that are found very useful in the natural sciences (and other areas), but this also convinces it that the world is really composed of the elements described exhaustively and precisely by these conceptions. In other words, the old materialism does not consider the atom of matter at its simple location merely a useful mental abstraction, but regards it as the real existing simple element out of which everything is composed.

In a similar fashion, Hobbes and other thinkers, when they composed their contractual theories about the origin of social life and the role of political authority, did not regard these theories as very useful mental abstractions whose purpose was to rationalize a new class's appropriation of Europe's economy, leadership, and destiny, but rather regarded these theories at the time (as some still do today) as if they gave us a realistic and

---

17 See *Science and the Modern World*, chapter six.

accurate description of the emergence of social life and the history of its development. Engels summarized this kind of criticism of static materialism and its ramifications for thinking and explanation in the following way:

> First of all we make abstractions of the real world through our minds, and then cannot know these self-made abstractions because they are creations of thought and not sensuous objects. Matter is nothing but the totality of material things from which this concept is abstracted, and motion, as such, is nothing but the totality of all sensuously perceptible forms of motion; words like matter and motion are nothing but *[A 140] abbreviations* in which we comprehend many different sensuously perceptible things according to their common properties.[18]

A few years after the death of Engels, Whitehead directed the same criticism at static materialism, accusing it of committing a grave error by replacing the actual corporeal realities out of which the world is composed with the mental abstractions out of which the theory is built.[19] According to Whitehead, these mental conceptions (like spatial points without dimensions, temporal moments without duration, static material masses that always remain the same, and the absolute movement of a single body in space) are useful abstractions but remote from the sensible, corporeal reality with all its riches, variety, and many complicated layers: it would be impossible to regard them as the real elementary units from which the world is actually composed. Therefore, Whitehead's view toward the task of philosophy resembles Engels' view when he claims that one of the chief functions of philosophy is constant criticism of the abstractions used in the different areas of knowledge in order to avert the confusing of totally mental abstractions with corporeal reality.

Thus philosophy is a constant warning against isolation within the framework of totally static abstractions and absorption into them as if they were true realities, and the constant appeal to return to dynamic, material reality, examining it carefully as the starting point for knowledge and the

---

18 *Dialectics of Nature*, 312-313.
19 What Whitehead calls the "fallacy of misplaced concreteness."

proper point of final return in order to verify the truth and effectiveness of the matter. As a result of this logic, dialectical materialism rejected all the basic principles of static materialism—absolute space, absolute time, absolute rest, and absolute motion—and insisted on the relativity of all these phenomena to the basic reality in the universe, and that is the materialist process. As an example, I will cite a short excerpt from the writing of Engels in which he rejects the idea of absolute movement (and absolute rest) as the real reality in the universe, as the old materialism believed.

> Constancy and equilibrium are nothing other than a relative state that is only meaningful to a specific type of motion…Motion of a single body does not exist – [it can be spoken of] only in a relative sense.[20] *[A 141]*

In fact, dialectical materialism's rejection of the idea of absolute rest and its advocacy of the relativity of time and space harbored a very serious implication that did not rise to the surface until after the emergence of relativity theory at the beginning of the twentieth century. Indeed, those who created dialectical materialism did not entirely realize (and they could not have realized) the kind of consequence, and its importance, arising from their rejection of the absolutes of the mechanistic theory. With this rejection, dialectical materialism made temporal and spatial relations inherent qualities of things and events (and not independent containers of them). This means that the nature of the spatial and temporal relations is defined in relation to strict causal laws covering the course of the materialist process and the interactions of its parts in a particular cosmological period. The establishment of this new relationship between the nature of time and space, on the one hand, and the process of material reality, on the other, has the following implications.

a) The invalidity of the classical materialist idea of bifurcating nature into a pair of absolute vessels (one temporal and the other spatial) and the finite number of things present in them.

b) Time and space do not have absolute necessary natures or eternal necessary qualities in isolation from their material contents. Therefore,

---

20 *Dialectics of Nature*, 329.

the Newtonian idea stating that time can be characterized by an absolute flow of duration and self-sufficiency is denied and its place is taken in relation to what we usually call "the rate of the flow of time" relative to qualities of the materialist process and the standards we use to measure it, as in general relativity theory.

c) As a result of these considerations, the old Newtonian account that "instantaneity," "succession," and "simultaneity" are absolute and real facts in the universe is found to be false. Another consequence is the relativity of the qualities of traditional space (homogenous space, Euclidean space, three-dimensional space, etc.) to the matter that we say exists and occurs in space.

d) The possibility of the existence of times that differ in their qualities from Newtonian time, as postulated by static materialism, and the possibility of the existence of non-Euclidean spaces whose nature differs from traditional absolute space, relative to the kind of developments that befall material processes and the complex forms that they take in their complicated transformations. These possibilities essentially entail the existence of non-Newtonian mechanisms and non-Euclidean geometries that conform to the qualities of the times and spaces mentioned.

3) Dialectical materialism rejects the intense reductionist tendency that characterizes static materialism in its attempts to explain phenomena, whatever their type and complexity, on the basis of the mechanistic paradigm alone. The reductionist tendency appears in the old materialism in these two aspects:

a) The attempt by the mechanistic theory to find the basis of all types of motion and change, including historical process, organic growth, and social transformation, in the shifting arrangements of the parts of atomic matter. This entails believing in the necessity of reducing processes with *[A 142]* more advanced, complicated, and higher structures to simpler motions, and without remainder. The best example of this reductionism is the argument that took place in the 19th century between two groups of specialists in biology: the proponents of Vitalism and the proponents of the school of pure mechanistic materialism. The mechanists among the biological scientists believed in the possibility of entirely reducing the laws of biology governing the growth and development of living beings to the laws of physics and chemistry (the laws of matter in general), and without sufficient remainder to distinguish the science of biology from chemistry and physics essentially and qualitatively and not merely quantitatively. Reductionism here entails the derivation of the living process, in all its complexity and high degree of refinement in the structure of its parts, from the simple mechanistic motions of atomic parts of matter. The proponents of Vitalism contested and rejected this claim, insisting on the impossibility of deriving biology entirely from chemistry, and emphasizing that biology was different in kind. However, the proponents of Vitalism were unable to offer any clear positive scientific explanation of the nature of the qualitative difference that was supposed to distinguish, in principle, biological phenomena from physical and chemical phenomena. Because of this inability, they were forced, under the pressure of their critics, to offer murky metaphysical explanations and hidden obscure forces to try to explain how living processes differed from the pure mechanistic motion of matter.

b) The second aspect of static materialism's reductionist tendency is located in its doctrine that if we had exact and exhaustive knowledge of the qualities of atoms of matter, then we would be able to predict with certainty what formations these atoms will take and all the phenomena that will arise from these formations. The best representative of this position is the French mathematician LaPlace, who offered the following example in order to explain the basic idea lying behind this tenet of mechanistic materialism: If we assume that there is a giant mathematical mind that has exhaustive knowledge of the speed of every atom of matter in the universe along with their exact locations in absolute space at each moment of mathematical time, then that mind could see the past, present, and future of the universe as one single fact present right now in front of it. In other words, it would know everything through "the mathematical principles of natural philosophy," as Newton termed them. Without these principles, there is no "science" taken in its strict and exact meaning.

The dynamic dialectical theory of the universe rejects the reductionist tendencies associated with the essence of static materialism and advocates the existence of dynamic reciprocal relations between the part and the whole, where the parts compose the whole and the whole has influence on the parts out of which it is composed. Said differently, the subordinate material parts that become part of the structure of a living cell are not "entirely blind in their course" but rather behave according to the system of the whole structure of which they are considered parts, and if they *[A 143]* become part of the structure of a different kind of body then their behavior is affected by the system of the whole structure of that body.

This entails that exhaustive exact information on the movement of atoms of matter does not suffice alone to predict the kind of formations and phenomena that will be produced by the aggregate of the atoms. For knowing their motions in this manner directly assumes that we have prior knowledge of the special kinds of complex formation and how the systems of their structures influence the motion and course of the atoms. In other words, the scientific knowledge of the part is not complete without some knowledge about the nature of the whole in which it forms a part of its structure. Therefore, LaPlace's idea about the giant mathematical mind and the knowledge it can gain from what it already knows about atoms of matter proves inconceivable. For in order for this mind to view the past, present, and future of the universe at once, it needs not only to know the velocity and location of every atom at every instant of time, but it must also know the nature of the universe that produces the motion of the atoms because their motion is affected originally by the nature of the whole that they form, within which they move, and whose system influences their behavior. Moreover, because dialectical materialism has left behind absolute space and time, it considers the idea of atoms of matter occupying a particular space and moving with a particular speed at any particular moment of time to be an empty idea that fails to apply to the dynamic reality of things and their factual nature. Without static materialist absolutes, LaPlace's idea crumbles.

Whitehead later criticized the reductionist tendency of static materialism from his dynamistic point of view, rejecting the possibility of viewing nature as a static reality in a durationless instant. On this basis, dialectical materialism rejects any strained reduction of the higher phenomena of growth and development along with the more complex structures in nature to lower and simpler phenomena without serious consideration of the new characteristics distinguishing types of existence at every level of development and complexity in structure, types generated by the material process. Thus, every scientific exertion must continuously strive to formulate specific laws that cover the basic distinguishing qualities at every one of these levels. This entails developing an appropriate research methodology for each level instead of applying a methodology copied from a different level in an arbitrary, strained, and automatic manner.

However, when dialectical materialism rejects the strict and comprehensive reduction of a particular science (like biology) to another science (like chemistry and then physics) considered prior to it, this does not entail the acknowledgement of absolute, essential, qualitative differences among the various levels under which phenomena of different natures are classified. In other words, it rejects the idea of absolute qualitative differences in nature and sharp, final distinctions between, for example, the levels of physical phenomena and biological phenomena, or the levels of biological and social-historical phenomena. It also emphasizes the integration, gradation, and contintuity of these levels: it stresses the unity of nature as a whole in this specific dialectical sense. *[A 144]*

4

The decisive blow that destroyed static materialism as an important world picture in the modern era came from the inside, that is, from physics itself, which was the source and the greatest mainstay for mechanistic materialism. Although scientists had accepted the conceptions, methodologies, and procedures of static materialism, this did not imply that they were entirely satisfied with it as a comprehensive world picture and instrument for giving causal explanations to natural phenomena for the sake of predicting and controlling nature within reasonable limits.

As time passed, theoretical differences began to emerge in the heart of mechanistic materialism, and empirical problems began to accumulate without it being able to explain or solve them as expected from a scientific theory. This situation made it necessary to make a total, comprehensive review of classical materialism and its founding assumptions. The review led to special relativity theory and subsequently to general relativity theory. I will offer three examples of the special kind of problems that static materialism faced and that led, in the end, to its being replaced by a new scientific theory that was more comprehensive and dialectical.

a) When embryology was placed on a sound empirical foundation in the nineteenth century (when it became a true science in the precise sense), the idea of a "mosaic" relationship between the ovum and the development of the embryo was ascendant. In other words, the prevailing theory at that time held that each part of the developing embryo grew from a particular and definite part of the ovum, and nowhere else. Thus if we destroy a specific part of an ovum, the organ that is supposed to grow from that damaged part will fail to emerge. This theory, it should be clear, is the application of the reductionism of mechanistic atomism to embryology.

However, the famous scientist Hans Driesch, near the end of the nineteenth century, discovered that in a great number of ova, we can damage a part without impeding the full and natural growth of its embryo. Driesch drew the lesson from his discovery that the mosaic relationship does not alone explain organic phenomena: the traditional mechanistic atomist paradigm fails to explain how the parts of the embryo emerge from the parts of the ovum, and fails to provide the causal, scientific clarification that would apply to reality and experience. Because the mosaic explanation was the only scientific explanation available at the time, Driesch went far in his imagination and attempted to offer obscure metaphysical accounts for the aspects of biological phenomena that the mechanistic atomist theory was unable to explain. That is why Driesch became a Vitalist.

The rejection of the mosaic relationship in this realm need not entail following Driesch and exiting the realm of science and its explanations in order to enter the realm of obscurities and occult forces. *[A 145]*

Instead, it ought to remind us that material molecules do not form ova (and thus embryos) as stones form walls or as atoms of gas are present in a closed vessel, where if we remove one of the stones there will be an immediate and inevitable gap in the wall. The material molecules in the ovum differ from the gas mentioned because they are influenced in their motion and behavior by the whole system of the unit of which they are a part, a living being that functions at a very high level of structural and organic complexity. Therefore, we find that the ovum is able to compensate for the damage done to some of its parts and fill the breaches that may have been caused.

b) Near the end of the nineteenth century, two scientists, Michelson and Morley, undertook an experiment whose importance in the history of modern physics lay in that it marked the beginning of the end of static materialism as an acceptable scientific world picture. The two scientists constructed a complicated apparatus that enabled them to measure the absolute velocity of the earth in its orbit through the "ether." Because the results of the experiment were entirely negative, scientists were forced to finally give up on the idea of the absolute speed of the body and withdraw it along with the idea of the ether in the new formulation of mechanics, as we find in Ernst Mach, for example. The theory of Einstein then arrived to finally rid physics of the conception of absolute time and the vessel of absolute space, demonstrating instead that spatial and temporal measures are relative to and derived from the flow of events in the material world.

c) The development of non-Euclidean geometry and the success of scientists in applying it in experimental and theoretical physics played a large role in destroying the pillars of mechanistic materialism since it made clear that the Newtonian conception of space as infinite, homogenous, three-dimensional, and Euclidean in character only applies to reality within certain limits (relatively short distances, bodies that are neither very large nor very small, and relatively low speeds). Since science has advanced beyond those limits, it now faces problems and questions that it can only solve and explain by adopting the new non-Euclidean geometries.

We cannot claim that the twentieth century has built out of its scientific triumphs and discoveries a perfect world picture to take the place of the materialist conception that has passed away. Such a conception ought to always be spoken of with caution and a spirit of approximation, likelihood, and flexibility, making allowances for revising and adjusting it in the light of future scientific successes and discoveries that will have an effect on our theory of nature and our ability to control nature. Dialectical materialism, certainly, is the most successful contemporary attempt to formulate an integrated world picture appropriate to this age and its science. This must be part of what Sartre meant when he said: "Marxism is the contemporary philosophy."

Appendix 1

Documents from the Trial of the Author and Publisher

December 1969-January 1970

1. The Indictment

We, Atif Fayyad, the Investigating Judge in Beirut, after examining the documents and the petition number 16837 (dated December 17th, 1969), charge the defendant, Dr. Sadik Jalal Al-Azm, 35 years old (whose mother's name is Naziha), arrested in absentia on December 19th, 1969, imprisoned January 8th, 1970, and released on January 15th, 1970, with the following offense: in Beirut and within the period of legal accountability, undertaking the publication of the book *Critique of Religious Thought*, which tended to instigate confessional strife. The Public Prosecutor has also charged the Defendant, Dr. Bashir Al-Daouk, the owner of Dar Al-Talia Publishing House, on January 2nd, 1970, in accordance with Articles 219 and 317 of the Penal Code and Article 62 from the Press Law.

First: Factual Findings

The Defendant, Dr. Sadik Jalal Al-Azm, published a book under the title *Critique of Religious Thought*, [A 147] composed of 230 pages and divided into a number of topics, summarized as follows: "Introduction," "Scientific Culture and the Poverty of Religious Thought," "The Tragedy of Satan," "A Reply to a Criticism," "The Miracle of the Apparition of the Virgin and the Eradication of the Traces of Aggression," "Deception in Contemporary Western Christian Thought," and "Introduction to the Scientific-Materialist Conception of the Universe and its Development."

In treating the majority of these topics, the Defendant addresses the revealed religions in general and Islam in particular, and in so doing raises doubts, disparages, ridicules, and scorns these religions and their doctrines and teachings, to the point of departing from pure scientific research and trespassing into the region that is punishable by law.

Since this study contains accounts and statements that involve the raising of doubts in and the disparagement of religious doctrines, and scorn and ridicule for religious teachings, we will examine as examples some of the statements that tend to agitate for confessional strife and incite sectarian conflict.

A. Some Examples Drawn from the Chapter "Scientific Culture and the Poverty of Religious Thought"

In this section of the book *Critique of Religious Thought* the Defendant shows scorn and ridicule for the Qur'anic verse that states the following: "God created Adam from clay, then ordered the angels to prostrate themselves before him, which they all did except for Satan, which is why God expelled him from paradise." The author then wonders with scorn whether this story constitutes a legend or not?

The Defendant answers his own question, stating:

> If this Qur'anic story is entirely veracious and true to the facts and history of the world (for it is revealed), it is clearly incompatible with

our scientific knowledge, and thus we must conclude that modern science has gone astray in this case. However, if this Qur'anic story is not true to the facts, what can it be (for the reconciliatory orators) but a beautiful legend? (p. 25).

In another discussion about the reconciliation between Islam and science, the author shifts from ridicule to raising doubt and disparagement about the Qur'anic verses concerning the Islamic belief in the real existence of creatures like jinns, angels, and Satan, asking aloud the following: "Should a Muslim today believe [in the existence of such creatures] just because they are mentioned in the Holy Qur'an, or is he allowed to consider them as mythological creatures like the Greek gods, mermaids, ghouls, and griffins? (p. 26) Then the Defendant shifts from raising doubt and disparagement about these religious doctrines to instigating the destruction of the pillars of concord and affection _[A 148]_ among the sects, since some of their religious doctrines appear not to be compatible, and then attacks with malicious intent the long-sought reconciliation between Christianity and Islam undertaken by people of good will, and especially the dialogue between Sheikh Subhi Al-Saleh and Father Joachim Bitar[1] (and others) concerning this issue. The Defendant presses further with his demonstration of the conflict between Christianity and Islam by citing Original Sin, the Holy Trinity, the Incarnation of Christ, and the Crucifixion and Resurrection, stating that "Islam rejects these beliefs and regards some as blasphemy." He then raises the question whether the God composed from the Father, the Son, and the Holy Spirit, Who was incarnated on earth and sent his Son to save humanity, is also the God Whom Muslims worship?

The Defendant concludes from all of this that the God that Muslims worship is not the same God that Christians worship, and other statements and discussions on page 41 and 42 of his book.

---

1   Joachim Mubarak is meant not Joachim Bitar (as appears in the indictment).

B. Some Examples Drawn from the Chapter "The Tragedy of Satan"

The Defendant discusses under this title the status of Satan according to what is in the verses of the Qur'an and the traditional Islamic interpretations of the meaning of Satan: "Satan was a favorite angel of God and was of great consequence in the order of the heavenly host until he disobeyed God's order and was expelled from paradise, incurring eternal damnation." (p. 56)

The Defendant only addressed this issue in order to be free to instigate blasphemy and to attribute cunning to God. Continuing in this vein, he says: "If God is the Creator of all things and the One who predetermines good and evil for His people, why then does He want people to believe that Satan is the cause of all evil and sin? And why does He want to burden Satan with the sins of those He had created evil and made to do evil?" (p. 79) The divine characteristic that he is discussing is that of cunning.

The Defendant elaborates that "although God had since eternity decided who would be the people of Paradise and who would be the people of Hell, He nevertheless sent messengers, revealed Holy Scriptures, filled them with command and interdiction; and distinguished between *halal* and *haram.*" (p. 82) In his words, "This means that God's sending of messengers and Holy Scriptures and His distinguishing between halal and haram are no more than tools of His cunning in order to carry through the decrees He had already willed for people." (p. 82) The Defendant concludes that we need to regard Satan again as an angel who served his Lord and "we must desist from heaping abuse and insults on him, forgive him, seek forgiveness for him, and ask people to think well of him, after we have falsely and slanderously made him responsible for all faults and abominations." (p. 85) *[A 149]*

C. Some Examples Drawn from the Chapter "The Miracle of the Virgin's Apparition and the Eradication of the Traces of Aggression"

The Defendant Sadik Al-Azm states under this title that "there is hardly a village around the world that is free of such stories and tales, which the people circulate as the absolute truth concerning the nobility of their forebears, the miracles of the saints, and strange, extraordinary events," (p. 99) and criticizes the pronouncements made by the clergy on the occasion of the apparition of the Virgin in this sarcastic manner:

> I can frankly say that the intellectual, cultural, and scientific level of the clergy in the Egyptian Coptic Church is exceedingly low and incapable of being described as composed, cautious, and intellectually responsible in how it handled and administered these issues.... I found that nothing that the Bishop said about the pictures of the Virgin has any basis in truth, solid historical support, or rigorous scientific argument, and that it does not add up to anything more than religious legends and stories woven by the imagination...Everything said about the existence of an original picture of the Virgin by the hand of Saint Luke is false. (p. 110-112)

The Defendant was not satisfied with all this criticism and doubt about the Virgin but tried, in the course of his discussion of Her, and with the aim of agitation, to exhibit the aspects of conflict among Christians themselves and also between Christians and Muslims regarding the status of the Virgin and Her sanctity, which fill some other pages of the book.

D. Some Examples Drawn from the Chapter "Deception in Contemporary Western Christian Thought"

Under this title, the Defendant made statements that raise doubts about the Christian message and doctrines. In his opinion, the modern world can live without this message, as he states:

> The representatives of contemporary Christian thought acknowledge this fact and convey their realization that the contemporary world is able to survive and live quite easily without them and their institutions. In reality, Christian thinkers find something embarrassing in this acknowledgement and that is that the modern world is able to muster systems and theories appropriate for the life of contemporary society and man without taking into consideration the Christian message and its doctrines and institutions. (p. 117, 118)

There are other statements and discussions that aim at instigating doubts in God, the prophets, and the revealed books in the context of a call for scientific investigation, atheism, and conflict. The Defendant Sadik Jalal Al-Azm denied the charge made against him before the court and stated that he had published these studies previously and without any intention to instigate confessional strife or what results from it. His attorney requested in a digression that his crime be included under the amnesty *[A 150]* of February 17th, 1968 (no. 69-8) or that of April 24th, 1969 (no. 969-14).

The other Defendant, Bashir Al-Daouk, stated that he published the book and agreed to pay Sadik Jalal Al-Azm twelve percent of the book's revenues.

According to the Law

Whereas, a person has absolute freedom to express his opinions and thoughts by any means, and the Lebanese constitution guarantees him freedom of speech and thought as long this freedom does not interfere with the rights of others and he does not commit what the legislator considers a crime punishable by law.

Whereas, a judge in a criminal court is not allowed to refrain from applying the legal text to the incident presented before him no matter how much goodwill, support, or favor the case presented for investigation finds among the public. If he does not apply the text, then he is placing himself above the doing of justice. More so, even if the general public criticizes or derides the relevant article in the law, the judge is obliged to apply it and to abstain from discussing its legitimacy or illegitimacy or its rightness or wrongness. The legislature alone has the right to make, modify, or annul the laws: the job of the judge is to apply it. The Lebanese constitution has established the separation of the three powers, and if a judge exceeds his authority, then he usurps the legislative authority.

For this reason, Article Two of the Law of Civil Proceedings clearly states that "The judge is not allowed to have an opinion on the correctness of the legislative acts, whether that involves comparing the law in question to current international legal norms or formulating his judgments as legislative acts."

Whereas, commencing from the constitutional guarantee of freedom of thought and opinion and from the principle that the judge has a legal obligation to apply the text to the matter before him and to which it is applicable, it is the right of the Defendant to think with full freedom and judge by the opinion he wants and which he believes is true, unless these rights infringe on the rights of others also established and protected by these laws.

Since the Defendant, if he does not believe in the existence of God, for example, or does not accept some beliefs and considers them superstitions and myths, is obliged, when he publishes these views among the people, not to disparage their feelings about what they believe, ridicule what they hold sacred, deride their teachings, and scorn their revealed books, even when they conflict with his opinion.

Since the Defendant has stated plainly in his book that in his view it is impossible to reconcile the essence of Christianity and Islam, and has undertaken the kind of studies that make *[A 151]* the doubter an apostate in the eyes of his religion, and has employed a mocking style that opens up a space for discord and inciting each sect against the other, criticizing those thinkers of good will who reconcile the essences of the two religions that meet on the way to truth, good, and beauty.

Since the Defendant has, through his actions, agitated to sow discord and aversion between the various sects, which exposes the safety of the state to danger and destroys what Lebanon enjoys of freedom of opinion and belief, the sanctity of its values, and concord among the different creeds (even if incompatible in appearance), on which the existence of Lebanon rests.

Since Article 317 of the Penal Code, which the defendant ignored but which apply to his actions, states that "any action, writing, or speech that intends or results in the inciting of confessional or racial strife or the inciting of conflict between the sects is punishable by imprisonment."

Since the studies, statements, and inquiries are replete with ridicule, scorn, disparagement, and doubt in Islam and Christianity and incite atheism, they have the effect of instigating religious factionalism and inciting sectarian strife, which has nothing to do with pure scientific research.

The subject of this charge is the issue that provoked both Christian and Muslim public opinion and moved the citizens to protest and present complaints because of the publication of the book. Were it not for the awareness of the citizens and the intervention of responsible people, the safety of the nation would be exposed to danger.

Since Article 317 of the Penal Code and Article 62 of the Press Law apply to the action of the Defendant, Sadik Jalal Al-Azm.

Since the two laws granting amnesty, of February 17th, 1969 and April 24th, 1969, to which the representative of the Defendant referred, are inapplicable to the present case, for the *Critique of Religious Thought* was only published and appeared on the market in November 1969, after the two amnesties, and that with the knowledge and consent of the Defendant Sadik Jalal Al-Azm.

Since the Defendant Bashir Al-Daouk published the study in question, he is an accomplice to the criminal act, and thus Articles 219 and 317 of the Penal Code and Article 62 of the Press Law apply to his action.

On the basis of the findings, our decision is the following:

1) The Defendant Dr. Sadik Jalal Al-Azm is indicted in accordance with Article 317 of the Penal Code and Article 62 of the Press Law.
2) The Defendant Dr. Bashir Al-Daouk is indicted in accordance with Articles 219 and 317 of the Penal Code and Article 62 of the Press Law. *[A 152]*
3) The legal fees are assessed to the two Defendants.
4) The two Defendants must appear before the Press Court in Beirut.

2. Interrogation Before the Press Court[2]

The Open Hearing of Wednesday, May 27, 1970

---

2   We have tried to recall the events of the oral interrogation that took place at the court in the way presented here based on the following sources: the official court clerk's minutes for the session proceedings (although he made only brief notes), the ample

Plaintiff: Public Prosecutor

Defendants: Sadik Jalal Al-Azm and Bashir Jamil Al-Daouk

Defense: Joseph Moghaizel, Edmund Rabbatt, Bassem Al-Jisr, and Abdullah Lahoud.

The Defendant Sadik Jalal-Azm was asked to repeat the statements he made before the Investigating Judge.

The Defendant answered affirmatively and added that he wished to discuss some of the issues that appeared in the Indictment since it had raised matters that the Investigating Judge did not address in his interrogation. For the indictment was composed after the interrogation and after the recording of the Defendant's statements in front of the Investigating Judge, and not before it.

The Defendant was asked to make a statement about the charges against him in the Indictment.

The Defendant answered that his aim in writing the book was to discuss what some Christian and Muslim thinkers say about religion and religious beliefs. In other words, the aim was not to criticize religious doctrines as a matter of free personal faith but to discuss how some thinkers and other people regard these doctrines.

The Defendant was asked what he meant by the word "myth" in his book.

The Defendant answered that the word has two meanings. The first as a popular term of reproach: when *[A 153]* we want to undermine something we call it a "myth." The serious and scientific meaning of the term, on the other hand, refers to the mythological heritage of peoples. The Defendant stated that he did not use the word "myth" in his book as a term of reproach but in its scientific sense, which entails the sum of the imaginative products that a particular culture leaves to us. This is what we

---

reports of the interrogation that were published in the newspapers *Al-Nahar* and *Al-Nawar*, extensive notes written by the main Defendant during the indictment process which he later relied on directly for his answers to questions raised in the court, and notes about the events of the interrogation taken down by some of those present. [Dar Al-Talia]

mean when we say that the *Iliad*, the *Odyssey*, and the *Epic of Gilgamesh* are myths. We study such myths in order to derive facts about the life of these people, and understand their reality. Thus, the study of the *Iliad* and the *Epic of Gilgamesh* reveal important facts to us about the Ancient Greek and Babylonian societies.

The Defendant was asked whether he meant that religious books are myths and products of the imagination.

The Defendant answered that he meant that religious books contain sections and segments that express mythic ideas and narrate stories that are mythic in the meaning defined above. For example, the story of the flood in the ancient epics of the Babylonians is repeated word for word in the Torah and the Qur'an.

The Defendant was asked whether his book claims that the story in the Qur'an that says that God created Adam from clay, then ordered the angels to prostrate themselves before him, and all the angels obeyed except Satan, and thus God drove him out of Paradise is a "beautiful myth." Did he intend to instigate sectarian factionalism?

The Defendant responded that he meant to say that the story of Satan is a myth in the scientific meaning of the term, as he defined it earlier, and therefore like the legend of the flood, in that its importance lies in its symbolic and ethical meanings and not in its detailed correspondence with reality. I wrote about this topic in order to demonstrate the existence of an element of tragedy in Arab-Islamic heritage because it has been accused of lacking the tragic element found in the Greek mythological heritage, for example, or in the Christian heritage and European culture. I tried to demonstrate that the story of Satan, as it appeared in the Qur'an, includes enough of the elements of drama to form a genuine tragedy, just like any other classical tragedy.

The Defendant was asked if he mentioned this clarification in his book.

The Defendant answered that he did this to a certain extent and especially in his reply to his critics. I made the clarification after and not before the criticism. It was only after I was criticized that the clarifications crystallized in my mind.

The Defendant was asked if on page 15 of his book he raised the question whether a Muslim in the twentieth century can believe in the real existence of Satan, jinns, Harut and Marut, and other creatures mentioned in the Qur'an, or must he regard them to be imaginary beings like ghouls and griffins and mermaids. Did he mean to ridicule religion, raise doubts, and instigate as was stated in the indictment?

The Defendant answered absolutely not. I raised the question in complete seriousness. Having been a university professor *[A 154]* for almost ten years, it appears to me that one of the greatest intellectual difficulties for a wide segment of Arab students with whom I am familiar with in Damascus, Beirut, or Amman is how to reconcile intellectually the contemporary scientific culture that they receive in the schools and universities and the religious culture that they grow up with at home and in elementary school. Any one of them with any glint of intelligence and sensitivity has to ask himself or herself the following question, even if in a naïve and obscure manner: How do I regard the story of the jinn, for example? Do I believe in it or not, especially after studying the methodologies of Descartes, Darwin, etc? I tried to raise with total clarity the question that the student gropes around, avoiding the disguises, displays of tact, and maneuvers that many take refuge in order to evade the brunt of the question and the psychological pain it usually inflicts. The other Arab writers who attempt to handle these issues are rarely frank or direct. Anyone with some learning, it bears repeating, must pass through this stage one day and ask himself: I am the son of this century and thus how do I regard the story that states that Moses split the Red Sea with his staff?

The Defendant was asked whether his purpose in raising this topic was to raise doubts or to explain.

The Defendant answered that his purpose was, first, to assist all of those who ask themselves these questions in a naïve, obscure, or fruitless ways in finding them means to ask them with clarity, precision, and scientific logic. Second, I wanted to make an approach to answering the questions and distinguish my approach from the approaches of others. It is the duty of each reader, nevertheless, to reach an appropriate response on his own, without being compelled by anyone.

The Defendant was asked if he would clarify what he said on pages 39–46 during his attack on the process of reconciliation that some Christian and Muslim clerics undertook in Lebanon and what he said in explaining the differences between the beliefs of Christians and Muslims. Was he looking to instigate factionalism and destroy the pillars of concord between the sects?

The Defendant responded that when he inquired into the Muslim-Christian dialogue in Lebanon, he discovered that intellectual deception played the leading role and that those who participated in the dialogue did not address clearly the heart of the matter but instead followed the Arab tribal way of affecting agreement in front of others and pretending that there were no differences between their beliefs. I wanted to expose this deception in order to demonstrate that the best way to achieve this concord in Lebanon is to stand on secular grounds when facing the country's problems, and that these grounds are national not religious. The only way to achieve this concord is with clarity and frankness about the points of conflict and agreement instead of misrepresenting the situation and pretending that there is nothing but agreement. I presented my frank opinion about the problem and made efforts to demonstrate the best way to achieve this understanding. The senior legal scholar Mohammed Jawad Mughniyah *[A 155]* published an opinion in the newspaper *Al-Muharrir* in which he completely agreed with everything I said about the phenomenon of the Muslim-Christian dialogue in Lebanon, writing the following:

> I agree with the remarks Dr. Al-Azm made on pages 42 of his book about reconciliation between Islam and Christians, and that the most appropriate and fitting way to achieve understanding between the Lebanese is on national and not religious grounds. I also agree with Al-Azm with what he says on page 44 about the current regime in Lebanon and the conspiracy of some small wealthy groups exploiting the miserable majority under the slogan of the higher interest of Lebanon and concord between religious beliefs.[3]

---

3   *Al-Muharrir* newspaper, January 8th, 1970. It is necessary to point out that Sheik Mohammed Jawad Mughniyah is not in agreement with the rest of what appears in the book *Critique of Religious Thought*, although he held an honorable position when

As for the comparison among some conflicting Christian and Muslim religious beliefs like the belief in the divinity of Christ and his crucifixion, etc., I did not do anything except state the reality of the situation as it is without deception or disguising differences in religious belief between the two religions. Every student attending school in the Arab world knows this and it is written in the books they study in Lebanese schools. Every Muslim student knows that Christians believe that Christ was crucified just as they know that their own religion denies this belief and considers it a blasphemy, and vice versa. I did not invent anything in comparing these beliefs of the two religions but confirmed reality in a descriptive and declarative manner without a touch of provocation. Everyone who reads my book knows that its style is far from that of instigation and fomentation. Here I would like to present a book to the honorable court that I bought in Lebanon entitled "This is the Truth: A Reply to the Slanders of the Christian Priests," written by Mohammed Ibn Al-Khateeb, and published in Cairo. The book, widely available in Lebanon, states that "The Christian does not believe in what the Muslim says, just as the Muslim does not believe in what the Christian says." (p. 11) He also addresses the topic of the crucifixion and its denial by Islam (p. 49–51) and the belief in the Trinity and Islam's rejection of it (p. 51, 57, 59). He also confirms that, in the view of Islam, Christ is not divine (p. 63–64, 75–76, 82). Finally, his book contains a chapter whose title I will read to you: "Mohammed the Warrior and Christ the Deserter." (p. 84–86) All of this is in the language of exhortation and instigation.

The Defendant was asked about what he said on pages 79–83 of his book concerning the cunning of God.

The Defendant answered that he was not the first to attribute cunning to God but that verses of the Qur'an assert it and attribute it to the divine essence. There are, in fact, *[A 156]* two theories found in Islam. The first grants man the ability to create his own actions: the *Al-Qadariya* and *Al-Mu'tazila* schools adhere to this theory. The second states that it is God

---

he said elsewhere that "it is better to allow Dr. Al-Azm and those like him to express their views as they like" (*Al-Sayyad*, December 25, 1969, p. 40)." [author's note]

who creates the actions of mankind: the *Al-Jabriya* and *Al-Asha'ri'a* schools adhere to this theory. I do not believe that the matter has been decided yet in favor of either of these two theories, and the Investigating Judge's perspective on the topic of cunning suggests that he belongs to the school of the Al-Mu'tazila and Al-Qadariya. As for myself, I treated the matter from the perspective of the Al-Jabriya school, which gives the quality of cunning a special importance. For if God has predestined everything for His creatures from eternity but the unfolding of events makes it appear to them that He had one purpose while, in reality, having an entirely different purpose, then He is practicing cunning, since man is unable to see the divine plan in its entirety.

The Defendant was asked about the purpose of his writing about the miracle of the apparition of the Virgin.

The Defendant replied that the article about the Virgin was more political than religious since it addressed the political exploitation of a mass event whose basis was supposed to be the appearance of the apparition of the Virgin. I directed my critique at what the newspapers, media, and official sources in Cairo said about this phenomenon, as a response to the political claims built on it. As for the accusation directed at me for criticizing the intellectual level of the Coptic clergy, I have no regrets since the clergy are not infallible and targeting them with criticism does not constitute a crime. Furthermore, their thinking is liable to discussion and criticism just like any other intellectual activity.

The Defendant was asked whether the purpose of his writing a chapter about deception in contemporary Christian thought was to spread doubt in religion and heresy.

The Defendant answered that European and Christian thinkers have no need of us in order to successfully criticize Christianity, and raise doubts about it, since they have a long heritage of fierce critics such as Renan, Strauss, Nietzsche, Marx, and Russell. My intent was to discuss a number of Christian thinkers who came from Europe to hold a conference in Beirut and to criticize some views they expressed about the role of Christianity in the contemporary world. The statement attributed to me in the indictment that "the contemporary world is able to do without Christianity" is, in reality, a direct quotation from the German Christian cleric and theologian Bonhoeffer, whom the Nazis killed because he was a member of the Resistance.

The Defendant was asked if he was inspired by the scientific methods that he borrowed from Western scientists alone in writing this book, or did he also rely on the tradition of freedom of criticism in Islam that lasted from the dawn of Islam until its period of decline?

The Defendant answered that after the establishment of the Islamic state, several schools of thought spread within the compass of this state, discussing and disputing openly in the courts of the Caliphs, and with their encouragement and patronage. For example, Imam Ghazali *[A 157]* wrote a book entitled *The Incoherence of the Philosophers*, responding in it to the philosophical opinions of a number of famous Muslim philosophers because their opinions were considered to be atheistic and heretical and outside the borders of religion. As is well-known, Imam Al-Ghazali reduced the views of the philosophers to twenty issues, accusing them of heresy in seventeen of them and charging them with unbelief in the other three. However, Al-Ghazali did not call for confiscating their books or summoning them before a judge.

The Defendant was asked what was the reaction of people when he expressed these opinions in his lectures: Did they approve or disapprove?

The Defendant answered that there was intellectual disapproval from some groups and intellectual approval from others, especially the educated.

The Defendant was asked if he wrote this book as a defender of religion or with the spirit of a heretic and doubter in religion.

The Defendant answered that he obviously did not write the book in defense of religion. I wrote it in the spirit of what is called the "critical scholarship" that treats the topic of religion or the phenomenon of religious thought. For example, there is a sociology of religion and a science of comparative religion. Were these sciences established for the sake of defending religion or raising doubts about religion? My goal was to write about religion in the spirit of these critical sciences.

Maître Abdullah Lahoud [one of the defense attorneys] asked the Honorable Court to note that the Indictment that transferred Professor Al-Azm to its jurisdiction relied on Article 317 of the Penal Code (inciting confessional strife) but that Al-Azm was, in fact, being tried on the charge of raising doubt and disbelief, and thus it was freedom of opinion and belief that was on trial. Maître Lahoud requested that the following witnesses for the defense be heard: Sheikh Abdullah Al-'Alayli, Sheikh Muhammad Jawad Mughniyyah, Professor Constantin Zureiq, Father Gabriel Malek, Professor Hasan Sa'ab, Micha'il Na'imy, Professor Sheikh Subhi Al-Salih, Father Joachim Mubarak, Muhammad Al-Niqash. The prosecution left the matter to the court, which decided to add the request of Maître Lahoud to the proceedings.

The Defendant Bashir Jamil Al-Daouk was asked to repeat the testimony he gave before the Investigating Judge.

The Defendant stated that he obtained the approval of the Ministry of Information to distribute the book on December 1st, 1969. He also stated that he was sympathetic to its argument. He stated that the period between its distribution and its confiscation on December 15th, 1969 was fifteen days and that since during that period there did not appear to be any reaction to it from anyone in Lebanon, the book could not have incited confessional strife. It was the general manager of the Dar Al-Ifta who filed a complaint with the Public Prosecutor after one of the newspapers published an article about the book and its author, and it was the Islamic Religious Institute that tried to provoke public opinion and instigate against the author, although it failed in this.

The Attorney General repeated the charges and requested a ruling. The session was postponed until June 10, 1970 *[A 158]* in order to hear the arguments of the defense.

3. The Decision of the Court

In the Name of the Lebanese People

The Penal Court of Appeals in Beirut, which oversees cases involving publications, after close examination and careful deliberation, found that the Investigating Judge in Beirut in his ruling of January 26, 1970 indicted the Defendants, Dr. Sadik Jalal Al-Azm and Dr. Bashir Al-Daouk, according to Article 317 of the Penal Code and Article 62 of the Press Law, to be arraigned in Beirut without delay, for the publishing and being an accessory to the publishing of a book entitled *Critique of Religious Thought,* which tends to the incitement of confessional strife.

As a result of the public trial proceedings:

The Facts

Both of the Defendants denied the charges made against them. Dr. Al-Azm stated that the book that is the subject of the charges was meant to be a scholarly critique and that he did not believe that the studies that appeared in the book contained incitement to confessional strife or derision of revealed religions. He had been preceded in this effort by Arab and foreign scholars, who had not been led before judges to stand trial for what they had published. Moreover, the Lebanese constitution guarantees freedom of expression and criticism to authors.

Whereas, upon review of the book, it contains the following studies:

1) The material that appeared in the chapter on scientific culture about the Qur'anic verse that states that God created Adam from clay and then ordered the angels to prostrate themselves before him, which they all did but Satan, and thus God drove him from paradise.
2) Some material about the tragedy of Satan.
3) Some material about the miracle of the apparition of the Virgin.
4) Deception in contemporary Christian thought, including the raising of doubts in the message and doctrines of Christianity.

Whereas, this court is not trying the Defendants for freedom of religious belief or thought, or for raising doubts in religion, since the Lebanese Constitution guarantees freedom of opinion, thought, and belief.

[A 159]

Whereas, the mission of this court is limited to the Investigating Judge's indictment of the Defendants according to Articles 219 and 317 of the Penal Code and Article 62 of the Press Law.

Whereas, the Defendant Dr. Sadik Jalal Al-Azm in November 1969 collected and compiled several lectures he had previously written and published in cultural journals in a book he named *Critique of Religious Thought*, which the Dar Al-Talia, a publishing house owned by the other Defendant, Bashir Al-Daouk, published.

Whereas during the Public Hearing, the two Defendants proposed that the alleged crimes fell under an amnesty and requested the expansion of the investigation and the calling of the following witnesses: Sheikh Abdullah Al-Alayli, Sheikh Muhammad Jawad Mughniyyah, Professor Constantin Zureiq, Father Gabriel Malek, Professor Hasan Sa'ab, Micha'il Na'imy, Professor Sheikh Subhi Al-Salih, Father Joachim Mubarak, and Muhammad Al-Niqash.

Whereas, the Public Prosecutor repeated the charge and requested that the Defendants be found guilty in accordance with the indictment.

According to the Law

1. Concerning Amnesty

Whereas, it appears from the documentation of the charge that the book in question was published after the issuance of the Amnesty Law of April 24th 1969, and thus the request is denied as invalid.

2. Concerning the Defendant Sadik Al-Azm

Whereas, the examination of the sections that the Investigating Judge made the grounds for the indictment, and all the articles comprising the book in question, show that it is a scientific and philosophical study containing scientific and philosophical criticism, discussing religious thought without the intent to incite confessional and racial strife, provoke a struggle between the different sects in the nation, or insult religions.

Whereas, the provisions of Article 317 of the Penal Code and Article 62 of the Press Law are only met when the author's intent or goal is to insult religions, incite confessional strife, or to urge conflict among the sects, and that this conflict takes place actually and openly.

Whereas, the provisions of those two articles are not met, it is necessary to drop the charges against the Defendant, Sadik Al-Azm. *[A 160]*

3. Concerning the Defendant Bashir Al-Daouk

Whereas, after the dropping the charges against the primary agent, the court must drop the charges against the second Defendant, Bashir Al-Daouk, as an accomplice to the two charges named.

Whereas, we no longer need to expand the investigation and hear the witnesses listed by the Defense.

In Conclusion

After hearing the announcement of the Public Prosecutor:

The Court declares its agreement with the dropping of the charges against the Defendants Sadik Al-Azm and Bashir Al-Daouk since the provisions of the criminal charges against them were not satisfied and with the waiving of the legal fees. The verdict was announced and understood openly and in the presence of the representative of the Attorney General's office on the date of its issuance on July 7th, 1970.

Councilor Albert Samaha
Councilor Ibrahim Shuqair
President Issam Albaroudi

Appendix 2

Statement of the Mufti of the Republic [Lebanon] about the Book "Critique of Religious Thought"

The Writer of the Book and All Those who Support him are Outside of Islam. A Duty of the State is to Apply the Laws to Punish the Antagonists of Religion.

Recently, a publisher issued a book by the name of "Critique of Religious Thought" that provoked Muslim public opinion because of what it contained of obvious contradictions of Islam and brazen defamations of what it holds holy.

The Office of the Fatwa in the Lebanese Republic referred the matter of this book to the authorities to take the necessary steps in accordance with the law, as his Eminence the Mufti of the Lebanese Republic received inquiries from many Muslims concerning the judgment of Islam concerning the content of the book in question.

Exposing the facts and placing the issues in their proper place, his Eminence issued the following statement concerning this book, which is an example of those destructive cases that are compatible neither with worldly nor religious decency. Placing the truth in its proper place and silencing the wicked, we direct the attention of our people to the following:

First: Islam is a religion that guarantees freedom to the individual in all its aspects so that he may act by means of it according to his absolute will. However, freedom has limits in the customs and rules of the people, as it has in the customs and rules of religious law, limits to be observed lest freedom turns to disorder, harm the individual himself, harm his community and cause the idea of the Absolute to lose its sanctity and value. Everyone knows that an individual's freedom ends at the boundary of the freedom and dignity of another individual. This way the community is protected from shocks, tremors and unrest.

Second: There are holy things in Islam that cannot be infringed or disparaged for any cause or reason. God, his angels, the djinn, heaven and hell, judgment and reward and punishment, Adam's creation from earth, the exalted and mighty God's commanding Satan to prostrate himself to Adam in a way that expressed reverence and veneration, the refusal of Satan to obey the command of his God, all of this, and other similar things that appear in the Qur'an and Sunnah, are absolute, immutable truths in Islam. Faith in them is an obligatory religious duty for every Muslim, and doubt or the encouragement of doubt in them or some of them is a blatant blasphemy that places a Muslim outside of Islam.

Third: The refusal to grant these unseen truths and others like them, confirmed by valid, immutable evidence handed down in an uninterrupted manner, under the pretext that they contradict science is a slander on science itsellf. For positivistic science still contains a large amount of the Unseen whose secrets science has not managed to penetrate. Still, science grants all this spontaneously, as the author acknowledges. So how can he cast blame on religions for acceptng what is unseen? Moreover, human science, despite its force and power, was not able to discover the Unseen that belongs to God and His knowledge alone. For, the failure of human science to discover one thing or another does not imply that it does not exist. Also, what science has been able to discover up until our day is insignificant in comparison to what is still unknown. The exalted God spoke truth when He said: "What I bestowed on you of knowledge is but a little".

Fourth: Following the deniers going along with them, supporting their ideas and justifying all that by invoking the freedom of opinion is a rejection of God's command and thus a straying from Religion.

Fifth: Based on the facts mentioned, because the book "Critique of Religious Thought" denies the Unseen and slanders religion and the Qur'an, its author is considered as outside of Islam and an apostate, and likewise those who support him and follow him in his view.

Sixth: It is among the duties of the state to thwart these kinds of misleading, destructive thoughts that damage the Umma in its core and expose it to dangerous divisions and great strife, to an extent only God knows. It is up to the state to apply its unambiguous laws to punish all who meddle in religious rituals and what is holy in order to injure them.

Seventh: It is imperative for our people to take caution against these injurious, poisonous thoughts that fail to abide by any law or religion. The core direction of these thoughts agrees with the thoughts of World Zionism whose aim is to wage war on religion in order to weaken the citizens and seize their homelands and dominate their destinies.

(Published in *Sawt al-'Uruba*, Beirut, 8 January 1970)